Nancy Now

Theory Now Series

Series Editor: Ryan Bishop

Nancy Now

EDITED BY
VERENA ANDERMATT CONLEY AND IRVING GOH

polity

First published in 2014 by Polity Press

Polity Press
65 Bridge Street
Cambridge CB2 1UR, UK

Polity Press
350 Main Street
Malden, MA 02148, USA

ISBN-13: 978-0-7456-6166-7
ISBN-13: 978-0-7456-6167-4(pb)

A catalogue record for this book is available from the British Library.

Typeset in 11/13 Bembo by
Servis Filmsetting Limited, Stockport, Cheshire
Printed and bound in the United Kingdom by T.J. International Ltd, Padstow,
Cornwall

The publisher has used its best endeavours to ensure that the URLs for external
websites referred to in this book are correct and active at the time of going to press.
However, the publisher has no responsibility for the websites and can make no
guarantee that a site will remain live or that the content is or will remain appropriate.

Every effort has been made to trace all copyright holders, but if any have been
inadvertently overlooked the publisher will be pleased to include any necessary
credits in any subsequent reprint or edition.

For further information on Polity, visit our website: politybooks.com

Contents

Notes on Contributors

Georges Van Den ABBEELE is Dean of Humanities at the University of California at Irvine, and previously served as Founding Dean of Social Sciences and Humanities at Northeastern University and as Dean of Humanities at UC Santa Cruz, after having taught at UC Berkeley, UC Davis, Miami (OH) and Harvard universities. A native of Belgium, he earned a bachelor's degree from Reed College and the PhD from Cornell University. His books include *Travel as Metaphor, Community at Loose Ends, A World of Fables,* and *French Civilization and its Discontents*, as well as numerous articles on travel narrative, tourism and immigration, contemporary philosophy and critical theory, human geography, early modern science, cartography and Renaissance literature. He is a member of the European Academy of Sciences and 2008 recipient of its Blaise Pascal medal for outstanding contributions to the human and social sciences. A former NEH and Mellon Fellow, he has lectured extensively throughout North America, Europe, and Asia, and has served as a consultant and reviewer for a range of colleges and universities, publishers, professional organizations, and government agencies.

Giorgio AGAMBEN is an Italian philosopher who teaches at the University of Venice. He is the author of numerous key works in continental philosophy, many of which have been translated into English. They include *The Coming Community*, *Homo Sacer: Sovereign Power and Bare Life*, *State of Exception*, *The Open: Man and Animal*, and, more recently, *The Highest Poverty* and *Opus Dei: An Archaeology of Duty*.

Isabelle ALFANDARY is Professor of American Literature at the Université Sorbonne-Nouvelle (Paris-3) and Directrice de Programme at the Collège International de Philosophie (CIPH), where she teaches seminars at the intersection of philosophy and psychoanalysis. A specialist of American poetry and critical theory, she is the author of a book on e. e. Cummings (*e. e. Cummings. La minuscule lyrique*, 2002) and on American modernism (*Le risque de la lettre*, 2012). Her next book, on Jacques Derrida and Jacques Lacan, is forthcoming.

Etienne BALIBAR is Professor Emeritus of moral and political philosophy at Université de Paris X-Nanterre and Distinguished Professor of Humanities at the University of California, Irvine. He is also Visiting Professor (2012–2014) at Columbia University. His most recent publications include *Violence et civilité* (2010), *La proposition de l'égaliberté* (2010) and *Citoyen Sujet et autres essais d'anthropologie philosophique* (2011).

Verena Andermatt CONLEY is Long-Term Visiting Professor of Comparative Literature and Romance Languages and Literature at Harvard University. She works at the intersection of the humanities and the environment. A recent publication is *Spatial Ecologies: Urban Sites, State and World-Space in French Cultural Theory* (2012).

Irving GOH is currently Visiting Scholar at the Society for the Humanities at Cornell University. He obtained his PhD in Comparative Literature from Cornell, having written his dissertation under the direction of Dominick LaCapra, Timothy Murray, Jonathan Culler, and Jean-Luc Nancy. His articles on contemporary continental philosophy have appeared in journals such as *diacritics*, *MLN*, *differences: A Journal of Feminist Cultural Studies*, and *Cultural Critique*. His first book, *The Reject*, is forthcoming.

Ian JAMES completed his doctoral research on the fictional and theoretical writings of Pierre Klossowski at the University of Warwick in 1996. He is a Fellow of Downing College and a Reader in Modern French Literature and Thought in the Department of French at the University of Cambridge. He is the author of *Pierre Klossowski: The Persistence of a Name* (2000), *The Fragmentary Demand: An Introduction to the Philosophy of Jean-Luc Nancy* (2006), *Paul Virilio* (2007) and *The New French Philosophy* (2012).

Gregg LAMBERT is Dean's Professor of the Humanities at Syracuse University, and author of many works in contemporary philosophy and theory, including *In Search of a New Image of Thought: Gilles Deleuze and Philosophical Expressionism* (2012). The present chapter is part of a series of critical reflections on the question of "the return of religion" in continental philosophy.

Ginette MICHAUD is Professor in the Department of French Literature at the University of Montreal. She is a member of the Editorial Committee in charge of Jacques Derrida's *Seminars* of which she has co-edited two volumes, *La bête et le souverain* (2008 and 2010 respectively) translated as *The Beast and the Sovereign* (2009–2011). She has also co-edited a volume of Derrida's writings on the arts, *Penser à ne pas voir* (2013) and published numerous texts based on the work of Jean-Luc Nancy, among which the catalog of the exhibit *Trop. Jean-Luc Nancy* (2006) and *Cosa volante. Le désir des arts dans la pensée de Jean-Luc Nancy* (2013).

Jean-Luc NANCY is Professor Emeritus of Philosophy at the University of Strasbourg. His major works, *The Inoperative Community*, *The Sense of the World*, *Being Singular Plural*, and *The Experience of Freedom*, including the two volumes of *The Deconstruction of Christianity*, have been translated into English. Translations of *Identity: Fragments, Frankness* and *Being Nude: The Skin of Images* are forthcoming.

Prelude:
The Silhouette of Jean-Luc Nancy

Giorgio Agamben

If there exists for each author a decisive experience – something like an incandescent core that he or she incessantly approaches and flees from at the same time, where must we situate this experience for Jean-Luc Nancy? Without a doubt, it involves an extreme experience. Nancy is not, as has been suggested, a tender thinker. The landscape of this Chthonian thinker is one of lava, as at the foot of Mount Etna. In pushing to the extreme one of the most aporetic points of Heidegger's philosophy, he thinks of abandonment – the condition of existing entirely and irrevocably abandoned by Being. His ontology is one of abandonment and of the *ban*.[1] Few pages in twentieth-century philosophical prose express this abandonment with as much rigor and harshness as those, under the heading of "Abandoned Being," that seal *The Categorical Imperative*, through the invention of a new genre of the transcendental which dissolves all transcendentals:

> Without us knowing, without us being able to really know it, abandoned Being has already begun to constitute an unavoidable condition for our thought, perhaps even its sole condition. The ontology that is demanded of us from then on is an ontology in which abandonment remains the unique predicament of Being, or else transcendental, in

the scholastic sense of the term. [. . .] [That is,] Being [thereby] considered to be abandoned of all categories, and of transcendentals. [. . .] From what Being was abandoned, from what it *is* being abandoned, and from what it abandons itself, there is no memory. There is no history of this abandonment, neither knowledge nor account of how, where, when, and by whom it was abandoned. [. . .] Being *is* not its abandonment, and it abandons *itself* only in not being the author or subject of abandonment. [. . .] It is by an abandonment that Being comes to be: there is nothing more to say.[2]

It does not matter if, in the final pages of this text, something – a Law – seems, in contradictory fashion no doubt, to precede abandonment and survive it. What matters is that ontological difference, i.e. the apparatus [*dispositif*] that oversees [*gouverne*] occidental culture, attains its critical mass here.

There is an inclination to regard Nancy as the thinker of touch. But how must touch be understood, if it is not to remain an empty metaphor? Aristotle seems to accord to touch a particular prestige when he states that, without touch, the living would not exist. But what defines the very character of touch in relation to the other senses is that it lacks a medium or an exterior milieu. In touching, as Aristotle says, tangibles are sensed not by the action of a medium, but sensed at the same time (*ama*, 423b) as the very medium of touch,[3] hence rendering touch hidden [*caché*] (*lanthanei*, 423b).[4] The milieu of touch is not something with an exteriority, as air or the diaphanous are for sight; instead, it coincides with the flesh that perceives. The flesh is simultaneously the medium and the subject of touch.

If one wants to grasp the thought of Nancy, it is necessary to follow, and once again push to the extreme, the Aristotelian analysis, far beyond what recent readings have done. Giorgio Colli has given a very wonderful definition of contact when he writes that there is contact when two points are separated individually by the absence of a representation. While Aristotle has expressed the latter in saying that "we think that we in fact make contact with things directly and that there is no intermediary" (423b),[5] this absence of representation, this ruin of the medium, is probably Nancy's very own thought. This ferocious mystic stubbornly remains in contact, in the dark and blinding night where all medium and all representation are wrecked.

Translated from the French by Irving Goh

1

Introduction: Time in Nancy

Irving Goh and Verena Andermatt Conley

As with every great philosopher, there is something inexhaustible in Nancy's writings. In that respect, one can immediately refer to his prolificacy: indeed, publishing his major philosophical writings since the 1970s, for example, *La Remarque spéculative* (1973), *Le Discours de la syncope* (1976), and *Ego sum* (1979), followed by what Derrida considers to be Nancy's "most powerful works" – *Corpus* (1992), *The Sense of the World* (1993), *The Muses* (1994), and *Being Singular Plural* (1996)[1] – Nancy shows no sign of stopping today, given the appearance of recent titles such as *Tombe de sommeil* (2007), *Identité: fragments, franchises* (2010), *Dans quels mondes vivons-nous?* (written with Aurélien Barreau, 2011), *L'Équivalence des catastrophes* (2012), and *Ivresse* (2013). This is not to mention the great breadth of his writings, which encompasses the history of philosophy (Hegel, Kant, Descartes), aesthetics, ontology, politics, literature, psychoanalysis, religion, and "deconstructive" engagements with philosophical topics such as subjectivity, community, sense, freedom, and the world. The inexhaustibility of Nancy's writings also pertains to the fact that there always remains something to be explicated or elucidated further in his philosophy, which proves critical not only in making sense of contemporary issues, but also in suggesting political and ethical implications for the future of the contemporary world.

This present collection of essays testifies to that inexhaustible force. At the same time, we would also like to think that a certain preoccupation with time forms an implicit backdrop to this collection, thus setting it apart from other collections on the work of Nancy. That preoccupation can be said to exist on at least two counts. Firstly, it is almost inevitable to think of the time of mortality when we think of Nancy, who underwent a heart transplant operation more than twenty years ago. In light of that, we have a greater appreciation of Nancy's prolificacy, reminding ourselves that the inexhaustibility of his writing is neither a given nor absolute: instead, it is always threatened by finitude and contingency. The second instance that gives us occasion to think about time is the collection's title itself – *Nancy Now*. With the "now" of the title, one cannot help but expect this collection to touch in one way or another on the topic of time, especially that of the present. In effect, time is very much at the back of most of our contributors' minds: most of them readily took the cue from the title, which they knew in advance, and evaluate the state of Nancy's philosophy *now*, taking stock of how far-reaching his thoughts are, and assessing the stakes for philosophy and the world today. Or else, they foreground the philosophical motifs mobilized by Nancy in his recent publications and explore their future theoretical and empirical potentialities.

We will speak more about the individual essays later in this introduction. First, we would like to concern ourselves with giving an explication of time in Nancy, which is perhaps one of the most difficult aspects of his philosophy. Time, as a philosophical question, is already no doubt difficult in itself. The difficulty of speaking about time in Nancy becomes particularly striking when one takes into account his reservation in dealing with this topic in any explicit or extended manner in his writings, as compared to his sustained engagement with other topics such as community, sense, touch, *corpus*, and the world, not to mention that all of these apparently privilege the question of space. Symptomatic of this reservation before time is Nancy's "Finite History": there is indeed a discursion into the question of time there, but it is veiled by the question of history, which Nancy argues is still not really so much about time as about community or being-in-common. In that regard, one could say that the question of time constitutes some sort of limit in Nancy's writings, as if one were approaching the impossible in his philosophy. And yet, the limit, as Nancy would say in *The Sense of the World* for example, is not where everything ends. Instead, it is where everything has the chance to begin again, differently. In that case, one could argue that if the question of time is indeed the limit of Nancy's thought, it is perhaps also with the question of time that we could begin again, *now*, to look at Nancy's philosophy anew.[2]

Time for Nancy is not just any time. It is not time past that is of interest to him; neither is it future time, especially not that which is already programmed or calculated beforehand. Time past and time future, according to Nancy, are but "categories [. . .] relevant only to time already interpreted as social and historical."[3] In other words, they are but anthropological constructions, barely touching on time itself, or else concealing its very dimensions. Against such constructions, Nancy is preoccupied with present time, or more specifically, the time *of* the present, *now*, which is not of the order of chronology. Identifying this present that is of specific interest to Nancy does not alleviate the difficulty of speaking about time in Nancy, however. This is because, while Nancy appears, as we will see, to speak more favorably of the present in more recent texts, it is not quite the case earlier on. This is rather evident in the essay "Espace contre temps" (1991), whose title only immediately reinforces the impression that Nancy seems to privilege the concept of space over time. To be precise, though, the essay will make clear that if there is a disenchantment with time, it is not with time itself but exactly with how it has come to be understood and schematized, i.e. time as chronology, or time in endless succession, calculated, accumulated, and ordered, such that each second or even nanosecond must always be followed by the next second or nanosecond. Chronology is not time, according to Nancy: as chronology, time cannot take time, or it cannot have time to exist since it must always move on to the next chronological unit without delay. Time cannot breathe here: chronology or chronometry is "without respiration" or "irrespirable."[4] All this also means that the present in chronology has no real significance except as a step between the past and the future.[5] The very singularity of the present then is always glossed over by an imposed chronometric operativity: it is subject to a *passing* from the past to the future, never allowed to dwell in itself and to see what *happens* to itself in that dwelling.[6] It is this chronological present, which does not allow what arrives in the present *as the present* to take time to happen, that Nancy renounces, calling it even "a bad concept."[7] This is also where Nancy turns his back on (chronological) time and turns toward space instead, especially "free space," where "free disposition of places, openings, circulations of perceptions, conceptions, affections, volitions, [and] imaginations" take place or happen.[8]

The reduction of the present to the "bad concept" of chrono-logic present does not mean that we should henceforth abandon all thoughts of time, especially not time of the present *other* than its chronological conceptualization. That *other* present must still be a subject of thought, except, in "Espace contre temps," it is still articulated in spatial terms. As Nancy argues there, if (non-chronological) present time concerns the instantaneous, then "time itself is space."[9] This is because the instant, according to Nancy, is something spatial, circumstantial, contingent upon how things and beings gather themselves at a particular place: "The instant is not of time: but topical [*topique*], topography, circumstance, circumscrip-tion of a particular arrangement [*agencement*] of places, openings, passages."[10] Given the association between the instant and the non-chronological present, the latter then must also be thought of spatially, as a gap or opening–up, or simply an opening, where its coming-to-presence can happen: "there is only this opening–up [*écartement*] of the present, of its extemporaneous coming."[11] It is in that sense of space allowing the coming of time and the time of the present to take place that Nancy clarifies that "space is therefore against [*contre*] time only to free time," to "let it happen" as a "spa-cious welcome," while "refusing the duration, succession, the rule of causes, retentions, and propensities [*propensions*]" of "compact, unshakeable [*inébranlable*]" chronological time.[12]

But must the thought of non-chronological time, of non-chronological present time, be articulated in spatial terms, as if subordinated to the latter? Can it not be thought in terms closer to temporality, if not in its own terms? That possibility would take some time to materialize in Nancy's writings, and it appears to take shape in his more recent texts. One such instance is in *L'Équivalence des catastrophes* (2012), where Nancy will say unequivocally: "what would be decisive [. . .] would be to think in the present and to think the present."[13] As in the case of "Espace contre temps," Nancy says this in response, or rather in reaction, to chronological time. In *L'Équivalence des catastrophes*, though, Nancy adds to the problematic of what mankind has made of chronological time, or more specifically, what it has projected for human "progress" along the linear, homogeneous trajectory of chronological time. Writing in the wake of the 2011 Fukushima nuclear accident, Nancy has in mind the problematic turn to nuclear power for the supposed greater efficiency in the running of cities. The drive for that power, however, and this is Virilio's thesis as Nancy acknowledges, is only waiting for the general accident to happen, i.e. nuclear fallout, as testified not only by Fukushima in 2011 but also by Chernobyl in 1986. In other words, projecting "progress" in this way only risks sending cities with comparable nuclear ambitions toward similar, catastrophic ends. According to Nancy then, we live in such times where we let slip the present and project a supposed greater and better future, which, unfortunately, only awaits a catastrophe to happen. "Our time," in that case, is but "time capable of an 'end of time.'"[14]

Against such time, where the present is again chronologic, merely passing and therefore without its own temporality or dimension, Nancy calls for another thinking of the present. He calls for a present "in which something or someone presents itself: the present of a coming, an approach."[15] Initially, Nancy would still articulate this present in somewhat spatial terms, as "the element of proximity" or "the place of proximity – with the world, others, oneself," in contrast to the thought of time predicated on 'the end of time,' which "is always distanced [*éloignée*]."[16] This time, though, Nancy would go beyond spatial categories. The non-chronologic present must be thought of as "the non-equivalence of singularities: those of people and those of moments, of places, of a person's gestures, those of the hours of day and night, those of locutions, those of passing clouds, of plants that grow with a learned slowness [*lenteur savante*]."[17] We have then a more literary, or more precisely a Proustian, sense of the present. It is after all Proust who had written that "an hour is not just an hour, it is a vase filled with perfumes, sounds, projects, and climates."[18] The Proustian reference becomes explicit when Nancy goes on to say that this present of non-equivalence "exists by the attention attuned to these singularities – to a color, to a sound, to a perfume."[19] What we have effectively then is a present as a multiplicity of senses. It no longer restrictedly bears a chronometric sense, a chronologic unit awaiting its future projection. It now also bears visual, acoustic, and olfactory sensations, including sensations of touch and movement. One could even follow Nancy to say that the present, in short, is filled with the sense of the world. To be in touch with the non-chronologic present, the present where time is taken for singularities to come to presence, where singularities, including the singularity of the time of the present, have time to breathe, Nancy goes further, saying that it is all a matter of "a particular consideration, an attention, a tending [*tension*], a respect, what one can even go all the way to name an adoration turned towards singularity as such." All this is not subjected to a certain obligation or duty, but moved by a voluntary or even spontaneous esteem for the coming of singularities.[20] Only then can we have the present that "opens itself to the esteem of the singular and [which] turns away from general equivalence and its evaluation of time past and time future, and from the accumulation of antiquities and the construction of projects."[21]

Clearly, we are still rather distant from articulating a non-chronologic present in more temporal terms. We get closer to that perhaps in Nancy's interview with Pierre-Philippe Jandin, published as *La Possibilité d'un monde* (2013), when Jandin poses the question of the present in relation to the Japanese *hanami*, through which one takes time to admire the cherry blossoms, and to which Nancy, following Haruki Murakami, makes reference in *L'Équivalence des catastrophes*. In the interview, Jandin asks Nancy to speak a little about the sense of the ephemeral that one attains through the contemplation of the cherry blossoms, and Nancy's response here touches on the present in more temporal terms. The ephemeral, for Nancy, is not that "which only passes," or which "ends once and for all by conferring everything to a projection of the future that essentially renders it present in advance."[22] Rather, it is something rhythmic, of "moments of absence and presence," close to the quotidian rhythm of sleeping and waking, "a rhythm that is also of day and night," by which "we absent ourselves from the world and return to it."[23] According to Nancy, such a rhythm brings one away from chronological time: "one is no longer in succession [. . .]."[24] In other words, it is a rhythm by which one takes leave from regulated time and from the ordered routine of a life productive of future projects, so as to experience the ephemeral that is opening up in the present. It is the attention to this rhythm that draws Nancy to articulate time in the following manner: "I would readily say that 'time itself' is *tempo*: there is in the latter a very important matter of rhythm."[25]

Deleuze
body
who
organs
Spinoza's
intellectual
love of
God

Tempo, a common term in music, is indeed a time-marker. However, in the musical context, *tempo* not only sets the pace of the music, but also regulates its rhythm, keeping the music in time. In other words, it keeps the music flowing in succession in an orderly manner, not missing a beat. In that regard, *tempo* seems to run counter to Nancy's notion of rhythm. For that kind of arrhythmic rhythm, and to keep to musical references, perhaps it is more accurate to consider certain cadential points in music, for example, where a musical phrase, especially the last, finds its resolution. At times, a *rubato* may be marked just before the resolution of the phrase, allowing the music to deviate from the general regular and regulated *tempo* of the piece and to take its own time. At other times, this *rubato* may be expanded into a *cadenza*, where the music can breathe even more, or take even more time, by revisiting a certain motif of the composition (a *ritornello* here no doubt), contemplating it in a different *tempo* and allowing it to flourish with *bravura* even, hence giving the motif an entirely different air. To put all these in Nancy's terms, *rubato* and *cadenza* can be considered an extended syncope or syncopation with respect to chronometric musical time.[26] They are also no less ephemeral in Nancy's sense, given that the *cadenza* and/or the *rubato* are never permanent digressions, but always eventually return to the principal music or musical phrase. This is also not to mention that the *cadenza* especially is regarded with high *esteem* by both musicians and audiences, which recalls Nancy's claim in *L'Équivalence des catastrophes* that *esteem* is the proper mode of attention to singularities in the experience of the ephemeral. But to return to the question of a different air borne by the singularity of the *cadenza*: perhaps time could be thought in terms of a musical *aria*, which also means "air" in Italian, where all the above-mentioned *rubato*, *cadenza*, and even *tempo*, are at play. It is time's *aria* to which we must listen (*à l'écoute*, as Nancy would say in a text of the same title),[27] an attention to which we may experience the coming to presence, if not witness the *déclosion* or dis-closure,[28] of presents that sidestep chronological time, of presents taking their time with ephemeral *rubati*.

While the term *aria* lets resound the notion of a present that is able to take time to unfold, resonating as well with Nancy's conception of the non-chronologic present as "the time of inaudible songs,"[29] its operatic backdrop might nonetheless appear to privilege or demand a particular sense for the experiencing of ephemeral presents, i.e. the sense of hearing, or even an Italian sense of hearing. To avoid that sensory (and nationalistic) delimitation, should we just simply say *air* then? In both English and French, *air* still retains a musical sense, but it also points to its more quotidian sense: the ethereal matter that not only surrounds us, but also that which we take in in our respiration, in other words, that with which we are always in contact, regardless if we can or cannot hear, see, smell, taste, and even touch.[30] (One underscores here too that if non-chronologic present is "of *inaudible* songs," one does not necessarily have to hear it, in contrast to chronology or chronometry, by which "we hear time ticking away."[31]) As ethereal matter, one could also say that air is nothing tactile or concrete, and yet not nothing, nor without existence. This aspect of air seems to correspond to Nancy's characterization of time in "The Soun-Gui Experience": "Time is taken from nothing. It *is* nothing, and it is made from nothing."[32] Or, if there is always time, and Nancy would say that time "is always here," "its permanence is that of the *nothing* that is hollowed out and turned back on itself to become another nothing: a nothingness that is continually shifting while still remaining the nothingness that it is."[33] That means that the "nothing" that time is is not mere nothingness. Like air, time is there, around us, without us seeing it, without us seeing its passing. In any case, there is a materiality to the "nothing" of time; or, as Nancy puts it, there is [a] "matter of time," and "time is matter that spaces."[34] Furthermore, we sense this matter too, this nothing-that-is-not-nothingness: "A jolt of nothing is continually shaking us. This is the time of presence leaping ahead of itself, an always-new image, always ready to fade away; nothing imaginary but, quite the contrary, the unimaginable real."[35] More than air, shall we then consider time as *areal*? As Nancy notes in *Corpus*, *areal* signifies both a nonempirical or non-deictic real, and an area or perimeter. For our purpose, *areal* captures both breath and breadth, both time and space, where "the distinction between the two is untenable."[36]

Time as *areal* then is where *and* when the non-chronologic present of time can come to presence, take time to exist, or have time to breathe. In the esteem or dis-closure of time as *areal*, however, one must always be vigilant or attentive not to fixate on a particular present, reifying it into an immobile, unchanging, and permanent presence, immanent only to itself. And if we are inclined to call the non-chronologic present a *now*, then this "now [. . .] is not immobilized,"[37] as it "presents the present, or makes it *come*,"[38] always "offering [. . .] itself to another movement of coming."[39] Presence in that case is also never fixed, but is always happening in time, in rhythm, or in *tempo* with all "the *presents* of time that always arrive and always disappear."[40] In other words, the presence of each present is always accompanied by its withdrawal or retreat, just as sleep falls [*tombe le sommeil*] or one falls asleep after a period of wakefulness, or just as the *cadenza* will take its bow to return to the principal music for the resolution of the final cadence, and this is also how the present is ephemeral. Difference is at stake here, for the movement or rhythm of withdrawal is not only in recognition or esteem of *other* presents coming to presence, but also of the self-differentiation of a particular present. Time, if not "time *itself*," even though it is "utterly singular, always the same," is that self-differentiation, or *différance*, deferring and differing (from) itself, such that the "'same' is nothing but the continual movement and change of all time at all times."[41] Or, as Nancy writes in "Finite History," time is but "the radical alterity of each moment of time."[42]

The question that remains then is how to articulate or be attentive to time as *areal* in its "continual movement and change," to
its "radical alterity of each moment." Perhaps, alongside the consideration of time as *areal*, we must give thought to the notion of
à chaque fois or *at each time*, a phrase that Nancy turns to from time
to time in his writings. Sometimes, Nancy just writes *chaque fois* or
each time, and in relation to time, this *chaque fois* pertains to time's
difference, to the other present of time, or to another coming to
presence of another present: "each time another circumstance,
another instant, another topic [*topique*] of the instant."[43] But if
chaque fois concerns a coming to presence (of time, of another
present), then it is also a question of the freedom of existence
according to Nancy in *The Experience of Freedom*: "*each time* it is
freedom at stake, because freedom itself is the stake of 'each time.'
There would be no 'each time' if there were no birth each time,
unpredictable and therefore undeterminable surging, and surprise
of the freedom of an existence."[44] In other words, *each time* reiterates the very fact of freedom of existing, and of existing in ways
surprising to previous moments. For Nancy, the notion of surprise
constitutes the event of the event, or it makes the event an event,
in being the event's unthought-of, unanticipated, and nonpro-
grammed arrival or coming to presence.[45] How then does one
ensure the element of surprise in *chaque fois*, in *each time*? We will
say here that there is surprise only with the preposition *à*, that is to
say, when *chaque fois* assumes its iteration as *à chaque fois*. The French
preposition *à* is important, and this is effectively the case with
Nancy's thought in general. For instance, *à* attaches to the French
noun *attention*, which Nancy mobilizes to describe the regard for
the ephemeral.[46] As we have seen, Nancy also uses the noun *adoration*, and the verb form of *adoration* in less contemporary French in
fact attaches itself to the preposition, as in *adorer à*, which Nancy
is inclined to maintain in *L'Adoration* (2010), the second volume
on *The Deconstruction of Christianity*.[47] That inclination is due to
the semantic force that *à* bears. In itself, *à* can suggest a movement toward (and this is where the English translation into "to"
is precise), if not an opening to something or someone else (as is
the case of *adorer à* according to Nancy), to somewhere else, or
to some other time.[48] In relation to *à chaque fois* then, *à* points not

only to the present of the presence of that "each time," which can be surprising in itself, but also to the surprising opening to another "each time." This is why we insist, as Nancy does sometimes, on *à chaque fois*. *À chaque fois*, after all, is also an important expression for existing, the world, and being-in-common in Nancy's writings. As Nancy says in *La Possibilité d'un monde*, "existence desires to be in the world and be part of the world [*faire monde*]. This happens – or it must be allowed to happen at least – with each existence, *at each time* [our italics] of existence, for and by each existence."[49] Or, as he writes in "Finite History": "*at each time*, what is open[ed] is a *world*, if world does not signify universe or cosmos, but the very place of existence as such."[50] As we know from that same essay, this existence is also never solitary or unitary existence, but always an existing in relation, existing as community, or existing in or as the world, that is to say, the world of being-with or being-in-common, the world where one is always free to arrive *and* to depart. But to return to the question of time: if time for Nancy, as we have seen, is "the radical alterity of each moment of time," Nancy would also say that alterity happens only *à chaque fois*.[51]

It is in respect of the differences at stake *at each time* or in *à chaque fois* that we return to the inexhaustible force of Nancy's writings, especially in the eyes of our contributors. As demonstrated through their essays, there is always something different that we can read in Nancy's philosophy, at each unique time. Indeed, at disparate times, guided by distinct sensibilities that inflect each particular time, we highlight aspects of Nancy's philosophy that previously we did not think urgent or critical. It is in that vein that both Étienne Balibar and Gregg Lambert take on Nancy's question of community, which, as with the question of sense, is time-less for Nancy. According to Balibar and Lambert, Nancy's take on community still requires further explication and affirmation. Balibar revisits the historical signification of Nancy's "inoperative community" [*communauté désoeuvrée*], articulated in 1983, that is to say, three decades ago with respect to the time (*now* in 2013) of our writing this introduction, amidst all the discourses on community and communitarian ideas at that time. While those discourses tend to seek some form of community that is productive of certain defined goals and ends, such as the project to establish *a*, if not *the*, community, Balibar situates Nancy's "inoperative community" as polemically resistant to all these, hence highlighting its seldom acknowledged revolutionary dimension. Indeed, "inoperative community" has no need for any pre-given or fixed ideas of community. That is because "inoperative community" is but the affirmation, just by the fact of our respective existences, of our already being-in-relation with one another, if not our being-in-common, before any work on the part of our subjective consciousness to gather ourselves into, or as, a community. Despite Nancy's reiterations across his *oeuvre* of this fact of existence as an already "inoperative community," we still forget or ignore this fact. We put in place projects that endeavor to construct "better" communities, while neglecting the fact that these projects usually come at a cost to others whom they exclude. It is in order to resist such projects that Balibar insists we must not obscure the revolutionary contour of "inoperative community," even though some of us might find it "the uneasy idea of the revolution qua pure revolution."

It is no doubt with that revolutionary aspect of "inoperative community" in mind that Lambert poses the question of how writing or literature, in Nancy's terms, can approximate itself to a community-without-union or -fusion. Lambert also has time in mind behind the thought of "inoperative community." For him, the fact of "inoperative community" presents itself in a specific non-chronological present (which we have also shown to be at stake in Nancy's conceptualization of time). Lambert refers to Bataille to articulate this present. Following Bataille, he argues that this present is "a time that is founded on nothing other than its own present, which is to say, a present without before or after, without order, which causes us to become dizzy and disoriented, ecstatic in our horizons, beside ourselves in the very present." For him, it is this present, this "dizziness, vertigo, disorientation [that] also defines our passion before every other singular being with whom we share the present in the form of an essential absence of relation." The question then is how writing can inscribe that present and/or that absence of relation. According to Lambert, this is where Nancy's conceptualization of writing, with its double-excision, complements the thought of "inoperative community."

In Lambert's account, the double-excision works by first cutting into, and tearing apart, all myths of unitary communities. A subsequent incision then turns on writing itself, in order to free one from any textual delimitation, opening one instead to the event or experience of community either as it plays itself out in the world beyond all mythic delimitations, or as it emerges from the tearing apart of communitarian myths.

Like Lambert, Georges Van Den Abbeele too is interested in the relation between writing and time. More specifically, though, it is the *form* of writing that informs Van Den Abbeele's inquiry. He revisits Nancy's *Monogrammes*, which were published along a discontinuous time line between 1979 and 1993, and *Chroniques philosophiques*, published in 2004. His concern is whether the monogram is indeed the form of writing adequate to capture the sense or even mood of the present, or else the sense and mood of *now*, which can very quickly become what we call "history," and to which we relate differently as time goes by, hence altering our perspectives on it. In view of that, the question, for Van Den Abbeele, is: "how to give form or shape, then, to this changing relation to history?" At first glance, the monogram seems inadequate to the task, since, written at a specific moment on a particular occurrence or event, both its perspective and rhetoric can easily become untimely in a rather near future: "perhaps the monogram is always already out of date, out of time, anachronistic, unhinged or disjointed like the traces that make up its contours." And yet, in another way, when it does not task itself to make a conclusive remark on something, for example, but insists instead on its strictly intimating or suggestive nature, the monogram can free itself from any specific historical contextualization and open itself to the future, allowing itself to be contemporaneous to any future time. According to Van Den Abbeele, this is when the monogram "remains at the level of a pre-text, a not-yet inscription that is nonetheless a kind of de-lineation of lines; the hint of a determination in and as yet undetermined, incomplete, and unconnected *pinpointing* of place, direction and connectivity." It is on this note that Van Den Abbeele also uses the term *déclosion* to describe such a monogram. In all, Van Den Abbeele does not make a binary distinction between the two possible trajectories of the monogram (one located in an always already past present, and the other always having its sight on the future). Instead, he situates the monogram somewhere in-between the two possibilities, not unlike the Kantian schema, which he notes as "something in-between the understanding and sensibility or perception." We could consider the monogram to be in-between time [*entre-temps*] too, which, according to Van Den Abbeele, "anachronistically thinks the air" – which we have also discussed in relation to Nancy's *tempo* – "we 'now' breathe in common and dare the insurrectional invention of [future] forms," and by which we can unceasingly "make sense" of every *now* at present and in the future.

While Van Den Abbeele looks to the monogram's "de-lineation of lines," Ginette Michaud has other lines in mind. Following Nancy's writings on art, Michaud turns to lines that present themselves in drawing, arguing that it is the lines of drawing that are the form of inscription that could follow sense more adequately. Michaud also suggests that there is something contemporaneous in thinking about drawing, given that drawing has been a topic of interest lately in art circles from around 2010 to 2012 in both the United States and France especially (though Michaud also notes that Nancy's next venture into aesthetics will focus on the notion of color). In any case, she shows that the thought of lines, under the rubric of drawing, reflects Nancy's lines of thought. We thus find Nancy's concern for the philosophical motif of opening [*ouverture*] in drawing, if we take into account, as Michaud does, that drawing, as the beginning of the form of something taking form, is a movement that "goes out in the open," or is the "form of the opening par excellence." When Michaud speaks of lines, especially those that cross, as "interwoven, reticulated" or as a "form of shared presences per se, a conviviality," we also begin to see how such lines connect with the question of community in Nancy. Or, as Michaud argues, the thought of such crossing lines has implications for the thinking of politics – not just the politics of "the being-together or the being-with of democracy," but also one that goes beyond the spatial determination of peoples, which, according to Michaud, "calls for self-deployment in space," where that space "is that of relation, of the 'connection *to*.'" We have already seen the importance of the preposition "to" in Nancy's philosophy, so we will proceed to mention that Michaud relates drawing to a more recent term seen in Nancy's intervention in *Dans quels mondes vivons-nous?*, which is "struction." There, Nancy suggests "struction" as something that is always already in the process of formation, prior to every construction, destruction, and even deconstruction. We add here that "struction" for Nancy is also a question of "inoperative community," or "being-in-common," prior to and in spite of every project of community-building.[52] This is not to mention too, in keeping with the question of time, that "struction" for Nancy there is also "an outside of time at the heart of time," if not "the perpetual flight of the present instant."[53] More precisely, and we quote Nancy at length:

> struction opens less to a past and a future than to a present that is however never realized in presence. It deals with a temporality that can no longer decidedly respond to linear diachronicity. There is something synchronic in it, which means less a cut [*coupe*] across diachronicity than a mode of unity of parts of traditional time that is the very unity of the present as it *presents itself*, as it arrives, takes place, happens. The *happening* is the time of struction: the event whose value is not only that of the unforeseen or of the inaugural – not only the value of rupture or the regeneration of the line of time, but also that of the passage, of the fleeting [*fugitivité*] mixed with eternity.[54]

In Michaud's text, we also find a strong comparison between Nancy and Derrida. One nonetheless needs to respect and affirm the difference or singularity of Nancy's thought, and that is the primary concern of James's intervention. James's endeavor to articulate that difference begins from the notion of technicity, in which both Nancy's and Derrida's philosophy are ineluctably immersed. Technicity clearly underlies the Derridean arche-writing, which Derrida also calls *différance*, and which disseminates according to the logic of its iterability as a trace beyond its spatial and temporal limits. Or, according to James, arche-writing "is conceived as a technical prosthesis, supplement, inscription, or trace that, as an originary instance, acts as a condition of possibility (and impossibility) for presence, voice, meaning and concept." However, one finds a certain renunciation of materiality in the technicity of iterability, since, "as a fundamental opening, temporalization, and spatialization, the technicity of *différance* both precedes human life and consciousness and would continue to iterate, and, as it were, to 'differantiate' long after the disappearance of human life." As James argues, this gives the technicity of Derridean *différance* a "*dematerialized* instance."

In contrast to the Derridean technicity of *différance*, there is the technicity of Nancy's *écotechnie*, which, as Nancy says in *Dans quels mondes vivons-nous?*, is the technical working of nature that sees to the world's own perpetuation, in spite of and despite Man's technological intervention in the world. In James's reading, "the ecotechnical precedes bodies and technical objects even as it is a generalized articulation of the bodily and the technical," and "ecotechnicity is primordially disclosive of experience and of the possibility of a meaningful world." According to James, the critical difference between *écotechnie* and arche-writing lies in the notion of the *areal*, with which *écotechnie* finds itself coexisting originarily. "The areal," as James notes, "is that material space that infinitely exceeds the world of phenomenal appearance or presentation, but which, at the same time, is nothing other than that world." Or, "areality [. . .] precedes sensible spatial extension and opens or discloses it as such, [but], as is very clear, is always engaged with bodies that are 'made' within a generalized ecotechnical set of interconnections." In other words, in contradistinction to Derrida's technicity of *différance*, there is no renunciation of materiality or finitude here; there is no "quasi-transcendental" anxiety, desire, or ambition, but, according to James, a "logic of trans-immanence."

Apart from the need to articulate the difference between Derrida's and Nancy's philosophy, James also makes the point that Derrida's deconstruction must not become some sort of policing discourse that watches over post-deconstructive writings such as Nancy's, seeking to keep them within the discursive boundaries of what it considers to be "properly" deconstructive. The critique of Derridean deconstruction as a policing discourse can also be found in Isabelle Alfandary. For her, misreading [*mélire*], which she finds in Nancy's reading of Derrida, especially in the essay "The Judeo-Christian" in the first volume of *The Deconstruction of Christianism* (2005), might be a potential strategy against that policing. As

Alfandary makes clear, misreading is not about deviating from the text or author in any textually uninformed manner, driven only by the reader's arbitrary idiosyncrasies. Instead, it involves "reading Derrida faithfully (in the name of fidelity to the friend and to the (ad)venture of deconstruction)," which at the same time "implies reading against [Derrida] and exposing the Derridean texts to unforeseen contexts – to a high-risk to-come." Alfandary puts this another way, too: "misreading could be understood as the ultimate and sublime form of fidelity – one that is ready to run every risk up to, and including, injustice." It is only reading as misreading, Alfandary also argues, that there can be a "proper" reading of a text: "misreading would become the paradigm of reading, conceived as a replacement of a text written in the absence of its author." That statement is at the same time revealing of a thought of mortality – this time that of Derrida – that belies the question of misreading. It suggests that "the paradigm of reading" can be fully in place only when the author is no longer present, if not passed on: (mis)reading can have "the effect of a lifting of inhibition" – the inhibition, for example, put in place by decon-struction's policing of post-deconstructive discourses – only "in the wake of the demise of a quasi-paternal figure." According to Alfandary, that "lifting of inhibition" also marks the time of·the reader's sovereignty.

The question of sovereignty in Nancy, particularly the question of being "sovereign otherwise" [*autrement souverain*], is taken up in Irving Goh's contribution. There, he argues that another sover-eignty otherwise of a Schmittian sovereignty, i.e. one that no longer predicates itself on a singular, monarchical sovereign who not only decides on the exception but also monopolizes the use of violent force through that exception, is possible by responding to the earlier question of *who comes after the subject* that Nancy posed sometime in 1986. His response is the *reject*, which perhaps finds some resonances with Giorgio Agamben's prelude to the collection. Agamben there reaffirms Nancy as probably *the* thinker of touch at present; and we recall Balibar's intervention here, as Balibar also suggests that touch is important to the thinking of a community-without-fusion, espe-cially when one keeps in mind Nancy's thinking of touch as the tactful movement of contact *and* withdrawal, never hypostasizing touch into a death grip. Agamben, however, also underscores Nancy's ontology of the ban or abandonment, based on Nancy's earlier essay "Abandoned Being" (1982) in *L'Impératif catégorique* (1983), and this is where the *reject* may be a figure of thought that is close to the notion of abandoned Being. At this point, we note here that abandonment, if not rejection, is related to time in Nancy too. According to him, "time abandons itself: that is its definition."[55] But to go back to the question of the *reject*: it also resonates with Balibar's piece, since, according to Balibar, the question of rejection is not foreign to Nancy's thought of community, as Balibar finds there Nancy's "double rejection" of, on the one hand, the terms individualism and collectivism and the setting up of these terms in binary opposition, and, on the other, Bataille's community of lovers as either exemplary of a community to come or absolutely detached from any society. But perhaps the *reject* can also be found in Nancy's contribution, which closes this present collection. Nancy's piece, written in the form of a dialogue in 2011, reflects on the heart transplant procedure he had twenty years before. The time of mortality haunts this piece. Indeed, all the questions he had surrounding that procedure, i.e. the question of surviving [*sur-vivre*] or existing after the expiration or even unworking [*désoeuvrement*] of one's own, "original" heart, all of which he had explored in *L'Intrus* in 2000 and 2010, preoccupy once again the dialogue. But the dialogue also deals with the question of the intruder and of rejection – not only the intruder in the form of a foreign organ transplanted into oneself, which can reject the body as much as the body can reject it, but also the intruder that is one's own heart, which rejected one's body when it decided to stop functioning. In that sense, there is always also the intruder that is in oneself, acting like an other of oneself, who refuses to coincide with all the enunciations and imaginations that one projects in order to render oneself a fixed, singular *subject*. This intruder, in other words, is always untimely, *at each time*, in relation to one's subjectification.

We will now leave the time of careful reading of each essay to readers. To conclude, we would like to simply return to the notion of *at each time*, or *à chaque fois*, and state that we are still left with the question of inscribing that *à chaque fois*. Should we, following Van Den Abbeele's essay, turn to the monogram? Or, along the lines of Michaud's reading, draw lines, that is to say, lines that are not only the lines of drawing, but also the lines of an inaudible, infinite melody, lines of a "chronomorphic poesy" or of "poetry without letters or words"?[56]

References

Derrida, Jacques. *On Touching – Jean-Luc Nancy*, trans. Christine Irizarry. Stanford: Stanford University Press, 2005.

Nancy, Jean-Luc. "Abandoned Being," trans. Brian Holmes, *The Birth to Presence*, trans. Brian Holmes et al. Stanford: Stanford University Press, 1993, 36–47.

Nancy, Jean-Luc. *The Experience of Freedom*, trans. Bridget McDonald and foreword by Peter Fenves. Stanford: Stanford University Press, 1993.

Nancy, Jean-Luc. "Finite History," trans. Brian Holmes, in *Birth to Presence*, trans. Brian Holmes et al. Stanford: Stanford University Press, 1993, 143–66.

Nancy, Jean-Luc. "The Surprise of the Event," in *Being Singular Plural*, trans. Robert D. Richardson and Anne E. O'Byrne. Stanford: Stanford University Press, 2000, 159–76.

Nancy, Jean-Luc. "The Soun-Gui Experience," trans. Simon Sparks, *Multiple Arts: The Muses II*. Stanford: Stanford University Press, 2006, 207–19.

Nancy, Jean-Luc. "The Technique of the Present: On On Kawara," *Multiple Arts: The Muses II*. Stanford: Stanford University Press, 2006, 191–206.

Nancy, Jean-Luc. "Espace contre temps," in *Le Poids d'une pensée, l'approche*. Strasbourg: Phocide, 2008, 85–8.

Nancy, Jean-Luc. "De la struction", in Aurélien Barrau and Jean-Luc Nancy, *Dans quels mondes vivons-nous?* Paris: Galilée, 2011, 79–104.

Nancy, Jean-Luc. *L'Équivalence des catastrophes (après Fukushima)*. Paris: Galilée, 2012.

Nancy, Jean-Luc. *La Possibilité d'un monde, entretiens avec Pierre-Philippe Jandin*. Paris: Petits Platons, 2012.

Proust, Marcel. *À la recherche du temps perdu*. Paris: Quarto Gallimard, 1999.

2

*Nancy's Inoperative Community**

Etienne Balibar

It is important to recall that 1983, the date when Nancy published his first essay and to which Blanchot reacted immediately,[1] was the year when a number of truly extraordinary books were published. They put the problem of "community," and, more generally, that of "being-in-common," with the antithetic orientations they include (e.g. the antithesis of *communication* and *community*) at the core of their discourse. This is in no way to diminish the original-ity of Nancy's intervention, but rather to explain why it acquired (and keeps acquiring) such an astonishing resonance. Here is a provisional summary.

The same year witnessed in France the publication of Jean-Claude Milner's *Les Noms indistincts*, probably the most remarkable effort on the Lacanian side to renew the problem of "identification" and address the issue of "paradoxical ensembles" (*rassemblements*) as universalistic ensembles made of irreducible singularities.[2] Claude Lefort also had published his collection of essays, *L'Invention de*

* This essay is an edited and abridged version of a seminar taught at the John Hope Franklin Humanities Institute at Duke University in March and April 2009. I express my deep gratitude to the Institute, its members, and its direc-tor at the time, Srinivas Aravamudan, for their wonderful hospitality and their many useful suggestions in the discussions.

la démocratie (1981), where he developed the idea that totalitarian
regimes are those that "fill" the empty place of the democratic
sovereign, and launched the debate on a "politics of human rights"
as permanent insurrection, while in an almost exactly opposite
manner, Regis Debray, in his *Critique de la raison politique* (1981),
addressed the necessity of a "supplement of the sacred" (a civic
religion, in fact) to ground historical and political communities
affected by an intrinsic "incompleteness." And in 1985, Deleuze
published *Cinéma II: L'image-temps* (in which he associated some
of the new cinema in Africa and Latin America with an aesthetics of the "missing people" that went beyond the antithesis of
historical myth and revolutionary consciousness). But above all,
1983 was the year in which Lyotard published *Le Différend*, where
he discussed especially what he called, in quasi-Kantian terms, the
"transcendental illusion" associated with performative uses of the
first-person collective pronoun (as in "We, the people"), a notion
to which Nancy refers, and which also underpins the later critiques
of Derrida against any recourse to categories of the "common" or
of "having in common."[3] This is already impressive. But looking
beyond the French borders, 1983 is also the year when Michael
Walzer published *Spheres of Justice*, considered to be one of the
founding texts of the "communitarian" point of view in contemporary political and moral philosophy. Benedict Anderson published
Imagined Communities, together with other seminal contributions
to the history and political theory of nations and nationalism.
This suggests that similar issues are addressed on the one hand in
speculative terms and, on the other, in empirical terms. And if we
are willing to expand the time frame slightly, we can add a couple
more significant references: first and foremost, Jürgen Habermas's
Theorie des kommunikativen Handelns (1981), which, taken together
with Lyotard's *La Condition postmoderne* (1979), would introduce
what I call here the "conjuncture of 1983," a pragmatic question
of "communication" involving the technological as well as the
ethical and the political. Without these references, we would not
understand why Nancy was eager to retrieve in Bataille a concept
of "communication," which is every bit opposed to the emergent
discourse of "communicative action" – being independent of both
rationality and the norms of civility.[4]

All this is certainly not sufficient to define concepts, but it indicates a conjuncture where both the *construction and the deconstruction of community* are central questions, to be addressed from opposite philosophical points of view. The semantics of the name becomes subjected to a kind of *écartèlement* or dissection. This is rooted indeed in philology and history: from "common," one can derive *community*, but also *communion* (whether religious or aesthetic), *communication*, *common-wealth* (a classical name for the "republic", the community of the citizens), *communism*, and *communitarianism*. Altogether, they delineate not only a semantic network but also a field of ideological tensions.

Some historical dates are also useful to remember here. I will inject three of them. First, there is 1968: the whole debate is haunted by the memory of events that combined the evidence of the internal decomposition of state communism and the spectacle of the spontaneous uprisings and new emancipatory movements in search of a common language in the realm of imagination and fiction. Nancy and Blanchot will recall it as the irruption into history of one idea of "communism" when another one becomes a living corpse. Then, there is 1981: in France, this was the year of the election of a "socialist" president, which raised immense hopes of "change." But in the United States, it was the election of Ronald Reagan to the presidency, who declared not only communism and socialism, but also every collective or "public" intervention in the economy, anathema. It had been preceded by the arrival of Margaret Thatcher as prime minister in the United Kingdom who famously declared that "there is no such thing as community." Finally, there is 1989 that in France marked the usual return of debates about revolutionary principles (equality, liberty, fraternity), but that above all coincided with the actual collapse of "really existing" communism (with the "exception" of China . . .). Soviet communism may have already been a living corpse, but a dead one is something else, the more so as it can start "returning" as a specter or a ghost, as Derrida would explain a few years later, suggesting that, after neoliberal capitalism had triumphed in a seemingly irresistible manner, what would begin was the haunting of this triumph by its dead other. . . .

I conclude that the background to our debate is a conjuncture in which the development of "individualistic" ideologies and the corresponding reduction of the political to a juridical formalism call for a critique that can no longer be achieved in terms of existing models of communism, but whose renovation can take the route either of a discourse of *communication* or a discourse of *communitarianism*, and finally a discourse of a *communism to come*, which all react against the history of twentieth-century communism. It is in this conjuncture that we will return to "the debate within the debate." Starting with Nancy's original essay on community, it took the form of a reconstruction of Bataille's ideas about the *desire of community*, and a *communication* opposed to the Hegelian (and Marxian) idea of a "collective praxis" that *produces the common* – and therefore the political – in an immanent manner.[5] To name this project, Nancy borrowed from Blanchot the category of *désoeuvrement* ("unworking" or "inoperative"), and he described the result as a "negative community," insisting in quasi-Heideggerian terms on its "finitude," whereby it is associated not with communion or eternal life, but with the experience of death, as was already the case in Bataille's conception of love. It is not surprising that Blanchot, among other reasons, would react to this essay in part to clarify his notion of *désoeuvrement* and the possibilities it opened to connect literature and politics. Hence his "replica" (*La Communauté inavouable*), plus Nancy's "replica to the replica," represented by the new chapters of "*Inoperative community*" (published in 1986), and, with some delay, Derrida's *post-factum* rejoinder (in the "seminars" later published as *Politiques de l'amitié* (1994), which altogether created a *displacement* of the problem of the political, where the deepest divergences emerge from the closest affinities and agreements.[6]

I will now return to Nancy's formulations, which I think can be organized in the form of four constellations:

> *First constellation*: the critique of "immanentism," a generic term that Nancy substituted as a name for the principle that transforms communities into a "work of death." I believe that it was largely deployed as a reaction to the work of Claude Lefort on *totalitarianism* as the reversal of a democracy whose "empty center" (which is also the place of the impossible representation of the common) would become filled with

a material or symbolic "incarnation" of the Sovereign.[7] To be sure, Nancy makes an idiosyncratic use of the category "immanence," where its antithesis is not "transcendence," but "communication" in the ecstatic sense proposed by Bataille.

Second constellation: the category of the *relation*, which in the metaphysical tradition was always secondary to that of "substance" or "subject." Nancy's understanding of the "ecstatic relation" assumes that in the *pros ti* of the relationship (its "toward it/ what/whom"), the *ti* (or the *tina*: someone, somebody), albeit always implicitly human, remains essentially indeterminate: an "escaping other" who is irreducibly *singular*. This entails a complete recasting of the ontological discourse, albeit not, from Nancy's point of view, a departure from ontology since it is only by proposing an alternative ontology that you can radically challenge the opposition of the "individual" and the "community" as mirroring images of self-sufficiency, which necessarily arise from the classical ontology of the subject. It would be in agreement with a reading of Heidegger's "existential ontology" that radicalizes his critique of the transcendental subject, while avoiding its incarnation in the figure of the *Mitsein* or "being together."

Third constellation: Blanchot's *désoeuvrement* as the horizon that allows us to read Bataille's concept of the *sacred* (therefore his reversal of classical figures of sovereignty) as the permanent exposure of community to its own destruction from the inside, or else in terms of its own radical finitude – again a convergence with Heidegger's discourse, provided we include a critical discussion of their antithetic understandings of the anxious exposure to death, more precisely the "death of the other."

Fourth constellation: Bataille's other theme, *la communauté des amants* [the community of lovers], and its generalization as the limit-experience (or the experience of limits) that evokes the idea of a deconstructive "community without community," or a sharing that can never really be shared – the essential "solitude" of singularities never to become *identified*, or transformed into complementary *parts* of a single whole or totality. It also therefore provides a principle of *resistance* against "immanence" that at the same time *comes from within* community and *objects to* it (to its sacralization, its hypostatization). The community of lovers would appear as irreducible to "immanence," albeit without bringing in any "transcendence" (and in fact it would only be the experience that it provides – the "desire" that it embodies – that would allow us to disrupt this traditional symmetry).

This schematic summary makes it possible for me to identify some important turning points in Nancy's original essay (1983) that will inform the discussion to follow. At the opening of Nancy's essay, it is important to notice the reference to Sartre's celebrated formula on Marxism as an "unsurpassable horizon of our time."[8] Nancy joins the Althusserian critique of every form of communitarian humanism, albeit for contrary reasons: not in the name of a Marxist science, but in the name of the "desire to discover or rediscover a place of community at once beyond social divisions and beyond subordination to techno-political dominion," whose emblematic name would be "communism." In fact, he tries to reopen the dilemma wrongly formulated as an opposition between humanism and antihumanism, which does not allow us to understand the "unbearable burden" carried by the name "communism" today. On the one hand, communism is a dream of redemption, the remedy for a death deprived of meaning (should we say the malady of death?). On the other hand, it stands in absolute contradiction to the political (and historical) reality of "communism" as *state* communism. The root of this contradiction is to be looked for in the understanding of communism as a self-realization of the common essence of the human through economic transformations, therefore a combination of *humanism* and *economicism*.[9] "It was the very basis of the communist ideal that ended up appearing most problematic: namely, human beings defined as producers . . . and fundamentally as the producers of their own essence in the form of the labour of their work." At the roots of "totalitarianism" (or the fusion of the political community into a mystical body around the sacralized or bureaucratized figure of the leader) is "immanentism." But immanentism is not proper to communism. In fact, the communism that "betrays" the dream of emancipation is the one that "absolutizes" modernity or democracy as the self-realization of the human (on this point, Nancy does not disagree with Lefort).

Hence the question: why is it impossible to think of the community as the common action/operation of "human" individuals (and conversely of individuals as expressions or parts of the community)? This is because community can fulfill its desire, or live up to its desire, only inasmuch as it represents for the individuals an exposure to what Bataille had called a *déchirure* (translated into English as "rupture," or "being separated," but bearing a meaning that is in fact more radical: being *internally torn apart*, experiencing the separation from their "own" being). This is what, under the umbrella category of *ecstasy* and the wordplay that it allows ("ecstatic experiences" of pleasure and pain, and "ek-static" existence in time), permits Nancy to bring together a reference to Bataille and a reference to Heidegger, and to propose a joint criticism of *individualism and collectivism*, both of which essentially ignore ecstatic being and *déchirure*, while promoting a metaphysical model of self-sufficiency. Bataille's violent separation of the "human" from itself as *a form of relation* to the other performs a simultaneous critique of individualism and communitarianism as "immanent" or "self-reproducing," that is to say, self-sufficient beings, or *subjects*. But we can notice right away that the proposed equivalence between the two languages, however partial, is not innocent: it also involves a departure from the *anthropological* understanding of Bataille's categories that he always retained (such as sovereignty, the "sacred" and the "religious," the "exchange" and the "expenditure", etc.) and a "translation" of these categories into an *ontological* understanding: "And so, Being "itself" comes to be defined as relational . . . *as community* . . . *Community, or the being-ecstatic of Being itself?* That would be the question." But we may also add that this "translation" produces a never-ending tension: it means that the Heideggerian problematic of Being remains subjected to an experience of *déchirure* that is far more violent than any notion of existential anxiety or *Sorge*.

Let us now pass to the philosophical consequences that Nancy derives from the idea of communism as a "transgressive" experience incompatible with the Marxian eschatology of the "end of history," which in fact only a *literary experience* could match. In these developments, he is concerned with a consideration of the aporia of community in Modern Philosophy, which is centered on Rousseau and Heidegger – that is to say, through an unusual comparison, on the intrinsic relationship between love and death in the representation of community, whose major political expression is *patriotism*, allowing it for a state and a people to become fused in a single "communitarian" idea. According to Nancy, Rousseau, and Heidegger, in parallel ways, *reversed* what could be considered the primary logic of their systems. Rousseau seems to be a nostalgic theorist of the loss of an originary community, but in fact he proves to anticipate a much deeper recognition that the community as such is not "lost," but arises *in the form of a loss*, absence or absent common substance. (Nancy will later write: "Rousseau was the first . . . the thinker par excellence of compearance."[10]) Conversely, Heidegger who seems mainly to be a theorist of the inconsistency of the subject, in fact sacrificed his deconstructive views for a project, if not a decision, to identify the meaning of "being for death" with the archi-authenticity of one people's (namely, the "Greek-German people") "community of fate." The crucial experience resides, accordingly, in the interpretation of death as "the other's death," which affects the subject and disrupts it. Or else: either it dissolves the subject's self-consciousness, pushing it to an unbearable limit (as is precisely the case in Bataille with the seminal "inner experience" of the eroticized contemplation of images of torture), or it generates an elation of the subject from the individual enunciation of the "I" to the collective enunciation of the "We." We should understand, I believe, that this "operative" form (which could also be understood as *work of death*) is precisely the figure under which the community is *narrated*, in order to "close the circle," or to recreate *in the future* the "transparency" or "fraternity" that was lost imaginarily at the origin.[11] This is what Nancy himself – probably borrowing from discussions with Lyotard before the publication of his own book – would call the "transcendental illusion" of the community, which takes the form of institutional "We utterances." This is also what indicates the possibility of a *bifurcation*. Once again, Bataille provides a crucial indication: his literary account of the irreducibility of the *death of the other* as a limit or "inner" experience, or the "truth" that disrupts every humanism and theologism, presents us with a reality that *cannot be sublimated* or "overcome," an experience of finitude as such.

In the central paragraphs of his essay with epigraphs from *Acéphale* or the headless "literary community" fantasized by Bataille, we observe the development of a critical reading of Bataille in which his analysis of the "sacred" or the transgressive phenomena of "sovereign desire," both antinatural and anti-economic, is tentatively separated from Bataille's discourse on "subjectivity" and from his nostalgia for archaic forms of power as recourse against the utilitarian ideology of modernity. This would call for a detailed confrontation with Bataille's texts, in which "sovereignty" is essentially described as *non-power*, or *renunciation of power*, or demise from power (abjection), therefore producing a fissure within the archaic images of sovereignty. Nancy would associate the critique of this nostalgia – which he believes he finds in Bataille, despite Bataille's most profound tendency – with an increasing awareness of the failure of historic communism, as a form of "anti-individualism" that is itself utilitarian and productivist, and therefore humanist. This leads to a rigorous critique of every form of "communitarianism" or community as "participation," such as membership or belonging to a substantial "common good," be it material or symbolic: "thinking its insistent and possibly still *unheard* demand, beyond communitarian models or remodellings." What is striking in such a "Bataille pushed to the limits of Bataille himself" is a short-circuiting of formulations concerning *sovereignty* as the "exposure to nothing," or the "risk of the nothing," and the "impossible" equivalence of equality and liberty, which, at least in a French context, evoke the Revolution itself, where Sovereignty and Revolution are reverse sides of the same medal. This short-circuiting determines the central idea of "ecstatic community" as that excessive movement which disrupts and dislocates the self-sufficiency of every "subject" without (or without yet) "filling the gap" with a compensatory representation of the good. It is the uneasy idea of the revolution qua pure revolution, reduced to its insurrectional moment and independent from its political goals . . . .[12] With this reference, we are in a position to better understand how the key terms *finitude, désoeuvrement, partage* are correlated. These notions go together because each is the condition for the combination of the other two, but on the condition that each presents itself in antinomic terms, i.e. as the negation of what they "commonly" mean: "the similar is not the same (*le semblable n'est pas le pareil*) . . . community is that singular ontological order in which the same and the other are similar: that is to say, in the sharing of identity." This is described not so much as a "fact" than a "passion". It is exactly what Derrida will repeatedly object to . . . But it is also where Nancy, with Bataille, will "hesitate" between the terminologies of *community* and *communication*, or rather, he will use both against their common uses, in order to explain what a "common" that implies having nothing in common could be, i.e. nothing representable, substantial, objective, durable, recognizable . . . except the communication of limit-experiences of finitude itself.[13] This is what ultimately Nancy calls *comparution* or "compearance" as exposure to the exteriority of the other prior to any "bond," including the political bond (the *zôon politikon*). We might say that it is "archipolitical", in either of two meanings: it could represent an essential community beyond politics (if it forms, above all, an "origin") or it could represent an anti-community that "interrupts" politics, in the form of an event, or a moment (e.g. an "absolute" revolutionary moment). Nancy will have to choose between these two possibilities, and the fact that the choice, or the distinction, is not easy will be reflected in his continuous return to the issue, rephrasing it as the "negative community" as such.[14] But the reference to Blanchot would already point in the direction of the second possibility, rather. *Désoeuvrement* would be the true name and solution to the riddle of what Bataille called in his anthropological language *le sacré* (the sacred) It would replace a dichotomized separation of realms (sacred and profane, transgression and normality, exception and rule) and the idea of jumping from one realm into the other, with the idea of an *internal void* or negativity that destroys *from within* any "collective work" as communitarian project, or the production of one's unity, by unraveling or disclosing its own excess or incompleteness. The allegoric figure of this internal disruption, at the borders of the sacred, eroticism, and revolution, is *crime*: the Sadean idea of a society or "republic" based on crime; or the antinomic notion of a substitution of transgression for the rule of law, which reveals their secret complicity, not to say identity, and which Blanchot had commented upon in his reading of Sade's revolutionary pamphlet *Français encore un effort* . . .[15] Is this also not the point of Bataille's own misrecognition, where he proves to be not entirely liberated from a metaphysics of the "free" subject (qua transgressive subject, who is absolutely liberated from prejudices, obligations, constraints)? Not quite, in the end, precisely because his *non-Sadean* notion of the "community of lovers" points in the direction of a different understanding of "transgression," whose "subject" (if it is one) is not a hero (not even an infamous one), but a relationship or *compearance.*[16]

We are thus prompted to comment on Nancy's final developments, where he returns to the issue of Bataille's equivocal fascination with the "archaic" or premodern, pre-utilitarian forms of community inasmuch as they build their mythical representation around the *sacralization* of their own violence (nonproductivity as excess or expenditure). How can Bataille escape a repetition of this mythical element (*"in spite of Bataille, and yet with him . . ."*)? What is it that, in his texts, leads to an internal dissolution of the idea of the *sacred*, which is at the same time a necessary path for the critique of the "transcendental illusion" of the "We," inasmuch as it shows that "immanence" can also become projected into a *transcendent* realm? What is it that leads to "the sacred stripped of the sacred"? What is it that *makes the difference* between the "sacred" as *sacrificial* murder or staging of the murder of the Sovereign, and the "finite exposure to death"? According to Nancy, this is the recurring model of the *communauté des amants*, which in reality forms an *anti-community*. It is the true locus of the desire of community, or the locus of the *partage* both in the sense of a crucial experiment and exposure to "nothing." We cannot but ask the question: is this not the archi-mythical romantic idea of "fusion in death" of the lovers who form one in two, which is also the permanent reference (not so hidden in fascist regimes) for the representation of the political bond of the community *as a bond of love* (be it mutual love among the citizens, or love of the citizens for the country, or for the leader, or all of that)? Isn't it haunted by the idea or the myth that the *achievement of love is a Liebestod* as in Tristan and Isolde, to which Blanchot will return, or *sacrifice of love* as in Héloise and Abelard? There is one element, however, that explicitly goes in the opposite direction, against every form of sublimation: this is Nancy's reference to the paradoxical experience of *touching* as a *material* but also *elusive* phenomenon. *Le toucher des corps* must be compared with this remark: "in the City, men do not embrace."[17] In the end, he apparently has some difficulty relating the analysis he proposes with a "political" practice or orientation.[18] However, one cannot say that Nancy has "forgotten" the issue of communism, or "retreated" into a "meta–political" discourse, where the name "communism" as a political name would become irrelevant. This is because of the reference to the idea of *resistance* that is associated with *désoeuvrement* and gives it an "active" meaning (and there are probably here implicit references to the problematic of *in-soumission* with which Blanchot himself at some point, during the Algerian war, linked *désoeuvrement* and resistance).[19] Does Nancy suggest it to pass, with Blanchot, from a Bataille of transgression to a Bataille of resistance? And yet, there must always remain an element of transgression in resistance because revolution (or democracy) is the limit of politics just as eroticism is the limit of love. It is the limit of the *communauté des amants* that the lovers *strive not to escape*, from which they would not "hide" themselves in the rituals of love as a "private" or "family" matter. Still, I would say, there is something not only enigmatic, but problematic, in the "experiences" that Nancy brings together in order to illustrate the idea of a *communauté sans communauté*. In several passages, it is a question of the "resistance" of the community in the form of singularities or differences perceiving each other before death in the concentration camps. And it is generally the "phenomenology of love," which, again, and this is important for the understanding of the *negativity* at stake here, is related not so much to the rather banal idea of the *impossibility of fusion* than to *love as quest for the limit*, which would precisely be the "touching" or the impossible fusion, a limit that is reached or experienced in a painful manner in the experiences of absolute love: perhaps as a glimpse of destruction or death in the middle of bliss. Nancy is certainly right in describing the kiss as the privileged allegoric case of this experience, which really illustrates *partage* in the oxymoronic sense of the French term (sharing/being separated). The lovers are divided or separated in the very moment in which they are "sharing themselves," or uniting.

I will add two remarks on this point. First, what is conceptually (and perhaps also morally) problematic is also illuminating as a conceptual "topography": I am thinking of Nancy's insistence on the *double rejection* of the idea of "love" or a "community of lovers" as a "kernel of society" (in the bourgeois sense, but it was already there in Aristotle, as Derrida will insist) *and* as an "anti-society" in the romantic sense. This is consistent with the idea of "resistance" as a disruptive or irreducible movement within the community. Second, there is a latent problem with this "rectified reading" of Bataille that puts aside his "ambivalent" fascination for self-destructive sovereign power, which betrays a "remainder" of nostalgia for the "lost community." Nancy stresses that the problem of "sovereign" cruelty joins the problem of the "work of death" that combines fascism and eroticism as alienated forms of the denial of finitude, which are neither instances of "communication" nor of the "literary" in that sense. Should we say that, to avoid the possibility of fascism, or its dangerous vicinity, Nancy has considerably *reduced* the function of eroticism and cruelty in his presentation of the "community of lovers"? I am not going as far as suggesting that his view of this community of lovers is too "Christian," but I do believe that Blanchot reacted to that possibility, and it was one of his reasons for granting a central role to the commentary of Marguerite Duras's short story (*La maladie de la mort*), an *erotic novel*, perhaps in the manner of a parody, and for discussing more precisely the "communitarian" experiences of Bataille based on a transgressive conjunction of "private" passions and "public" (or secretly public) concerns: *Contre-Attaque, Acéphale*, and the *Collège de Sociologie . . .*

To summarize, what I have emphasized thus far is:

(1) The trajectory of Nancy's essay is a critical movement passing from a representation of community (called "humanist" or "immanent"), which sees it as the common work of individuals who are overcoming their separation (or individualism), to an aporia of community, which is the exact negative of this positivity. It rests on a *double rejection* of "individualism" as atomism, and

"collectivism" as holism or totalitarianism, both of which form two sides of the same medal, namely the metaphysical representation of the subject as self-sufficient reflective unity underlying its own properties, thus "mastering" or "organizing" its own relations and communications. This double rejection is performed in the name of a questioning about the originary aperture of the singular to its opposite (other), which is always exterior to it. It is based on a simultaneous reading of Bataille's *déchirure* (or violent separation from oneself) and Heidegger's *ek-static being* of the *Dasein* (being "there" means being "thrown" into the world in a radically contingent manner, which Nancy understands as being immediately "exposed" to the otherness of the other).[20] In a sense, community is not a "problem to solve," no more than it is a result or a good to achieve through work or *praxis,* as Sartre would believe it after Hegel (and Marx), because it is always already "resolved." Rather, it inheres in the aporetic form of an "impossible" completion, a completion of the impossible unity or fusion that will never take place as such in the "reality" of institutions, but only as its own "desperate" or "anxious" *lack,* which is also its own irrepressible desire. This is where the "bifurcation" of authenticity and inauthenticity takes place: acknowledging or denying the finitude or incompleteness of the community.

(2) The "ontological" modality of this originary community (the community that "unworks" its own work in order to retrieve the authentic relation as resisting its own "subjectivation," is called in different ways (apart from the pure negative formulas: community without a community, etc.). Essentially it is called *communication* in Bataille's sense, which particularly emphasizes the logic of "relating to" and "sharing with"; and it is called *compearance,* which particularly emphasizes the "ontological" primacy of a "shared presence," the "immediate presence" of something that will remain inexorably absent, or elusive (an idea "schematized" in the phenomenology of touching as elementary experience of what we might call the "intimate separation," or the intimacy of the separation). It can be noted that both terms form antitheses to the (religious, aesthetic or political) idea of "communion." But the second allows it to understand better the otherwise disturbing idea of a communication that includes neither reflexivity nor

reciprocity, that is to say, neither a meeting with oneself, nor a meeting with an image of oneself, a "recognition" of the *alter ego*.

(3) There are two great *bifurcations* – "ontological" but also "ethical" – that are involved in this construction. They are latent in the sinuous critical confrontations with Bataille, or attempts at reading "Bataille against Bataille." The *first bifurcation* concerns the authentic or inauthentic community as a "relation to death." The *second bifurcation* concerns the authentic or inauthentic community as a "perfection of love." Indeed, it is their overdetermination that concerns the political, as indicated by permanent references to fascism as the "extreme" realization of the communitarian model of the institution of the "We," and the politization of the affect, which is replicated, if at a lesser degree, in many other political regimes, for example, communism as state communism, and democratic republics that are staging their popular or "patriotic" unity. This is also a negative way, at least, to understand that, from the point of view of the community, *"death" and "love" are not separate issues.*[21] Let us be more precise, in posing our final questions.

What does the "bifurcation," associated with the reflection on community as relation to death, establish? There are two sides to this, each opposing the other. On one side, there is a representation of community built around death, or even built *upon* the symbolism of death as *sacrifice*, particularly the "Christian" narrative of the articulation of death and resurrection as sublimated presence, eternity, and the idealization of the notion of incarnation.[22] But in fact, for Nancy, this production of the sacred in terms of sacrifice is anything but purely Christian.[23] It is always mythical, but it is not purely "ancient." On the other side, there is what we would call a "finite" experience of death, or an experience of the finitude of death, as the *absolute limit of symbolization and idealization*, which does not recover the full meaning that the notion of the sacred bears, but just the opposite – should we say the "kenosis"? That would raise again the issue of a "religious critique of the religious" . . . – or the actual impossibility of "making sense of" (as the myth of resurrection makes sense of the event of death). I am tempted to say that this is also one point that Blanchot, with the help of a different understanding of the "death of the other" (drawing on

Levinas), but also revisiting it in the romantic tradition, will try to complicate further. . . .[24]

And what is the bifurcation associated with the "perfection of love"? Again, we are faced with a dilemma. *Either* the scheme of "fusion" of the two into one single being, which the common concept of love associates not only with the overcoming of finitude (since there seems to be something actually "infinite" in the experience of love, or at least it is dreamt of that way), but also with the overcoming of the *intellectuality* of the human (or social) relationship, which establishes or re-establishes the primacy of "affect."[25] *Or* the "ek-static" experience of the lovers who "share" in a devastating manner (certainly again physical, but not necessarily devoid of *thinking*) their incapacity to become *one and the same*: to "understand" each other, to "live" within one another, to remain "indivisible." Although Nancy does not use the word, there is clearly a "melancholic" element here, which Derrida will take up in his theory of friendship as the anticipated mourning of the friend. But above all, there is the idea of a radical and paradoxical "solitude," proper to the experience of love, because the lovers experience their separation "only for themselves," or, *they share it only with themselves, and nobody else*. It is this despair of oneness that they really have in common. One wonders, of course, if this is only another modality, perhaps "negative," of the melancholic element that is always there in the romantic idea of love. Therefore, it is crucial to assess the place of the *erotic element*, which carries love away from the notion of "pleasure" in the direction of *enjoyment*, a jouissance of shared separation rather than imaginary fusion, which Nancy both includes and displaces, or perhaps seeks to limit, for much the same reasons as he seeks to limit the importance of the "sacred" and the "archaic."[26]

References

Balibar, Etienne. *Citoyen Sujet et autres essais d'anthropologies philosophiques.* Paris: PUF, 2011.

Blanchot, Maurice. *L'Entretien infini.* Paris: Gallimard, 1969. *The Infinite*

Conversation, trans. Suzanne Hanson. Minneapolis: University of Minnesota Press, 1993.

Cadava, Eduardo, Connor, Peter and Nancy, Jean-Luc (eds), *Who Comes after the Subject?* New York and London: Routledge, 1999.

Nancy, Jean-Luc. *La Communauté désoeuvrée.* 2nd edn. Paris: Christian Bourgois, 1986.

Nancy, Jean-Luc. *Une Pensée finie.* Paris: Galilée, 1990.

Nancy, Jean-Luc. *L' "il y a" du rapport sexuel.* Paris: Galilée, 2001.

Nancy, Jean-Luc. *La Déclosion. Déconstruction du christianism 1.* Paris: Galilée, 2005.

Nancy, Jean-Luc. *La Communauté affrontée.* Paris: Galilée, 2011.

Nancy, Jean-Luc. *Politique et au-delà: entretien avec Philip Armstrong et Jason Smith.* Paris: Galilée, 2011.

3

"Literary Communism"

Gregg Lambert

In the following reflections on the philosophy of Jean-Luc Nancy, I will address the theme of "community" (including the literary and philosophical form of "negative community") that appears frequently in his writings throughout the period of the mid-1980s. Here, I am specifically referring to the writings collected in *La Communauté désoeuvrée* (1986), which take as their overt subject a conception of community that is found in the prewar writings of Georges Bataille, the French sociologist, philosopher, bibliophile, and co-founder between 1937 and 1939 of Le Collège de Sociologie. In *La Communauté affrontée* (2001), Nancy himself describes this period of his work actually beginning in 1983 with the publication of the original essay version of *La Communauté désoeuvrée* in a special issue of *Alea* around the themes of the "community" and the "number" (i.e. the mass, the crowd, but also addressing the new political concepts of the assemblage, the multiplicity, and the multitude). As he recounts, the return to Bataille's concept of community, and particularly to the early writings on the "sacred sociology" and the "absence of myth," was an effort "to discover another possible resource for the concept of the political."[1]

Before this moment, Nancy writes, "community was a word

that was ignored in the discourse of thinking."[2] In other words, philosophical discussions of the concept of community were infrequent and mostly took place in the public press around the formation of the European Union, especially with the passing of the Single European Act in 1986; moreover, from the immediate postwar period through the end of the Cold War, the Left had maintained an allergic reaction to any mention of this theme, given the historical association with the German *Volksgemeinschaft*. (For example, Nancy reports that the 1988 German translation of *La Communauté désoeuvrée* was labeled "Nazi" by a leftist journal in Berlin.) However, following this period and coinciding with the dissolution of the Soviet Union in 1991, Nancy also describes a sudden and dramatic shift in the polarity of the concept's meaning over the next ten years, as a result of which the term is gradually associated with the "return of/to communism" in France and Italy through the writings of Agamben and Esposito, or else with the positive aspirations of the multitude and a new "communitarian" discourse in the United States following the publication of Hardt and Negri's *Empire* in 2000.

By drawing a circle around these three decades – the 1930s, the 1980s, and the 1990s leading up to the current moment – I am highlighting a certain return of and to the theme of "community" in each historical moment, a theme that in each case either privileges, on the one hand, the communist community and communism, or, on the other, a quasi-religious secondary community or "community of affect" (*Bund*) as primary sociological notions. (In other words, perhaps the multiple returns *of* and *to* "community" may be a more accurate determination of the underlying issue in what is often and, in my view, mistakenly referred to as "the return of religion" in western philosophy.)[3] Taking account of all these transformations over a brief twenty-year period, Nancy himself summarizes the different and even opposite meanings that are ascribed to the concept as the expression, symptomatically, of a more fundamental problem confronted by modern leftist political theory in general: the impossibility of founding the concept of the political on an actual instance of community; more precisely, the problem of establishing the rights of a particular expression of community on the basis of a politics that is assumed *a priori* to be truthful and just.[4]

In Bataille's own sociological research from the 1930s, the anthropological and religious notions of the sacred and sacrifice are explored to raise the possibility of an "abandonment" of the form of individuality to the group (as an act of donation, or as a gift) in a manner that is fundamentally different from the idea of "substitution" of individual identity for the identity of the leader in modern fascism, or the negation of individual particularity for the collective identity according to the communist ideal. Nevertheless, Bataille's notion of community is offered as a critical rejection of the sociological principles belonging to the formations of fascism and communism in his time, even though he retains the essential problem of community that is at the basis of each political form.[5] Perhaps the immediate distinction we might make concerning the return to these themes in the 1980s is that in the postwar societies of France and Germany, and especially for a younger generation of intellectuals, any discussions of the sacred would immediately evoke an association with the community of fascism, and thus, would simply be "unthinkable" in all the senses that this term implies – unless, that is, it was presented in the form of a "negative community," as in the case of Nancy's writings. As for the idea of communism, in addition to assuming a more progressive and discursive form of "communitarianism," as already mentioned above with regard to the works of Hardt and Negri, it has either evolved into a utopian expression of "the coming community" (Agamben) – that is, into yet another expression of negative community, if not simply negative theology in Agamben's case – or, in the case of Badiou's "return to communism," into a more millenarian and "post-leftist" expression of "elective community" (i.e. "elective fidelity to the event") that in some ways recalls the motives behind Bataille's own communitarian projects in the 1930s. In this regard, we might recall the epigraph from the first issue of *Acéphale* that appeared in 1936, taken from Kierkegaard's comment on the revolution of 1848: "What looks like politics and imagines itself to be politics, will one day reveal itself to be a religious movement."[6]

Finally, a third development that appears specifically in Nancy's resuscitation of Bataille's writings during the 1980s, which will be the primary focus of my reading, is the manner in which Nancy

sometimes reduces some of the excesses that belonged to Bataille's
original themes of community and the sacred (including ecstatic
and intoxicated states of ritual experience) to the more "literary"
forms of depersonalization and subjective abandonment that will
determine the experience of "literature" – or "writing" [*écriture*],
that is, if we adopt, as Nancy suggests, "the acceptation of this
word [today] that coincides with literature."[7] Here, we find the
basis for Nancy's proposal of a "literary communism," one in
which neither "communism" nor "literature" should be understood in their habitual linguistic or overtly ideological senses, since
it would not necessarily assume the form of a community of letters,
but rather refers to a community that constitutes its understanding
of "being-in-common" through the experience of writing and
"the communication of works." This "coincidence" that Nancy
inscribes into the concept of community informs my interroga-
tion of the subjacent concepts of "literature, or writing" from this
period. Given that this emphasis on literary community in some
important ways contradicts Bataille's own view of the revolutionary possibilities that belonged to the literary movements of his
own time (e.g. "the Surrealist community"), I have also chosen to
reformulate Bataille's earlier reproach, cited as the first epigraph to
this essay, as a question: Can "literature" (or "writing" today) again
assume the task of directing collective necessity?[8]

The "absence of myth," or the myth of writing?

After this all too brief and cursory summary of the history behind
the term "community," let us first return to Bataille's original
notion of community from the prewar writings. Being somewhat
distinct from "society" or "the social," the notion of "community" for Bataille always refers to something mythical, that is, the
expression of the sacred as the implicit presupposition of every
social form. According to Bataille's original thesis of "the absence
of myth," there are societies, including our present one, where a
subject (an individual, a collective) *can* exist without community,
or where the necessity of the sacred as the most intense expression

of "being-in-common" is discovered to be absent, lost, destroyed, or simply forgotten through the historical processes of colonialism, modernization, or globalization. Following Bataille, Nancy, in *La Communauté désoeuvrée*, calls this a time of "myth interrupted," where the very mythic sense of community is suspended between two times so to speak: between the "no longer," referring to what was formerly determined by ritual, and the "not yet" of the "community to come," which can (and in some ways cannot) simply be understood as the anticipation of a new mythic foundation of the social bond. The question I will return to below is the presumption of myth itself as a form of necessity for the idea of community.

Nevertheless, Bataille also claims that the time of a society that exists in the absence of myth (i.e. the absence of community) is itself a modern myth, if not the myth of modernity itself. In other words, this is *our myth today* and we are present to it in the sense that we live in a time without origin, a time that is founded on nothing *other* than its own present, which is to say, a present without before or after, without order, which causes us to become dizzy and disoriented, ecstatic in our horizons, beside ourselves in the very moment. This dizziness, vertigo, disorientation, also defines our *passion* and our *passivity* before every other singular being with whom we share the present in the form of an essential absence of relation. In other words, it is as if every social relation is struck by this dizziness, brought about by its absence. In other words, according to the foundational principle of capitalist societies like our own, *no social relation is absolutely necessary!* Neither family nor kinship ties, blood or racial membership, class or social caste can any longer be said – that is, in an absolute sense that constitutes a general case of collective identity – to determine the location and ultimate destination of each singular being in its relation to others.

In the early writings on what he called "the Surrealist religion," Bataille focuses on the possibilities of the *Bund*, social organization or secondary community, in his list of collective forms that appear in modern post-industrial societies, and marking an essential antagonism between what he called, following the sociological research of Jules Monnerot, the "community of fact" (race, nation, language) and the "community of affect" (sympathetic, or elective community):

The belonging of fact cannot satisfy us, since it does not allow our relation to others to be founded upon what is, according to the choice we
make, most important for us. We are complete only outside ourselves,
in the human plenitude of assembly, but we become complete only
if, as we gather together, we do so in a way that responds to our most
intimate demands. To the extent we no longer want to become ridicu-
lous or disfigured in our own eyes [i.e. incomplete, solitary beings
apart from community] we are in search of a secondary community
whose aims are in complete accord with our own intimate being.[9]

Bataille calls this desire for secondary community, without irony,
our "sociological tendency."[10] In explaining this tendency, he
emphasizes the social organization of the *Bund*, or secondary community, as a peculiar quasi-religious form of community and the
expression of a sociological tendency that will become a constant
and ever-increasing feature of modern societies. As he writes:

It may be the consciousness of this radical difference, to which we are
brought by more and more rapid subversions in the forms of social
life, may introduce a new possibility into history: possibly people will
finally realize clearly that there is no internal debate so profound that
the historical movement of human societies cannot give it a *meaning*,
and recognize at the same time that the *meaning* of this movement is
not exhausted unless it is taken to the source of its intimate echoes.[11]

In the case of the Surrealist movement, which is a prototype
of the "literary commune," it is a secondary community that is
marked by its subversive characteristics and by the expression of
the heterogeneity of its "being-in-common" in opposition to that
of the surrounding society (*Gesellschaft*) to which it belongs. What
distinguishes the space of this secondary community from society
is the fact that – radically differentiating itself from the public,
which is formed by the interactions of similar individuals – its
members form a *finite whole* (a set within a set) that is heterogeneous with the surrounding social space and values. As Bataille
writes, "it is a whole limited by individuals forming a whole
that is different from a crowd."[12] Consequently, the particular
subversive character of the avant-gardes from Surrealism onward

can be sociologically explained by the creation of heterogeneous and "non-exchangeable" values that exist in relation to the larger society, which is governed by the principle of exchange. Nevertheless, its initial formation simply represents the sociological principle of the *Bund*, which is also found in most historical religions as well, and thus its expression contains the presumption that the unique values of the community are heterogeneous, or even posed as transcendent, to the larger society. Thus, in the case of the Surrealists who are the object of Bataille's earlier reflections, it is the expression of collective revolt against the "community of fact"; and its affective community is manifested in the creation of new values that will constitute the reversal of everything that the larger society has cast away (e.g. dreams, mystic trances, drugs), and specifically by a mode of communication that is determined as completely useless as information or work – namely, *literature.*

Here, we might understand the modern notion of "negative community" as a sociological form of *Bund* that actually precedes the various literary and philosophical movements that will institutionalize it as a dominant and partly mythic vehicle of culture, which is partly responsible for its generic determination associated with "the ideal community of literary communication" from Romanticism up to and even including the various expressions of communitarian discourses and literary communisms that belong to the present moment. Of course, Nancy writes:

> This can always make for one more myth, a new myth, and not even as new as some would believe: the myth of the literary community was outlined for the first time (although in reality it was probably not the first time) by the Jena romantics, and it has filtered down to us through everything resembling the idea of "a republic of artists," or, again, the idea of communism (of a certain kind of Maoism, for example), and revolution inherent, *tels quels*, in writing itself.[13]

For Nancy, however, the word *literature* designates the very possibility that enters into "an epoch of our history"; it is employed as an act of incision (or interruption) that constitutes the very scene of myth today, but in the same stroke, erases the very traces of writing by means of which it has cut into its own myth.[14] If one excuses

the overtly Derridean tones of this definition (although these over-
tones are everywhere in Nancy's own exposition), "literature" can
be grasped as both the scene and the event of a double *ex-cision* of
the foundational myth of society. It is an act of literature (that is to
say, writing) that must first cut into all previous myths of community, and then in a second incision (which is actually an *ex-cision*),
manages to cut away any traces of its own mythic performance,
even performativity, as the scene of a modern myth. In other
words, after the second stroke, the sense of this event no longer
appears as literature (as writing), but rather as a new foundation for
the experience of community itself, which accounts for the nature
of its presentation as an interruption and suspension or deferment
of the relations that compose actual existing society. Is this experience, then, merely a fiction in the negative sense of an essential
deception or alibi? No. Because in wiping away all its own traces as
writing it no longer appears as a fiction, and thus cannot be determined merely as a metaphor of lived experience, nor as its abstract
or imaginary representative as in most common interpretations of
ideology. Writing *is* lived experience, but an experience that is first
of all founded upon an aporia. To cite a passage from Blanchot
that I will return to explicate below, writing is "the sharing of
'something' which, precisely, seems always already to have eluded
the possibility of being considered as a part of the sharing: speech,
silence."[15] It is this *aporia* that will concern Nancy (and Blanchot,
in a different manner, as we will see below) in a sense that it would
not for Bataille, who saw the "literary community" as only one
possibility of the *Bund* – and not even the most privileged expression of this "sociological tendency" – since, for him, modern
cults and other secondary communities of culture and identity are
too multiple to reduce to one sociological principle of collective
experience.

In order to illustrate this last point, let us return to Nancy's own
definition of "community." He writes, "community means, in
some way, the presence of a being together whose immanence is
impossible except as its death-work."[16] Here, Nancy is not simply
referring to the subjective and psychological states of mourning,
nor even to the existential state of solitude and "being towards
one's own death" (*Dasein*), but rather to the collective and ritual

work of mourning as the performative and social character of speech and silence that this work enacts "in common" (*Mitsein*). Thus, this experience of community can only be present in the act of mourning as the presence of being together. We might ask, however, what is it that presences itself in a work of mourning that names a kind of being-together that is not possible in any other social relation, or possible mode of being together? This would presuppose that the being together of family or ethnic belonging would not encompass or approach this presence, nor the being together of a social project, or even of any type of activity including political activity.

What is it that is present in the being together of mourning, that is, *necessarily*, which may or may not be present in these other modes of being together? Nancy immediately reveals this exceptional trait as "the Word" (which remains capitalized in his own discourse). In the work of mourning the Word still retains a living relation to one who, by dying, is absented from every other form of belonging, and it is only through "the Word" that our being together is still preserved, even as a form of intimacy. As he writes elsewhere: "But in point of fact *désoeuvrement* itself cannot be understood otherwise than by starting out with the resurrection of death, if, by means of *œuvre*, 'the word gives voice to death's intimacy.'"[17] In "a Word," our being together transcends death, but in a manner of immanence (or intimacy) that cannot be achieved within any other social relationship (i.e. neither in sexuality, nor work, nor in politics, etc.); therefore, in turn, this mode of presence, or of being together, exposes every other social relationship to its own constitutive limit, to an essential experience of its finitude or impossible coming to presence as a community. Therefore, as in the case of mourning, the work of *désoeuvrement* affected by "literature, or writing" (Nancy) suddenly appears to transcend every other social form of community, as if constituting the sovereign limit of every other manner of *being-in-common*.

Following Nancy's argument, however, at this point we might ask whether or not all writing is in some sense founded in mourning-work? In fact, we must allow this as a possibility. However, accepting this hypothesis, we must also allow the possibility that this represents a fundamental bias that belongs to

Christianity, with the establishment of a *necessary* relationship between the presence of the Word and the presence of community that is encrypted within writing. Moreover, not only must we allow for the possibility that this relationship between "*the* Word" and "*the* Community" is a bias inscribed in the Christianized West, but also recognize it as an alibi or diversion invented by a particular notion of community that absolutely refuses the death of the individual and thus the loss of the demand of community itself – a demand for presence that exceeds even the biological death of its individual members! In other words, this is the danger specific to the transcendence of "the Word." Is the still current bias toward literature as a privileged site of collective experience something that precedes us, as Nancy says, "from the very depths of community"? Yet, in asking "what community?" or rather "where is community?", we find ourselves before a tautology, that is, before a mythological statement concerning origins, since the original community is precisely what is lacking, and it is this absence of community that is now only present in the form of a myth that belongs to writing itself, that is to say, our *graphocentricism* today.[18]

On "literature," or the insufficient principle of insufficiency

Let us now turn to Bataille's original statement concerning the relationship between "literature" and collective existence: "Literature [or writing, that is, according to Nancy, if we accept the coincidence of these two terms] cannot assume the task of directing collective necessity." In taking up this statement, I will now refer to an early commentary by Blanchot in *La Communauté inavouable* (1983), which appeared in the same year as the earlier version of *La Communauté désoeuvrée* and was written partly in response to Nancy's text, and in another respect, will represent what Nancy later calls its "*désoeuvrement*."[19] It is the occasion of this extremely elliptical and secretive communication by Blanchot to Nancy – so secretive that Nancy himself confesses to not quite knowing what Blanchot was saying to him – concerning the earlier even more secretive relationship that existed between Blanchot and Bataille. Nancy writes: "I was immediately struck by the fact that Blanchot's reply was, at the same time, an echo and a resonance or replication, a reserve, and even in some sense a reproach. Nevertheless, I have never been able to completely clarify this reserve or reproach, neither in the text, for myself, nor in correspondence with Blanchot."[20]

Turning to Blanchot's text, therefore, let us rephrase once more Bataille's original statement in accordance with Blanchot's commentary: *Literature is insufficient to direct collective necessity for the idea, much less the actual existence, of community.* Thus, the word *"insuffisance"* is underlined throughout Blanchot's commentary in reference to Bataille's primary thesis concerning what he defines as the governing principle of community, as well as our "sociological tendency": *the principle of insufficiency*. According to Bataille, "there exists a principle of insufficiency at the root of each being": "a being, insufficient as it is, does not attempt to associate itself with another being to make up a substance of integrity," but rather, from the awareness of its own insufficiency, needs the other in order to place its own being in question.[21] Although this might appear counterintuitive at first glance, since we usually or habitually imagine that a being that perceives its own insufficiency will seek in another the basis for its own completion, "integrism," or "fusion" (Nancy). And yet, because "insufficiency cannot be derived from a model of sufficiency," what Bataille calls "our own intimate being" must already be encompassed (and preceded) by the presence of another, or by a plurality of others (not yet a community) whose presence "triggers a chain reaction in each singular being."[22] In other words, the principle of insufficiency is nothing other than the presence of others whose presence triggers this chain reaction in each separate individual and causes the idea of community to come into being, especially since "a being is alone or knows itself to be alone only when it is not."[23]

Turning now to Nancy's reading of the term "insufficiency," it is also equated with the experience of "literature" (for which, we also recall, there is no name that is yet sufficient). However, in his commentary on Nancy's text, Blanchot, somewhat anxiously, calls into question this analogy, even going so far as to refute

Nancy's central thesis that the nature of the separation effected by
the movement of writing could in any way express the principle
of insufficiency that determines each singular being in relation to
community. As he argues:

> It does not follow that the community is the simple putting in
> common, inside the limits of what it would propose for itself, of a
> shared will to be several [*à plusieurs*], albeit to do nothing, that is to say,
> to do nothing else than maintain the sharing of "something" which,
> precisely, seems always already to have eluded the possibility of being
> considered as a part of the sharing: speech, silence.[24]

The above passage contains an allusion to the phrases that appear
throughout Nancy's arguments concerning what has eluded the
part of the sharing [*part à un partage*]: speech, silence. How so?
First of all, the material and psychological partitions that determine the speech and silence are not "parts" of our experience
(*Erfahrung*) of *being-in-common*, but already attest to the fact of
our separate and isolated existence as singular beings. As Bataille
writes, "Communication is [already] ecstasy," the object of which
is defined as "the negation of the isolated being."[25] Of course,
Nancy also says that "communication is the constitutive fact of an
exposition to the outside that defines singularity," but Blanchot
calls into question whether this exposition can be identified with
"the simple putting in common, [i.e. the act of writing], inside
the limits of what it would propose for itself [i.e. a work, a text],
of a shared will to be several [*à plusieurs*]."[26] Therefore, to say that
writing is the privileged form of communication in which finitude
appears (in "com-parution," Nancy says at this point) would simply
risk producing yet another hypostasis of the Being of beings, or in
Nancy's own words, *the presentation of a "primordial structure," at once
"detached, distinguished, and communitarian."*[27]

Our question will concern, therefore, whether writing alone
is "sufficient" to trigger the chain reaction noted earlier. In other
words, is "literature, or writing" sufficient to represent this principle of insufficiency? Of course, it is true that writing can also be
determined as the effect of a chain reaction that expresses a principle of insufficiency in each singular being, causing this being to

actively expose itself to the other or a plurality of others – for recognition, identity, affirmation, contestation, work. Otherwise, why would writing exist if it did not testify to the insufficiency of the individual being, even in relation to its own "singular being," and open in us a supplementary and necessary dimension to our social existence? Nevertheless, does this exigency for writing express the principle of insufficiency, or does writing merely express itself as an abstract and superficial effect of a more primary principle of insufficiency, or "prime mover"?

What is this "prime mover"? Earlier we had described death as the event that calls forth or co-invokes a plurality of others to come into being qua community, but precisely in the finite number of those members whose presence actualizes the physical existence of a community. Writing, here, can only evoke this event *in absentia*, by memorializing it in the form of a simulacrum that may very well produce a chain reaction of effects that expose each singular being to a plurality of others, but is incapable of causing this plurality to come into presence as *a finite community*. Therefore, if "literature, or writing" is to function in any way as commanding or directive, then it must first be set within a concrete social relationship. For Blanchot, moreover, without any relation to a particular other (as in the case of his own friendship with Bataille, which he maintains as a "secret") or to a plurality of others who constitute the possibility of community (as in the many communities Bataille himself founded, only to see them all splinter and fall apart) writing itself can only function as a dead letter. It is according to this same argument that Blanchot will write in *L'Attente, l'oubli*: "We should understand then why it should be that speaking is worth more than writing. Speech bears within itself the fortuitous character which links the impact of chance to the game. It depends immediately on life, on the humours and the fatigues of life, and it welcomes them as its secret truth."[28]

Put another way, more provocatively, only the excessive presence of the Other is sufficient to represent a summoning *directive*, and only the other's absence *in particular*, and *qua particular*, that causes the solitary individual to live on as if "beside himself" (excluding even the substitution of the ego's own death as a model for this original *ekstasis*, thereby fundamentally calling into question Heidegger's conception of *Dasein*).

> Bataille: "This is what puts me beside myself, *this is the only separa-
> tion that can open me*, in its very impossibility, to the Openness of
> community."[29]
> Blanchot: "That is what founds community. There could not be a
> community without the sharing of that first and last event which in
> everyone ceases to be able to be just that (birth, death)."[30]

In the above passages, I have highlighted Bataille's and Blanchot's
arguments concerning the intimate relation between the death of
the other (qua particular) and the finite principle of community,
because here we are confronted with the most glaring contradiction in their exposition of these themes: if being present to
another "who absents himself by dying," even holding the hand
of "another who dies," is the *only* decisive event of separation that
opens the individual to community, then the actual condition of
community would be necessarily finite, that is to say, un-sharable
apart from those who experience it directly, and thus no principle
could be drawn from this "limit-experience" to communicate this
condition of being-in-common to others. Once again, this would
appear to be counterintuitive: how can the principle of community, which is normally understood to express the general or
universal condition of *being-in-common* (*Mitsein*) be founded upon
an event that is, by definition, in-communicable and un-sharable
outside those few who have experienced it, as if endowing its principle with an air of mystery and esoteric knowledge, and certainly
exposing it to a certain religious signification?

And yet, we might ask why would the death of the other, even
in only referring to a particular other, and to the most common
and insignificant death, be any less remote or mythical as a foundation for the idea of community than the death of a hero or a
God?[31] In other words, the death of the other is the only event that
separates me from myself, as an isolated being; that places the supposed self-sufficiency of my ego or my autonomy as a subject most
radically in question. However, this death must be particular if it
is to function as a summons of my separate existence, no longer as
an isolated being, but as a being who is fundamentally dependent
on the other, that is, a social being. This is why, ultimately, my
own death cannot serve as a model, which would simply reaffirm

my self-sufficiency and my autonomy, or my independence before others – even an indifference before the others' death, as if every other being was only a stranger and the ego remained locked in its own immanence. Moreover, if the only directive of collective existence is the death of a particular other – an other who, according to Bataille, must be "elected" from a plurality of others and whose social relation is not determined on the basis of a "community of fact" – then this is why the subject is always called to become part of a particular community, a finite community whose members "have a share" in death (always the death of a particular) as the condition of their being-in-common, even in those cases where community can number no more than two members, as in a community of lovers (which is the title of the second part of Blanchot's response). In other words, because community is always finite, and can even be composed only of a few, it cannot become a permanent foundation of the whole, but always remains partial and incomplete, which is to say, a secondary whole.

There are many dangers to this kind of formulation – too many to recount in the space of this analysis. First of all, it limits the possibilities of community solely to the relation between individuals and would not seem to allow for a general principle of society that could include populations, and most importantly, strangers and those social others with whom the subject has nothing in common – in short, a relation of and between multiplicities or the "multitude." Nevertheless, this is the "sociological tendency" that we have already established at the basis of the *Bund*, the secondary community or the "community of affect," which is defined as "a whole limited by individuals forming a whole that is different from a mass or crowd."[32] If we were to concede to this principle, however, then we must also acknowledge that the concept of community be *completely insufficient* as the directive principle of any political project that seeks to organize the masses, the crowd, the multitude, as well as any democratic presentation of an assemblage of individuals (e.g. "We the people . . ."). In other words, there can be no "politics of community," because the historical community – determined as a secondary whole that is differentiated from a multiplicity – is either formed in retreat from the society that excludes it (as if, constituting "a line of flight," or a

"becoming minor"), or, as in the example of the Nazi community
(*Volksgemeinschaft*), because the community totalizes the field of the
political and thus excludes all politics. Certainly, this leads to a critique of the collective politics of fascism and racism, as exemplified
in Bataille's own early analysis, but may also reveal a fundamental dehiscence between the modern concepts of community and
politics. In other words, as Nancy first observed, today there is the
presence of a generalized "decoupling" of politics (i.e. sovereignty)
with the experience of community (i.e. intimacy), and as a result
both aspects have seemed to withdraw to a limit that cannot be
totalized or assembled into one form. Although this may be good
news with regard to the threat of a return of totalitarianism (which
we now understand to belong to a historical moment of modernization), it exposes us to the idea of a multiplicity of politics without
any common horizon, without project, or universal genus – and
thus, to a politics based purely on calculation and strategy.

At the same time, modern expressions of community could only
have emerged alongside the equally modern notions of the masses,
or the crowd, As Blanchot writes, "theoretically and historically,
there are only communities of small numbers . . ." and this fact
exposes the principle of community to two dangers that are both
quantitative in nature.[33] First of all, this fact exposes the social body
of community to the problem of finitude that is not possible for
the masses or the crowd: either in the form of the loss of individual
members who are too few in number, or to the equal danger of
fusion of large numbers into the form of a supra-individual (the
nation, the race) that exposes the group to possibilities of collective
death, or genocide, and more recently, nuclear extermination. For
Bataille, "the tendency to fusion" only intensifies the presence of
death for each individual, for the society that is composed or fuses
itself into an aggrandized identification exposes every member
of society to the same death (e.g. the death of Christ, the death of
Hitler, etc.) As Blanchot writes, it is this "tendency towards a *communion*" described as "an effervescence of elements that give rise to
a unity (a supra-individuality) that would expose itself to the same
objections arising from the simple consideration of the individual,
locked in its own immanence."[34]

Again, let us recall the almost physical description of finitude as "a chain reaction" that the existence of the other or a plurality of others effects in the existence of every singular being, but in the form of community that must be maintained in a high degree of tension, which Bataille earlier equates with consciousness brought about by the death of another. If this chain reaction that Blanchot speaks of becomes indeterminate and trails off into the realm of higher quantities, it would "risk losing itself in infinity, or splinters apart just as the universe composes itself by delimiting itself in an infinity of universes."[35] According to Bataille, the only manner for a community to persist in being is to maintain itself in the consciousness of death and to manifest this presence to its highest degree of tension within each of its members, as if to constantly re-invoke death's directive as a foundation of the *Bund*. It is also around this commanding directive that we find Bataille's interest in the ritual forms of sacrifice in many primitive religions, but also the basis for his critique of these forms as well as his critique of the sociology of fascism as precisely a resistance of the truth of community itself: precisely its temporal finitude and its smaller quantities.

In the later writings during the period of the *Collège de Sociologie*, for example, there is a constant relationship demonstrated between the sociological form of fascism as a "mass phenomenon" and the necessity of war as the most prevalent means of manifesting the immanent presence of death, at its highest degree of intensity, within each singular being as a power "sufficient" to co-invoke the absolute directive of the fascist community. In this case, the group binds itself to the myth of community and consequently negates the entire principle of the number in favor of a fusional principle of identity, modeling itself in some ways after a community of souls, or a community of lovers, which only require a number of N + 1. Community, being founded on a principle of homogeneity, is constitutionally opposed to the heterogeneity of the number or the multiplicity, especially to any heterogeneity among its own numbers, however few.

It is around this phenomenon, finally, that we also discover that the same principles of finitude and number will also be responsible for the greatest threat of all: the loss of community itself in the death of all its members (at once), thereby ruining the habitual possibilities of immanence and transcendence for both the individual

and the group. Here we find the form of *communion* that threatens
to become a principle of sufficiency for community, and which
Nancy often evokes as the explicit threat of a "fusional fulfill-
ment in some collective hypostasis."[36] Among the examples of this
kind of "fusion," of which of the Christian Eucharist is given as a
primary symbol, Blanchot also invokes the contemporary example
attested to by "the sinister collective suicide in Guyana."[37] The fact
that the Jones community of Guyana made the symbolic meaning
contained in the Eucharist a literal expression of the sharing of
death by each of its members, almost as a grotesque parody of the
Last Supper, ruins the possibilities of both immanence and transcendence for both the individual and the community.

How is immanence and transcendence ruined? If the immanence
of community can only exist as a conscious idea of the death of the
other which "interrupts" the separate and isolated existence of the
ego, then the death of every particular (at once, in the act of collective suicide) would negate both the space of consciousness and
the necessity of community. In short, if everyone dies, then community is no longer necessary and exists from that moment much
in the same way ruins exist: as only the traces of a now extinct
society. At the same time, what Blanchot refers to as the "habitual
forms of transcendence" – meaning that there is more than one
form – are ruined by the fact that it is precisely the death of the
other as a particular (i.e. as a separate and isolated being) that makes
it possible for a community to transcend this event by sharing this
separation with all the others. Thus, the consciousness of community is extinguished only in the position of its separate existence in
the individual, but undergoes redistribution among the survivors
for whom the presence of others still causes a chain reaction that
interrupts the separate and isolated existence. In the case of the
collective suicide, however, transcendence is ruined, meaning
that it is no longer necessary since no one survives and the spark
that ignites the initial chain reaction is also extinguished, like trying
to light a match under water. Therefore, if the consciousness of
community is only immanent in the death of each particular, and
at the same time, transcendent in its separation from the death of
every particular, then the "fusion" of the death of the particular and
the collective in one gruesome act of collective suicide becomes

the highest expression of a model of sufficiency that haunts every finite community.

Returning to Nancy, it is not by accident that we find again the term "fusion" to represent the greatest threat, or that writing is offered up as our only possible defense. In other words, it is only writing that makes possible the idea of communication "without a bond *and* without communion, equally distant from any notion of connection or joining from the outside and from any notion of a common and fusional interiority."[38] This formulation is everywhere present throughout his work, even constituting a major "philosopheme" (as Derrida would also say in *Le Toucher*), in the sense that we could find in all his writings one theme that is stated repeatedly: *communication without the threat of communion, outside any common identity, or danger of fusional interiority.* In view of this dangerous and threatening horizon, perhaps the highest task of his philosophy is precisely to expose every living community to this limit, thereby making it unworkable; to de-mythologize all presumptions of community based on the presence of a "common being," that is, at the very moment when any collective threatens to convert its own substance into the epiphany of community – to effect a "revelation" of the singular plurality of "being-in-common."[39] It is in this sense that we might understand Nancy's concept of community as negative, but not in the usual senses accorded to this notion, which correspond to the *Bund*, or the secondary community. For Nancy, the negative is purely procedural or poetic, the manner in which he occupies the theme of community only to unwork it, to untie it from every social bond and every possible communion, even though Nancy will later acknowledge Blanchot's earlier criticism that this apotropaic gesture was perhaps too absolute in its negation of any "fusional intimacy," however brief and excessive, recalling that Bataille saw the collective experience of the *Bund* as a possibility of freedom from "the community of fact" (race, class, nation, language), or today, one might also say "the community of the number" (whether this is understood today as a political or an economic formation of neoliberal society).

On the "coming community"?

I conclude by returning now to the genealogy of the theme of community as it appears in Nancy's most recent reflections since 2001. Here, it is important to note that Nancy employs the term "community" less frequently in the writings that follow this period, and prefers instead to concentrate his work around the less graceful term "with" [*avec*], as in "being-with," or "being-together," in place of "community," which now appears to him to bear a new set of risks in association with the reemergence of fascist tendencies in European societies at the turn of the millennium, especially in France with the rise of Le Pen and the National Front in the elections that would take place just one year after Nancy published the following comments:

> In many respects I have come to understand the dangers posed by the use of the word community: its inevitable resonance with substance and a replete interiority, its just as inevitable Christian connotations (spiritual community, fraternal communion) or more broadly religious significations (Jewish community, community of prayer, community of believers), and its current usage only applied it seems to so-called "ethnicities" could only caution us.[40]

Again, in the context of the mid-1980s, Nancy had simply attempted to find in the unpublished writings of Bataille the conceptual resources around the theme of community that would escape both the dangers of fascism, on the one hand, and the coming neo-liberal society, on the other. In this context, he took the risk of invoking the word "community" at that moment, even if it was only in an effort to abandon the myth of community by reducing it to a "common limit where singular beings share one another" (i.e. to "literature, or writing").[41] Twenty years later, however, it seems, he had to return again to abandon the word itself in view of the return of its various associations to the new communities of fascism, or in relation to the potential abuses and dangers evoked in the term "ethnic community," but most importantly, in view of the tendency of the current neoliberal society to immediately ruin whatever new chances a renewal of the concept of community could provide to our political discourse today. In some ways, this repeats a similar set of circumstances earlier experienced by Bataille and Blanchot during the immediate prewar period concerning the concept of democracy, and may even indicate a new prohibition of the usage of the term "community" in current philosophical discourse, despite the promise of its association with new communitarian ideals, or to a "return of communism."[42]

Is the theme of "community" now running the risk of becoming, yet again, "excessive" and "inappropriate" as a *philosopheme* or as an element of our current political discourse? Is the "inappropriateness" of community something that is "proper to Man?"[43] Moreover, must the idea of "the return of community" (but also the "return of religion") always be destined to be associated with the dual horizons of fascism and communism, both of which are resolutely past, and yet, always still just over the horizon and yet to come – but always in a new sense that is both more promising and more threatening at once. Is there not a possibility for another horizon, a third horizon, perhaps? In reply to these questions, I think Blanchot understands this problem best when he reminds us that the concepts of fascism and communism, even in their common usage in the 1980s, were in no manner equivalent and could not even be said to have the same meaning as the concepts employed in the 1930s. As he writes, "the premonition of what is already fascism but the meaning of which, as well as its becoming, eludes the concepts then in use, [forces] thought to reduce it to what is common and miserable in it, or on the contrary, [points] out what is important and surprising in it."[44] Of course, it is not surprising to hear implicitly the defense of a certain historical difference of the situation faced by a European intellectual in the prewar period, or then again in the immediate postwar environment, especially given his own personal history; but more importantly, we still find the admission of a certain "conceptual ambiguity" and a suspicion concerning the "abandonment" of both concepts to their most common or vulgar historical meanings. Concerning both dangers he sees lurking in the uses of the terms "communism" and "community" in Nancy's text, he simply observes that while "dishonored or betrayed concepts do not exist, concepts that are not appropriate without their proper–improper *abandonment* (which is not simply their negation) do not permit us to tranquilly refuse or refute them."[45]

References

Bataille, Georges. *Absence of Myth: Writings on Surrealism*, trans. Michael Richardson. London: Verso, 1994.

Blanchot, Maurice. *The Unavowable Community*, trans. Pierre Joris. New York: Station Hill, 1988.

Hollier, Denis (ed.). *Le Collége de Sociologie: 1937–1939*. Paris: Gallimard, 1955. *The College of Sociology*, trans. Betsy Wing. Minneapolis: University of Minnesota Press, 1988.

Nancy, Jean-Luc. *La Communauté désoeuvrée*, 2nd edn. Paris: Christian Bourgois, 1986.

Nancy, Jean-Luc. *The Inoperative Community*, trans. Peter Connor. Minneapolis: University of Minnesota Press, 1991.

Nancy, Jean-Luc. *La Communauté affrontée*. Paris: Galilée, 2001.

Nancy, Jean-Luc. *Dis-Enclosure: Deconstruction of Christianity*, trans. Bettina Bergo et al. New York: Fordham University Press, 2008.

Nancy, Jean-Luc. *Politique et au-delà: entretien avec Philip Armstrong et Jason Smith*. Paris: Galilée, 2011.

4

Monograms: Then and "Now"

Georges Van Den Abbeele

Now and then

Between June 1979 and December 1980, Jean-Luc Nancy wrote what we would have called in a pre-internet world a "column" or a regular contribution to a journal, something like what we now call a web-log or "blog." And while these periodic essays do function as a kind of log, or more precisely what Nancy refers to as a "chronicle," the experiment in this kind of writing comes to a halt after a short eighteen months with the demise of the periodical *Digraphe*, for which those pieces were written.[1] The series begins anew a dozen years later, in February 1992, for another journal, *Futur Antérieur*, only to end just as abruptly some twenty months later in October of 1993.[2] All told, fourteen of these pieces, to which Nancy gives the name *Monogrammes*, were published over a total of fourteen years. Far from there being a continuous output over time (as the numerical equivalencies would suggest), they appeared unevenly in these two bursts of sustained activity broken by a long hiatus. After the last burst, they would seemingly disappear from his writing, never to be picked up again, at least as such.[3]

By "as such," I mean that Nancy is not necessarily a stranger to various forms of situational or occasional writing, and one should certainly note his many such contributions in this vein, including the series of radio lectures published in 2004 under the title *Philosophical Chronicles*.[4] A study of Nancy's *Monogrammes* is thus the occasion to broach a more general consideration of this untracked tendency in his work, not as a "break" or detour, or *détournement,* from his philosophizing in more traditional and abstract ways – viz. his monographs on individual thinkers, such as Descartes, Kant, and Hegel, or his theoretical works on such questions as community, democracy, or Christianity – but as a *distinct* approach that he charts for the practice of philosophy.

It is not my ambition or intention to uncover the archeology (historical, biographical, psychoanalytical) of this pursuit – now and then – of a form of writing made more familiar in our current media-saturated world. And it is no doubt a symptom of the prescience of Nancy's monogrammatic forays that at least those essays published in the now defunct *Futur Antérieur* have themselves been collected and made readily accessible on the website of the successor journal, *Multitudes*.[5] Rather, my interest has to do with coming to terms with the practice modeled by Nancy's *Monogrammes* as a novel and experimental kind of intellectual intervention that is at the same time a continuing *philosophical* reflection on the meaning of the *form* that this intervention takes, and more generally, on the occasion for the invention of *forms* that have creatively, and even classically, enabled the advent of certain ways of thinking (I'm tempted to say certain *worlds* of thought).

Definitions: singular plural

So, what are these "monograms"? The first one begins with a triple definition, and subsequent installments will add further examples, specifications, and definitions of what a "monogram" is. There is a fundamental pluralism here, not merely in the proliferation of formal definitions given at the beginning of each publication, but each of the fourteen is itself given the "singularly plural" title of "*Monogrammes*." And indeed, Nancy's approach is to include within each installment a number of different short texts on differing topics separated by blank spaces and triangulated asterisks. Each of the "*monogrammes*" is itself a *set* of monograms, a collection of "singular remarks" bundled together and signed according to date and often place.[6]

Of the three definitions proposed in the first paragraph of the first "*monogrammes*," the first is a personal one, to indicate what is meant *hic et nunc*: "*Monogrammes: ici, espèces de monologues écrits* [Monograms: *here*, some kinds of written monologues]." The monogram is first and foremost a "kind" of *written* monologue, with the accent on the "mono" or single-voice aspect of the form, i.e. this would appear to be not a *dia*logue between speakers but the uninterrupted utterance of one. That monologue, however, does not exclude, and indeed *a contrario* the situational context of these "chronicles" demands, dialogue with real or potential readers. Indeed, many of the subsequent *monogrammes* include various responses by Nancy to readers whose messages and identity remain typically absent. The acknowledgment of such responses cannot simply be occasional. Why would one write such a chronicle, if not precisely to elicit dialogue (like the "objections and responses" to Descartes's *Meditations*)? Or more boldly, to make operative a certain (philosophical) community? Either way, there is no "mono" without a "dia," the plural singularity of the mono-logic monograms calls forth the singular pluralities of dialogue (or a multi-logue). The "speaking with" precedes any "speaking to," the *co*lloquy comes before any so*li*loquy. It is as if the *monogrammes* presage or pre-stage the well-known theses of the *Inoperative Community* and of *Being Singular Plural*.

More tellingly, however, the *written* monologue is not a *logos* but a *gramma*, a mono-*gram*, the singularity of a trace, as suggested by the third of the three definitions that Nancy provides at the beginning of *Monogrammes I*. This time, the definition proposed is not a personal one but the institutional definition given by a standardized dictionary, in this case, the *Littré*: "*Terme d'Antiquité. Qui ne consiste que dans les lignes, dans les contours. Peinture monogramme* [Term from Antiquity. What consists only in lines, in the contours. A monogram painting]." The *graphic* nature of the monogram is thus underscored by its *painting* a picture by the mere deployment

of lines, by its consisting only of an outline, or a set of contours. But this is indicated as an outdated expression, a term from
"antiquity" and one that would appear to be as far removed as is
possible from the contemporaneousness or *"actualité"*[7] that Nancy
otherwise embraces for his "monograms" as a kind of "chronicle"
where current events, book reviews and philosophical reflections
intersect, where the lines between them cross and cross again in
a distinctive if undefined pattern, a monogram, a singular set of
traces whose outline remains sufficient unto itself, while perhaps
adumbrating something more. Far from being simply "mono,"
the monogram appears to be irredeemably plural, as its each time
plural title of *Monogrammes* suggests. But then the monogram(s)
cannot be a simple trait, not something simply singular but always
already plural, repeated and repeatable as per the nexus of lines
that out-lines the picture. The picture is the pattern recognized
from the retracing of lines whose linearity withdraws before the
instance, the instantiation of the image. The monogram is not a
simple trait, but always already a complex *re-trait*, a retracing that is
a withdrawal, a retreat that is also an emergence.

Finally, a monogram is also something whose traces the signa-
tory bears like a set of initials. It is both a decoration and a brand, or
as *Monogrammes IV* states, "Ornament and signature at once." The
monogram is also not a monograph: "It is not a ciphered message,
it's the Cipher itself, which does not cipher and thus does not
decipher anything." The monogram both reveals and conceals the
outline of a trace or the trace of an outline, an open "cryptogra-
phy," that is, "a secret displayed out in the light of day, or the light
of day itself in its cryptic nature." As such, the monogram recalls
the Heraclitean conundrum *phusis kruptesthai philei,* which Nancy
translates and comments upon in detail as follows:

> *phusis kruptesthai philei* – nature loves to hide itself, to encrypt itself –,
> this phrase which we cannot translate (but is Heraclitus himself able to
> translate it?), and which, for this reason, we cannot stop commenting
> on, speaks to the nature of the name as much as to the nature of light,
> or to the nature of nature. It speaks about what takes place in the light
> of day [*au grand jour*] in general, it speaks about the light of day. At
> Easter – in this moment – we learn anew the light of day, the bright,

dawning light of the sky that has not yet installed its closed reign of heat, its calefaction and all the work of fructifications. In the sky and on the ground, everything withdraws [*recule*] before the evidence of a budding forth [*éclosion*]. For this budding forth is a withdrawing, rather than a manifestation, a cipher rather than a declaration. Except for a few runaway flowers, the plants are still only their monograms. The freshly planted sapling and the recently pruned tree are their own initials; they hold the evidence of their ciphers. And all evidence is a cipher.

That's what Leibniz failed to understand, when he reproached Descartes for not having placed a sign upon the inn of evidence. Evidence is the contrary of publicity.

Leibniz notwithstanding, the "evidence" of the Cartesian *larvatus prodeo* is both a masking and an unmasking, the monogrammatic cipher that is both signature and evidence, the sign of spring and what it openly portends and secretly declares: the bud as monogram that brightly reveals what it hides inside, a withdrawal or retreat (*recul, retrait*) that is also an emergence or advance, a ripening that redraws the contours of an outline in germination, a re-tracing or *re-trait* for that which "consists only in lines," the monogram. (As for the concern about distinguishing evidence from publicity, that remark too rejoins a number of comments in the early *monogrammes* about the media phenomenon of the so-called "nouveaux philosophes" and the wider problem of what Nancy describes in *Monogrammes I* as the suspect desire to present a certain "figure" of philosophy, "to pass oneself off as a philosopher," to pass philosophy off as what can be given a certain "figure," all of which fail, *on philosophical terms*, to understand "the very question of philosophy" as a relentlessly calling into question of "figuration" itself.)[8]

This set of monograms (*Monogrammes IV*) that so effortlessly evokes the Easter moment as the key to unraveling the meaning of "monogram" is dated April 15, 1980, just days after that year's Easter Sunday (April 6), thus situating the philosophical reflection within the ground of a particular place and time, a *hic et nunc* that is not coincidental but rather the contextual frame, the *contours* if you like that form the out-line of the monogram.[9] Nancy signs his monograms with the date, his initials J.-L. N., and the place,

his home/retreat at Les Ayes. When he doesn't make that location explicit, he often as not describes it, as in the final section
of *Monogrammes III*, which is also a striking example of implicit
dialogue *within* the monologue: "Someone, a reader in sum, had
asked me to speak again about nature in this chronicle. I will
only tell him the following, today: winter is beginning, a little
bit of snow has fallen, just now, while I was working in the
garden. November 24, 1979 J.-L. N." Instead of a philosophical
reflection, we have the contours of the philosopher's dwelling,
the outlines of his being in retreat, working à la Voltaire in his
garden, cultivating what must necessarily already be at an end,
with the growing season cut short by the winter's first snows.
Although, to be precise, one cannot really say that the season is
"cut short" since winter's advent points to the final completion
of the ripening process, not a contingency or interruption except
in the sense that all change is contingent interruption, the sign
of finitude's inevitability, of the end always already inscribed in
the beginning. And what could one possibly be doing by way of
"work" in the garden at this time of year? Clearly, any effort at
planting would be most untimely and literally "fruitless." But
there does remain the job of clearing the dead vegetation and
of making one's little plot ready for the next season's germination, ready for the return of Easter's daylight, which we will then
"learn anew" along with its monogrammatic buds. Part of this
preparation, as any gardener knows, is to prune or cut back any
untoward branches or shoots so as to enable the new buds to
succeed come their spring, come the eternal recurrence of their
Ur-sprung. The growing season's growth must then indeed be cut
short for it to grow again later. But just like the spring's anticipation in/of the bud ("Except for a few runaway flowers, plants are
still only their *monograms*"), so too does the final autumn pruning
leave us with nothing more than the outline of the plant, its contours or initials, its monogram, which is not a cryptogram, but
the "evidence of a cipher": "The freshly planted sapling and the
recently pruned tree are their own initials; they hold the evidence
of their ciphers." The *monogrammes* are thus essentially marked
by a poetics of finitude: they chronicle a certain (outdated?
untimely?) time and place for philosophical reflections that them-

selves bear the potential for meaning beyond as well as within the context of their germination.[10]

Now and then

Monogrammes XIV (the last in the series!) begins by reflecting precisely on this potentiality of meaning given the non-coincidence between the *now* of publication and the *then* of writing:

> The spirit, as one says, of this chronicle should be that of a freewheeling commentary on current events [*un libre commentaire de l'actualité*], or even a commentary on the mood, as one also says. Experience indicates that the delays in the fabrication and publication of *Futur Antérieur* do not allow for staying close enough to the event. (Perhaps that's what the title of the journal is supposed to signify, by the way). . . . If I mention these details, it's not on their own account, you might suspect. It's because I cannot remove the bitter taste [*le goût amer*] left in my mouth by a chronicle I wrote about Bosnia in December 1992 or January 1993, which was only published four or five months later, and which, at the time I'm writing this (for the first time, by hand, in August 1993, then on the computer in September), has lost nothing, absolutely nothing, of a sinister freshness [*une fraîcheur sinistre*].

Monogrammes XIV appeared in *Futur Antérieur* 19–20 (1993/ 5–6); the piece on Bosnia was originally published as *Monogrammes XI* in *Futur Antérieur* 16 (1993/2). Reading these remarks some twenty years later (which further raises the question of what this means in the context of a volume dedicated to "Nancy *now*"), one can't help but be struck by the concern about the timeliness or currency of the text, its *actualité* relative to events whose distinctness appears significantly diminished with age, and yet whose "sinister freshness" paradoxically remains stronger than ever. For Nancy, this paradox is observed over a period of mere months rather than years. This anxiety about a six-month delay in publication would seem even more acute were such chronicling to occur in our contemporary social media and twitter-fed environment, where

a statement more than a few hours old may appear already hope-
lessly outdated — like that other outdated term from antiquity, the
monogram. Perhaps the monogram is always already out of date,
out of time, anachronistic, unhinged or disjointed like the traces
that make up its contours. This chronic anachronicity should not,
however, be understood as a simple state of being always out
of date, or as a kind of structural belatedness tarred with all the
nostalgia and melancholia of classic romanticism. For Nancy also
struggles here with a bizarre, unexpected and unsolicited kind of
actualité that makes what was written in either a recent or remote
past appear with an unparalleled contemporaneity, a "freshness"
that is all the more "sinister" for its marking a difference that
appears to make no difference at all. The *inactualité* of what was
written about Bosnia remains disturbingly more *actuelle* than ever.
It is this *unheimliche* and multiple, complex, unpredictable anachronicity of the chronicle that draws Nancy's attention.

The specific chronicle that is this installment of *Monogrammes*
(number XI) is both in and out of date, and it is even more relevant for its being not, i.e. an *inactualité* that is more *"actuelle"* than
ever. *Monogrammes XI* is even more peculiar for it being the only
one that has ever been republished as such,[11] and yet it is also the
only one absent from the *Multitudes* website, where all the other
monogrammes from the *Futur Antérieur* series are posted. As for the
text's "sinister freshness," that uncanny or untimely relation to
its own actuality is in fact bolstered by the content of the essay's
three sections, one on the relation between the "current" Bosnian
crisis and the context of the Yalta conference (itself an historical
analysis), a second section responding to media complaints about
the lack of involvement of "the intellectuals" in responding to that
crisis (which itself emerges as a properly philosophical discussion
of the ethics of intellectual involvement), and a final section about
Philip Glass's *Einstein on the Beach* (which also phrases the ongoing
aesthetic interest of that work, an aesthetic interest, we might
add, that has increased rather than diminished over the last two
decades). All three sections, while manifestly rooted in "current"
concerns, also speak deliberately and overtly to issues that in one
way or another transcend the moment of writing. Why, then, the
complaint in *Monogrammes XIV* about a few months' delay in pub-

lication when the piece itself is one that so clearly speaks beyond the currency of its context?

In any case, this paradox of an enduring (in)actuality leaves Nancy with a "bitter taste": how can the chronicle of a particular event (in this case, that of the war in Bosnia) remain so current? "How can one follow a current situation which has nothing current about it?" he asks a few lines later. There is a bitterness or a bitter realization here that can only be explained by a much larger set of considerations, one that exceeds the situation in question: "What pertains to Bosnia pertains in an analogous way to most of the former 'Eastern' bloc countries, but also to Iraq, Egypt, Algeria, India, Bangladesh, Somalia, South Africa and two-thirds of Africa, Brazil and Mexico, and Europe." Symptomatically, this list of trouble spots from the nineties seems scarcely different from the one we could make today, in the second decade of the twenty-first century. The last of Nancy's *monogrammes* (and curiously the only one that commences *without* listing various definitions of the word!) comes up against the very concept of a philosophical chronicle that launched his first *monogrammes* to the extent that such a concept would seem to presuppose a certain theory and philosophy of history, and indeed a certain *subject* of history:

> The actuality of these years, which seems stuck in disaster and regression, presents in sum a well-declared Hegelian aspect: the cunning of history [*la ruse de l'histoire*] shows itself bare and crude, but we can no longer call it *the cunning of Reason* without either laughing or crying, or else as a technico-economic reason that would be Marxist-Hegelian but deprived of its supposed rationality. What was once understood as process or as progress shows itself, more than ever, as a sequence of mechanisms, forces and calculations [*comme enchaînement d'engrenages, de forces et de calculs*], but the process as such no longer has any of the trappings of progression, it has only those of being carried along, of being carried away, and to finish, of explosion and implosion. How can we follow a current situation that has nothing current about it, which bears witness only to an enormous, obscure drift; emerging from the night of time and sliding into another night?

The "inactual actuality" of our times thus points to the collapse of the grand Hegelian narrative (to use Lyotard's well-known expression), where historical progress would be determined by a certain rationality, whose detours or "cunning" could be recognized and explained as the work of some Reason, whence a certain optimism in historical process as progress reflected in the feeling that "history is on our side." But history appears no longer to be on anyone's "side," if not that of bare "techno-economic" efficiency.[12] The trappings of progress are gone, leaving only the implosive or explosive cycle of brute force and reckoning, the tactical level of cunning, not cunning as a strategy of reason. Or even as a strategy of folly:

> But this aporia is but the flipside of the trust for which it expresses despair. We are haunted by process, and if it does not allow itself to be perceived as progress, we jump to the theme of degeneration. Perhaps it is necessary to arrive at the following understanding: there is no more of a mad cunning than of a rational one. Cunning is a word that presupposes a sly agent [*un agent rusé*], a clever subject who bets on ends [*un fin sujet qui calcule des fins*]. But what appears to us today as "cunning," or as the overflowing [*débordement*] of history, an overflowing such that neither history, nor eternity, can be found again, can only be as follows.
>
> Once history appeared, that is to say a finite destiny, we were quickly overwhelmed [*débordés*] by the absence of a subject of history, that is to say, a support, a henchman, an agent and a guide for it. The ordeal of the totalitarianisms would have been the ordeal of the *subjects* of history, or of the subject-histories. Henceforth, it is a matter of understanding that history is essentially without a subject, that *history* or *historicity* means, very precisely: neither destiny, nor subject, but the infinity of an always finite sense [*l'infini d'un sens toujours fini*].

To think history thus without a subject and not as destiny but rather as the infinite of an always finite meaning requires another form: "To this, form must be given." One can no longer write a chronicle in its "chronic" form in the spirit of a "freewheeling commentary on contemporary events" (*un libre commentaire de l'actualité*) since there is no longer anything "actual" in that actuality, nothing rigorously contemporary in what is happening *now*.

How to give form or shape, then, to this changing relation to history? Nancy indulges us then with a brief sketch, the mono-grammatic contours if one likes, of an intellectual history, the history of the giving shape to history, the history of the making of historical sense, and so the infinity of an ever finite meaning:

> In their time, this is what Montaigne, Cervantes and Shakespeare did. It's what the age of the baroque did, or wanted to do: in becoming worldly, Christianity gave figure and cadence to the arhythmically unfigurable (*l'infigurable arythmique*). Still it was necessary to believe, ultimately, in the birth of man. But during this time, the same Christianity engendered itself as the subject of history: the salvation of the human genus by the generic human being, and vice-versa. This was the subject against man, and the cunning of his reason.

This odd paragraph is not unlike the opening paragraph of *Monogrammes XIV* where the complaint about publication delays is countered by the persistence of the message's ongoing "fresh-ness." We seem to have gone from the need to invent new forms in the absence of a universalizing history to the very development of that history out of secularized Christianity in the guise of classic, enlightenment humanism. Nancy can't help but comment on the irony of his own historical sketch:

> All of this, this history that I am thus sketching out, is too perfect, functions too well through some kind of supreme cunning. This will one day have to be told otherwise, or else no longer told. Cunning and reason will only have been but a time in history. We are at the end. If history shows us its cunning in so ostensible a manner, it is because there isn't any cunning any more – nor reason either, any more than madness [*déraison*].

The problem is that trying to tell the history of the invention of forms responsive to the ever-finite meaning of the historical moment ends up falling into the very form of historical thinking (via the cunning of reason) that is being contested in the current

situation where nothing is "current" any more and where the calculated cunning of techno-economic power is only too obvious
(*ostensible*). Nancy concludes:

> Another form is to be invented. Cunning is useless, reasoning is useless.
> So too for spontaneous bursts (another version of the same cunning, a
> refreshing one). The only thing to do is to hold on well to the inven-
> tion of forms [*tenir bon, sur l'invention des formes*]. But to *hold on* well up
> to the point where there is neither support nor resistance [*Mais tenir
> bon jusqu'au point où il n'y a plus d'appui ni de résistance*]. To hold on well
> without knowing why or for what, nor what that *well* might be [*Tenir
> bon sans savoir pourquoi ni pour quoi, ni de quel bon il peut s'agir*]. To hold
> on well because humanity will always give itself a new form.

The challenge of finding the right form is not to be underesti-
mated, and we cannot simply rely on previous forms of cunning
and reason, nor even upon spontaneous expression, which merely
subscribes to the same ruse in another way (since such spontane-
ity presupposes the validity of a "naive" response to the moment
without thinking that what is in question is precisely how and
what we understand by "being in the moment"). But if one does
not rise to the challenge of "holding on well" to the invention
of some other form, then some other form will come to us since
"humankind always gives itself a new form."

But *what* that form is matters tremendously. How we think
about who we are could not be more consequential, and the last
of Nancy's *monogrammes* turns to a singularly devastating critique
of the contemporary social sciences (the explicit topic of that
entire issue of *Futur Antérieur*). In Nancy's view, the social sciences
have become organized primarily as an exercise in auto-ethnology
driven by surveys and statistics, and thereby have abdicated any
responsibility to think beyond the narcissistic self-affirmation of a
society complacent in the contemplation of its own image:

> These so-called social sciences hold exactly the place where the worn
> out or abortive form of this society is made. They are the form of
> what does not create any form. A society that no longer needs to
> invent its form, that has neither form, nor style, nor rhythm, is a

society that can do no more than mirror itself, admire itself and despise itself within an indefinite profusion of reflections of itself, of a *self that is fleeting enough to be merely the stringing along of these reflections themselves. That is what, ordinarily speaking at least, one calls* social sciences: a sociality that is conventional, preprogrammed, with no invention of sociality, of self-knowledge, of a self-image. By indulging in our own ethnology . . . , we project an image of ourselves as a society without history . . .

The social sciences thus mime the collapse of the historical narrative into mere technique and calculation. In the absence of any utopian or "exonomous" vision or the project of an imagined form,[13] the "science" of society such as it is abdicates any responsibility to (re)invent who we are and thereby abandons all sense of history as meaning-making ("the infinity of an always finite sense"), leaving only the narcissism of media-based self-display:

A society which thereby knows, or *believes it knows*, what it is qua society, which knows it and distributes this knowledge, that's what one calls the media, which are nothing other than the self-exhibition and the self-confirmation of the so-called social sciences, relentlessly displaying the anatomy of a social body that is itself defined by its capacity to anatomize itself, and hence by its cadaverous state. This takes place not only in gaudy magazines filled with opinion polls and tests: this also takes place in thick scholarly tomes, filled with surveys and statistics. This society is summed up by the exhibition of its own cunning to invent nothing other than itself. It is for itself and by itself the *absolute social science*: science as sociality and sociality as science, as if, in another register, physics were itself matter, and matter physics . . .

The social body thus construed is a dead one, incapable of "inventing anything other than itself," and its *science*, social science, consigned to the mere tautology of societal self-reflection. Nancy concludes the last of these *monogrammes* with an acerbic and monogrammatic call to arms: "What remains is insurrection, invention of forms [*Le reste est insurrection, invention des formes*]."

Kantian schematics

But the end of the series and the provisionary abandonment of Nancy's attempts to write a "philosophical chronicle," as well as the call to invent new "forms," send us right back to the first *monogrammes*. Let's recall the first and third definitions of the term "monogram", which open that entry: "kinds of written monologues" and an ancient, outdated term for "what consists only in lines, in the contours." I neglected to cite the second of the three definitions, something other than either the personal or the institutional (dictionary) definitions that frame and surround this middle definition. This second or middle definition is a philosophically technical one derived from Kant's *Critique of Pure Reason*: "monograms composed of isolated traits and determined by no given rule, forming a wavering design [*dessin flottant*], so to speak, among various experiences." This definition comes from the section on "The Ideal of Pure Reason" in the first *Critique* and rejoins the earlier chapter, "On the Schematism of the Pure Concepts of the Understanding," where Kant postulates the necessity of something in-between the understanding and sensibility or perception, something which can mediate between category or concept, on the one hand, and appearance or intuition, on the other, and which "makes possible the application of the former to the latter": "This mediating representation must be pure (without anything empirical) and yet *intellectual* on the one hand and *sensible* on the other."[14] Such a representation is what he then calls a *schema*, whose mediating function he then elaborates as follows: "The schema is in itself always only a product of the imagination; but since the synthesis of the latter has as its aim no individual intuition but rather only the unity in the determination of sensibility, the schema is to be distinguished from an image" (273). Kant gives the example, then, of putting five points down in a line as an *image* of the number five, whereas if we "think a number in general," such as the number five, "this thinking is more the representation of a method for representing a multitude . . . in accordance with a certain concept than the image itself." The expression "representation of a method for representing" is quite striking and at the limit of comprehensibility.

Given that a "method," as Descartes so famously refined the word (*meta-hodos*, what stands alongside a path, such as guideposts) is already the representation of a *way* of thinking, the schema would seem to be a "thinking" that is a representation *of* a representation *of* a way to make a representation, a tertiary form of representation, then, whose methodicalness or procedural thoughtfulness enables it somehow to serve as a pathway between sensibility and the understanding: "Now this representation of a general procedure of the imagination for providing a concept with its image is what I call the schema for this concept" (273); moreover, "we will call the procedure of the understanding with these schemata the *schematism* of the pure understanding" (273).

Kant elaborates that "in fact it is not images of objects but schemata that ground our pure sensible concepts," and here he gives another example, the canonical one, also drawn from Descartes among many others, of the triangle:

> No image of a triangle would ever be adequate to the concept of it. For it would not attain the generality of the concept, which makes this valid for all triangles, right or acute, etc., but would always be limited to one part of this sphere. The schema of the triangle can never exist anywhere except in thought, and signifies a rule of the imagination with regard to pure shapes in space. (273)

As such, schemata are "the true and sole conditions for providing [concepts] with a relation to objects, thus with *significance*" (276). But when it comes to differentiating schema from image, Kant demurs: "We can say only this much: the *image* is a product of the empirical faculty of productive imagination, the *schema* of sensible concepts (such as figures in space) is a product and as it were a *monogram* of pure *a priori* imagination, through which and in accordance with which the images first become possible, but which must be connected with the concept, to which they are themselves never fully congruent, always only by means of the schema we designate" (274).

Remarkably, the schema, which is the very condition of signification in the Kantian critique as what links object and concept, intuition and understanding, is "as it were" itself a kind of monogram, which is described in the chapter on "The Ideal of Pure Reason," among "creatures of the imagination, of which no one can give us an explanation or an intelligible concept":

> [T]hey are, as it were, *monograms*, individual traits, though not determined through any assignable rule, constituting more a wavering sketch, as it were, which mediates between various appearances, than a determinate image, such as what painters and physiognomists say they have in their heads, and is supposed to be an incommunicable silhouette of their products or even of their critical judgments. These images can, though only improperly, be called ideals of sensibility because they are supposed to be the unattainable model for possible empirical intuitions, and yet at the same time they are not supposed to provide any rule capable of being explained or tested. (552–3)

If schemata are a kind of monogram or "product of pure *a priori* imagination," they somehow represent the possibility inherent in the senselessness of the monogram nonetheless to *make* sense. They are the "condition of possibility for signification in general" while themselves remaining unsusceptible of being given "an explanation or an intelligible concept." They "*signify* a rule of the imagination" but are "not determined through any assignable rule." They are a "*representation* of a method for representing" yet seem to fall below the threshold of a representation: "more a wavering sketch . . . than a determinate image," "an *incommunicable* silhouette," etc.

Retraits

The monogrammatic schema thus inhabits a liminal space in Kantian epistemology, a space of lines, contours, traces, and *gramma*. Looking ahead to *Monogrammes XIV*, it is the not-yet formed possibility of other forms (invention, insurrection), and, as such, it evokes the infinity of an always finite sense. But it is back at the beginning of *Monogrammes II* that Nancy undertakes his most explicit commentary on the Kantian notion of the monogram:

The monogram is thus something traced before there is sense [*un tracé d'avant le sens*], neither meaningful, nor meaningless [*ni sensé, ni insensé*]. A wavering trace, not yet a figure, not yet an imprint, and not yet a writing [*Un tracé flottant, pas encore une figure, pas encore une empreinte, et pas encore une écriture*]. Its "wavering" is not for that matter pure and simple chaos; there is tracing [*traçage*], and trace (there is *gramme*), the sketching out of determination, of delineation; there is, not completed and not put together, a pinpointing [*repérage*] of places, orientations and connections.

The monogram remains at the level of a pre-text, a not–yet inscription that is nonetheless a kind of de-lineation of lines; the hint of a determination in an as-yet undetermined, incomplete, and unconnected *pinpointing* of place, direction and connectivity; a *repérage* or "repair" in the archaic sense of a place one goes back to, a place delineated or pinpointed by the plural singularity of a trace that is always a re-tracing, a *re-trait*, that is both withdrawal and emergence, *éclosion et déclosion*. A *retrait* or re-treat that is a "wavering," as in the "wavering sketch" or "*schwebende Zeichnung*," hence a *schweben* in Schlegel's romanticist sense as well.[15] It is not a "pure and simple chaos" but rather the lineaments of a schema, a de-lineation that is the condition of possibility for signification in general: "This – the schema, schematism – is thus not by itself sense – nor having sense," but "that which, before any sense is articulated (before any object is presented), articulates the possibility of any given sense [*"Cela, le scheme, le schématisme, n'est donc pas par soi-même sens – ni du sens" mais "ce qui, avant qu'aucun sens soit articulé (avant qu'aucun objet soit présenté), articule la possibilité d'un sens quelconque*]."

This bird has flown

What is the link between this pre-sense of the schema and the practice of writing a chronicle? What exactly is the project that unfolds in the series of *monogrammes*? In *Monogrammes II*, Nancy specifies: "The philosophical chronicle ought to be consecrated, as one says, to this: to what, in the era, in the mood of the moment – and in the mood of people – schematizes philosophy. To that which traces the wavering and fragmentary contours for philosophy [*La chronique philosophique devrait être consacrée, comme on dit, à ça: à ce qui, dans l'époque, dans l'air du temps – et dans l'air des gens – schématise de la philosophie. A ce qui trace des contours, flottants et fragmentaires, pour de la philosophie*]." This formulation suggests a different kind of chronicle, one that is neither a simple or "free-wheeling" commentary on current events, nor a rigorous decipherment of reason's cunning in the historical moment. Rather, it is an approach to what philosophy should be attending to in the current situation, what shaky bits of images that call for philosophical reflection, and the sense-making that is the schematism of the understanding at work in the realm of these disjointed traits that are not yet sense, i.e. monograms. Nancy makes clear that this philosophical *écoute* in the moment is not something "pre-" or "infra"-philosophical, not a "subordination of any kind," and certainly *not* "something like a philosophical potentiality or virtuality that philosophy and its discourse would be charged with actualizing."

Rather, Nancy argues, "The discourse of the philosopher only actualizes that which has effectively already been produced." He adds: "Hegel knew this well: the owl only takes flight at the end of the day." But how do we understand the role of this "poor owl?" asks Nancy.[16] It cannot simply be a question of reducing philosophy to the "useless and always belated registering of a history that always precedes it." Rejecting such a "masochistic" view on Hegel's part, Nancy clarifies what Hegel understood by the owl's flight: "Hegel knew (and this might even be exactly what he inaugurated within knowledge) that what is produced does not take place within the instant of its event (or, if you like, that there is no natural history), but only in the repetition of thought." This "repetition of thought," Nancy cautions, does *not* mean that "the event takes place if it is repeated 'in thought' (in the mode of representation, and of discourse), but that which, in it, takes place – that which truly *happens* – is what of it is repeated, what of it is thought." It is thus that philosophy, like the owl's evening flight, "actualizes" what happens, because what happens *actually* [*wirklich*], or "truly," is what can be repeated in thought, what can be thought. "Thinking," in this sense, adds Nancy, "no longer designates an intellectual faculty, nor the order of discourse (even if it must *pass* that way); 'thinking' signifies that what happens happens." Thinking" (or "being thought" Nancy stipulates) means that what happens actually *happens*, or "truly" happens. Without thought's repetition, the event doesn't truly happen, doesn't matter, or is inconsequential, and an event without consequences cannot, rigorously speaking, be said to be "eventful," is not an event. The task of thinking is therefore not inconsequential at all, but the very consequence of what happens, and it in turn makes what happens consequential. We return to the opening sentence, where we are told that a philosophical chronicle should be consecrated to what "in the era, in the mood [air] of the moment – and in the mood of people – schematizes philosophy [*dans l'époque, dans l'air du temps – et dans l'air des gens – schématise de la philosophie*]." It's a question of what's in the air (how else might the owl take flight?), or on people's minds, or of the moment (*époque*). "Thought" concludes Nancy, "signifies that what happens really happens."

A break is introduced into the text at this point, after which Nancy reflects on the preceding discourse: "What I just wrote does not belong to the philosopher." The philosopher cannot take credit for the owl's flight. "A given painter, writer, or musician knows quite well (that is to say, thinks) what is involved. (A given philosopher, on the other hand, knows nothing about it . . .)." Artists may know what they are making since it is they who make it (*poein*), but the philosopher cannot speak for others: "I dare not say it: everyone of us knows it, for it is precisely not true, it's not true in a simple and immediate way. 'Everyone' is not without some other form of adjudication, and at every instant, in *truth*. It depends upon what happens (to him/her)." It all depends on what happens, but what happens depends in turn upon "the schema, the monogram, that suspended, wavering trace . . . , through which or along which that happens." This is how philosophy is "schematized," by thinking what happens, by what happens to thought, at the end of the day, so to speak, through whatever it is that "traces wavering and fragmentary contours for philosophy," the monogram.

"Traits of another thought"

Another break is introduced, after which we are given an "example" of how this happens, in the explicit form now of a "chronicle of the most minute and most immediate actuality": "For example, and to make a chronicle of the most minute and immediate actuality [*pour faire chronique de l'actualité la plus mince et la plus immédiate*] – anachronistic by the time you read this – I'm writing these lines in the countryside, in the month of July, towards the end of the day (well, well! [*tiens, tiens!*])." So, the example of how philosophy is schematized turns us back again to the philosopher's "retreat" or repair, his isolated country home far from the urban commotion of the metropolis.[17] It is his "immediate" actuality because that is where *hic et nunc* he is writing, even if, as if in anticipation of *Monogrammes XIV*, the gap between writing and publication (not to speak of the gap that is the very event of writing) necessarily defers the so-called immediacy of this actuality, made no longer current and in the moment but always already "anachronistic," no longer chronic and thus underscoring the inalterable untimeliness of every chronicle (again in anticipation of *Monogrammes XIV*). Trying to write what is happening now may truly actualize it, may make it really, "truly" happen, but this writing from the outset always comes afterwards, at the end of the day. In noting the evening hour when he writes these lines, Nancy exclaims, "*tiens, tiens!*" as if in surprise before the coincidence that isn't, the moment for the owl to soar.

All chronicles are thus necessarily anachronistic, and never more so than when they seek to be as "actual," as current as possible. Perhaps this suggests Nancy's interesting use of the word "*mince*" to accompany "immediate" as adjectives qualifying "actuality." How can actuality be "thin"? *Mince* is of course related to the word *minute* as a thin or slender slice of time, a "mincing" of time if you will, hence my choice of translation. But it is the "thinness" of the minced moment that strikes me, that recalls the inescapability of the present moment not as presence, being present or present being, but as divided between the marker "now" and what both precedes and succeeds it. The thinness of the actual moment has no depth, being no more than the depthless depth of a line, a mere trace of the difference between "now" and *now*. And in trying to re-mark that trace, to grasp the presence of the "now," we encounter only the re-treat of time, of the finitude that in turn is the condition for what happens to happen, for there even to be something like an actuality to chronicle. For Kant, the monogram that mysteriously takes the shape of a schema, insofar as it is the "apprehension of an intuition" (or more verbosely, "the unity of the synthesis of the manifold of a homogeneous intuition": 274), is that by which the subject generates time itself as inner sense: "The schemata are therefore nothing but *a priori* time–determinations in accordance with rules" (276).[18] "*Mince,*" we might say! But what about all those other "individual traits not determined through any assignable rule," those "wavering sketches" and "incommunicable silhouettes," those monograms, in other words, which do *not* emerge as schema? What is the determining role "at the end of the day," of apperception, of apprehension, in the actually happening of what happens, in the *schematization* of the monogrammatical, in the flight of philosophy?

And what is it exactly that we get in the guise of this most minute and immediate actuality? The philosopher at home, or more precisely, a prodigiously detailed description of that remote country home in Les Ayes which we have already encountered twice (once at the break of spring and once at the break of winter). "Now" we have the midsummer heat of July, and the overgrown abundance of an old farmyard left unattended during the year, a vacation retreat where something happens, but what?:

The old farmyard, deserted during the year, is covered with exuberant vegetation, tall weeds, and grasses dotted with poppies and hairy willow herbs. A young ash tree is already able to bear the weight of the birds on its branches. Has something happened, is something happening? [*Est-il arrivé, arrive-t-il quelque chose?*] In the joyful sovereignty of the vegetation, in the flower-laden wisteria, and farther off, in those nettles as tall as a man, what is happening? Or else, in the flight of the swallows? Or in the secret presence, which only the dogs sense, of some wild animal, maybe a weasel [*belette*]? Does anything happen other than these very images, and this worn-out imagery [*cette imagerie usée*]? Anything other than a romantic or ecologicist sentimentality [*attendrissement*] that takes itself for a meditation on nature stamped with authenticity on account of its having taken place "within" nature? Anything other than the thrill of the philosopher out in the fields, who thinks this is coming cheek by jowl [*qui croit s'aboucher avec*] to the *Physis* (after all, we have on this subject an entire album of photos by Heidegger . . .)?

A beautiful passage indeed, and all the more so since the writer manages to wring out all the possible commonplaces of rustic idyll from what in point of fact appears to be an overgrown, weed-ridden patch of land, concealing and revealing a wildness emblematized by that indeterminate hint of a lurking weasel (a "*belette*," or "*belle petite bête* [lovely little beast]," he reminds us, allowing the etymology to convert the specific species into a generic animality). We remember from *Monogrammes III* that "nature likes to hide itself," but what is happening in this stunning *éclosion/déclosion* that is clearly attentive to something else lurking in "worn-out imagery" [*imagerie usée*]? The commonplace answers are all ruled out: the paroxysms of romanticist sensibility, the in-situ declaration of ecological "authenticity," the philosophical epiphany of an intimate encounter with the physical world that is nature. It is something other than Rousseau's tears or Heidegger's photos, and certainly something other than a "green" manifesto.

"Something else happens in fact," Nancy rejoins, something coming "through the grasses and fields, fireweed and weasels (and through the words of course . . .)": "Something wholly other happens, and it takes once again, as if by chance, the voice of Kant: at the end of a Mary McCarthy novel, whose action is situated in Paris during May of '68, Kant appears to the main character to tell him: "Nature is dead, *mein Kind*" [nature is dead, my child]." The contemplation of his unkempt farmyard leads not to the rapture of an immersion in nature but to a literary citation, specifically in the form of a ghostly prosopopoeia spoken by a philosopher, and not just any philosopher but Kant himself, "as if by chance." The citation schematizes the manifold of images into an intuition leading to a conclusion that is different from the simple meaning of the words:

"Nature is dead", that can be understood and commented upon in many ways, whose tally doesn't interest me. But something happens with "*mein Kind*," with that slight trembling of the German voice, of the philosophical voice. These two words exceed the variably interpretive abstraction of "nature is dead." They trace a wholly other schema, and that is the schema of a mourning. What thereby happens – and which renders, for us, something in the order of sense and truth – is less the death of nature than the announcement of the mourning which commences, and this news brought out like a child who has lost a mother, along with the pain, the tenderness and the courage that will be needed to accompany the mourning.

What makes this schema wholly other (*tout autre*) is not the content stating the death of nature (a commonplace susceptible to a rather predictable list of interpretations, as Nancy points out and rightly refuses to enumerate) but the *announcement* of the demise of nature spoken in the voice of Kant and addressed to a child listener, who is spoken *to* in English (the child's language) but addressed as such *in* German (the philosopher's language). It is as if the *auditory* dimension unified the visual manifold of images, "that slight trembling of the German voice," with its vocalic "wavering" in place of the sketch's *schweben*, and the paternal injunction to undertake that "painful, tender, and courageous" work of mourning, whose process Freud described as a conjuring of images, each called up in turn to be let go,[19] like the sequence of images Nancy himself details in describing the farmyard in Les Ayes, evoking one by one the images of nature painfully, tenderly and courageously: "Through the grasses – and the strange invention of a novelist – comes to me the mourning for a mother, whom one called in effect nature, and along with this mourning, in order to bear it and to follow through with it, the monogram of a painful, tender, and courageous thought." The mourning comes to him through the plant life and a novelist's "strange invention," comes about as something that happens and that must be borne by the philosopher, to whom it comes or happens, with a painful, tender and courageous thinking, a powerful monogram, but one he hastens to add, whose "adjectives are not very suitable, it would seem, for philosophy." That possible "unsuitability," however, and far from being in any simple way "inappropriate" to philosophical reflection, is rather what "schematizes" it, what traces – in whatever wavering or fragmentary way – that to which a "philosophical chronicle," like the *monogrammes* series, should be consecrated. "Here float the traits of another thought," writes Nancy in conclusion.

Kind/ *Kind*

If we recall Nancy's later summation from *Monogrammes XIV*: "What remains is insurrection, invention of forms," and the association of such formal inventiveness with the names of Montaigne, Cervantes, Shakespeare, and now Mary McCarthy, then we need to stop and examine the place of literature in the "traits" of that "other thought," in the disjointed monograms that somehow, in this instance, *hic et nunc*, rise to the level of a schema that links the sensible and the intelligible, that "represents a way of representing" what as yet remains unthought.

The "strange invention" attributed to Mary McCarthy as novelist is a citation of the last line of *Birds of America* (1965), a novel that begins, interestingly enough, with the death of an owl. Curiously, and despite his preceding reflection on Hegel's owl, and on the various birds in his yard, Nancy does not mention the novel by name. Much is at stake everywhere here in the possibilities and conditions of flight, metaphorical and literal, avian, and philosophical, in a kind of pervasive syllepsis. *Birds of America*, as I said, begins with the death of an owl and its emotional impact on a young American about to spend a year in Paris (the year is 1964, not 1968, as Nancy misstates, perhaps intentionally). The young man is obsessed with birds and the natural world in general, as well as with Kantian philosophy, and, in particular, with the possible applications of the moral imperative to his daily life. He is also deeply attached to his twice-divorced mother, who is herself associated with nature in general, and with birds in particular.[20]

The end of the story is triggered by the protagonist being bitten in the Jardin des Plantes by, of all things, a black swan. Unable to overcome infection and an allergic reaction to penicillin, he ends up delirious in the hospital. First, in flesh and blood, his mother appears from the United States, and disappears again. Then, in the novel's closing scene, he hallucinates a bedside visit by the philosopher from Königsberg in the guise of a kindly old man with an important message for him. The message is initially misunderstood to be that "God is dead," to which the boy protests "I *know* that," and "you didn't say that anyway, Nietzsche did." Kant leans forward to specify: "No what *I* say to you is something important. You did not hear me correctly. Listen now carefully and remember." Again he looked Peter steadily and searchingly in the eyes. "Perhaps you have guessed it. Nature is dead, *mein kind*" (344; *sic*).

In citing this final line, Nancy corrects the English text by capitalizing *"Kind"* as it should be in German. But the uncapitalized English version generates some different and unexpected outcomes. "Kind" in English refers also to *likeness* (as in the expression, the monograms are *"kinds* of written monologues," or to understand McCarthy's novel as "a *kind* of Bildungsroman"). *Kind*, in this sense, is also a *kind* of schema, a vague likeness or image, the representation of a way of representing. As such, *kind* also recalls the notion of "family resemblance," and indeed the German word for child (*Kind*) is etymologically linked to the English word for likeness of category. My "kind" is also my "kin." Or, as Hamlet says: "A little more than kin, and less than kind."[21]

There is, of course, another meaning to the English word "kind," and that refers to the affect of caring and generosity, of being *kind* to someone. Here, we can only evoke in passing both the importance of "care" (*Sorge*) in Heidegger's *Being and Time* and the Kantian moral imperative, which is also the key driver in the behavior of McCarthy's protagonist. He aspires to be kind throughout a series of misadventures, culminating in the swan's bite, all of which, and recalling again the incipit of the dead owl, point to a less than kind image of nature.

The death of nature thus appears more portentous than the misheard and banal death of God, and the weight of that announcement is mitigated by the polysemy of the word *kind*, uttered by the kindly old man who is also the character's philosophical ideal. To be greeted as his child or "kind" softens the blow of the dread announcement and of the task of mourning that must then begin, a mourning that is also a farewell to childhood and the affirmation of the protagonist's incipient maturity and consequent detachment from his mother. The polysemy of the word, kind, also motivates Nancy's characterization of the scene as not only "sorrowful" but also "tender" and "courageous."

The task of mourning the loss of a mother – in this case, what we call "nature" – is the "strange invention" of a literary text that beckons to philosophy while speaking in the fictive voice of *the* critical philosopher. It is not a question of how to be a philosopher in one's garden or out in the *physis*, but of the philosophical urgency to think beyond the *meta-physis* of some foundational identity, be it God or nature, or history, or nation, or self. Philosophy would *begin* with the awareness of loss, of finitude, of insuperable negativity. The mourning of metaphysics is the dusk that motivates the flight of Minerva's owl through the wavering, disjointed "traits of another thought," the not-yet sense of the monogram that signifies not merely the salutary strangeness of that other thought (that "strange invention," the "insurrection" of forms) but the very estrangement of thought itself, which exceeds any notion of philosophy as merely a technical competency in concepts and discourses.

Stranger than thought

In the final pages of *Monogrammes II*, Nancy continues to dwell on the necessary attentiveness to this *"schéma inédit"* or the strangeness of that "other thought." Reflecting on a recent colloquium at his home university of Strasbourg, he points to what is supposed to happen in a *col-loquium* (literally, a speaking together), namely the opportunity for thinking to take place in-between the closed idioms of specialized knowledge, on the one hand, and the open communicability of all discourse, on the other: "It is evident that a colloquium cannot take place – if it truly takes place – except in this 'in-between' ['*entre*']. But how? There again, wouldn't that suppose an unprecedented schema [*un schème inédit*] of pain, tenderness and courage?" The "traits of another thought" are

those that float or waver in-between the expressions of clarity
and obscurity, universality and singularity, ready comprehensibility and resistant obscurity. *Monogrammes II* closes with a review
of a work by his close colleague and friend, Philippe Lacoue-
Labarthe, for whom Nancy has no higher praise than his pursuing
"a constant, obstinate (even obsessive) practice of the *strangeness*
of thought": "Philosophy, for him, is not the completely localizable [*repérable*], if not wholly familiar, order of concepts and
their discourses. Philosophy, for that matter, is not above all the
terrain of difficult questions – but of strange questions, barely
questions, moreover, and often suspicions, worries, forebodings,
always strange."

Qualifying this further, Nancy adds that it is not the strangeness per se of the object studied that matters so much as the
concomitant *estrangement* of thought: "It's a thinking that never
stops becoming strange to itself, itself losing the very knowledge
it acquires. Thereby, it suspends itself, as if by interdiction, at the
limit of knowledge, and of the knowledge of self." Can this still
be called philosophy, or is it rather the "future of philosophy?"[22]
A future not in some progressive or anticipatory sense, much less
a developmental one, but rather as what is to come (*a-venir*), what
always stands resolutely *in front of* philosophical reflection, the
wavering contours and incomprehensible silhouettes that *fore-see*
other forms, the "strange inventions" of novelists or artists ("what
painters and physiognomists say they have in their heads" [Kant,
Critique of Pure Reason, 552]).[23]

The monogram signifies that future, that otherness of thought,
its very estrangement, the ongoing atmosphere ("*l'air du temps*"
or "*l'air des gens*") that is the limit condition of thinking (the
"incommunicable silhouette") and where philosophical reflection
can only take off owl-like in the twilight of its own mourning.
Elsewhere, Nancy describes the "exigency of reason" in the following manner: "that of illuminating its own obscurity, not by
bathing it in light, but by acquiring the art, the discipline and the
strength to let the obscure emit its own clarity."[24] At the same
time, this "requirement that carries thought beyond itself"[25] does
not suppose a solipsistic figure of the philosopher, on the contrary:
"'a philosopher' meaning here: not a technician of the concept,

but above all that which is expected, required, today, of the common consciousness."[26] As the practice of such an exemplary *écoute,* Nancy's *monogrammes* remain a chronicle of philosophy, if not a philosophical chronicle, that anachronistically thinks the air we "now" breathe in common and dares the insurrectional invention of forms, even or especially through the withdrawal (which is always also the emerging) of philosophical thought from the actualities and conditions of the world, be it the estrangement of that "other thought" staged within or without the philosopher's retreat, at Les Ayes, in Strasbourg, or elsewhere . . .

Postscript, kind of . . .

In 2002, nine years after the last *monogrammes* written in 1993, Nancy returns again to the genre of the "philosophical chronicle" in a series of radio lectures, gathered afterwards in a book by that title. There are nine of these short talks delivered over an eleven-month period.[27] The published version indicates the date (but not the place) for each of these texts. The term *monogrammes* seems to be abandoned, despite a certain similarity in the genre of discourse. One major dissimilarity is in the much greater argumentative cohesion of these "chronicles" than the more dispersed and fragmentary style of the *monogrammes* series. Nonetheless, the first of these published lectures discusses what Nancy now means by a "philosophical chronicle." The resulting text can be read as a commentary on the earlier *monogrammes*:

> A chronicle of philosophy. What can this really mean? A chronicle is a rubric indicating something punctual and periodical, whose content has to do either with a particular specialization (gastronomy, gardening, etc.), or with a subjectivity (the world according to the mood of the chronicler). But philosophy, in whatever manner we envisage it, aspires to be removed from specialization as well as from subjectivity. From the beginning and in principle, it demands the universal and the objective.

The "philosophical chronicle" appears as a perilous and insuper-able oxymoron. To philosophize is to reject every conditionality, to seek the unconditional, but that would mean an invariant that is utterly at odds with the necessary variability of a chronicle. To engage the form of the chronicle would not only be to abandon this philosophical imperative but also to risk the tendency "today" of a certain "cultural mode of 'philosophy' that endlessly warms up [a] very light broth [of 'values,' 'virtues,' and common sense], while letting the vague promise of an unconditional final truth float about in its vapor." The result is to accept "a cheap ethico-pragmatic consensualist ideology while boosting the market value quoted for 'the philosopher.'" But, as I hope these pages have shown, it is a distinctive *trait* of Jean-Luc Nancy's work to address the concerns of the here and now while maintaining a philosophi-cally committed approach to the questions involved, to pursue a philosophy that does not eschew but rather fearlessly engages the singular and the particular, the chronic and the anachronic, as a genuine philosophical problem.

I do not claim that I can avoid the cultural peril without remain-der or risk. I have chosen to brush up against this ambiguity because this cultural danger must be confronted on its own territory – by speaking on the radio, for example. This is not just a matter of strategy. It is also because the cultural development of philosophy itself opens up a question of some philosophical importance.

I could begin again by citing the very first of the *monogrammes*, written more than thirty years ago but under strikingly similar circumstances, during the first manifestations of the media-savvy *"nouveaux philosophes,"* whom Nancy takes to task in those first *monogrammes*. The challenge, then as *now*, is to engage the new venues and media while "holding on" to the invention of forms, while resolutely practicing the insurrectional strangeness of thought itself. Strangely enough, this engagement might not be something new at all but, in effect, a return to a certain "classical" form of philosophy, as Nancy writes at the beginning of *Monogrammes I*:

A philosophical chronicle, today, what could that be then? The oppor-tunity having been offered to me, my curiosity piqued, I seized upon it. I don't know if this venue is suitable, nor if I have the physical

stamina for the job . . . I dream of something that philosophy would
have lost: an existence that is *chronic*, precisely, following the thread of
time, tied to the rhythm of the seasons and reasons, partaking in our
history, periodized and syncopated, full of occasions and interventions.
I imagine classical philosophy existed like that. . . . Descartes, Leibniz,
or Hume circulated in every way.

The "circulation" of philosophy and philosophers circles us back,
then, to an existence that is demonstrably *chronic*, actualized in the
presence or absence of any given *actualité*, "full of occasions and
interventions" that, *now and then*, find their form, insurrectional or
not, in the disjointed traces or wavering designs of the monogram.

Post-postscript: the *impossible* now

Speaking of Nancy "now," in the last year, since the completion of
this study, he has again relaunched the *monogrammes* series, beginning with the number 10 issue of *L'Impossible* (February 2013), and,
as of this date (October 2013), continuing with two installments in
numbers 12 (April 2013), and 13 (Summer 2013). Nancy's reprise
of the *monogrammes* thus casts a rather obvious pall of anachronicity,
if not to say, inaccuracy, over my remarks regarding the definitive
abandonment of the term *monogrammes*. But then, it always was
within the potential of the "series" to begin anew and unexpect-
edly after a long hiatus (as happened before in the decade between
the contributions to *Digraphe* and to *Futur Antérieur*). And I did
speak of the "seeming" disappearance of the word *monogrammes*
from an experimental form of occasional philosophy that can just
as easily take on different names (chronicle, for example), as well as
different venues, times, and places. Appearing most recently in the
journal *L'Impossible*, the first of these latest *monogrammes* redirects
the name of the venue by taking the word "impossible" to mean
something other than what is "not possible" or "unrealizable,"
but rather as "what is foreign to the economy of the possible and
the impossible, to the calculation of what is (un)feasible, in today's
jargon." It is, once again, to pursue the strangeness of philosophy

to itself: "To think outside the possible, is to think the unstated, the unheard – what every existence bears along with itself and which is never given or deposed." For the "now" is never given simply, never simply given: "Nancy *Now*," an impossible task, to be begun ever anew as the untimely chronicle, the singularly plural *monogrammes*, of what is always yet to come.

References

Hegel, G. W. F. *Grundlinien der Philosophie des Rechts*. Leipzig: Felix Meiner, 1911.

Kant, Immanuel. *Critique of Pure Reason*, trans. Paul Guyer and Alan Wood. Cambridge: Cambridge University Press, 1999.

Lacoue-Labarthe, Philippe, and Jean-Luc Nancy. *L'Abosolu littéraire*. Paris: Seuil, 1978.

McCarthy, Mary. *Birds of America*. New York: Harcourt, 1965.

Nancy, Jean-Luc. *Chroniques philosophiques*. Paris: Galilée, 2004. *Philosophical Chronicles*, trans. Franson Manjali. New York: Fordham University Press, 2008.

Nancy, Jean-Luc. *La Déclosion. Déconstruction du christianism 1*. Paris: Galilée, 2005.

5

Extended Drawing

Ginette Michaud

Translated by Fernanda Maria Negrete

Le Plaisir au dessin (*The Pleasure in Drawing*)[1] holds a singular place within Jean-Luc Nancy's broad philosophical work on the arts, in which the question of sense —"*sentir*" [*feeling*], sensation, sensibility, sensuality — is increasingly intensified.[2] This reflection also takes part in the current revival of drawing in France as well as in the United States, where, if one considers the attention paid to drawing — drawing and its extension, drawing extended[3] — one notices a desire "to invigorate the discourse around drawing."[4] As proof, I shall discuss two books published in 2010, almost at the same time as *The Pleasure in Drawing*, already revealing a most significant conjunction of interests. On the one hand, in France, the exhibition catalogue appropriately titled *Lignes de chance. Actualité du dessin contemporain* [*Lines of Chance. Actuality of Contemporary Drawing*][5] (it even sounds like a Nancean title!), which gathers the accounts of fifty artists, writers, researchers, poets, and philosophers (among them Jean-Luc Nancy[6]), foregrounding the desire for experimentation currently sparked by this practice that borrows from very diverse paths of creation and knowledge. On the other hand, calling upon impressive means and tackling a huge breadth of theoretical and aesthetic perspectives, there is the important MoMA retrospective *On Line: Drawing Through the Twentieth*

Century, whose catalogue commands attention due to its theoretical quality as much as its statements regarding drawing, to which I will return further along.

What is striking about these two multi-authored books, which from the very beginning find a surprising meeting point with the layout chosen by Nancy in *The Pleasure in Drawing*, is the highly dynamic montage, in each of these books, set up between the drawings and the critics' and artists' own propositions concerning the art; as if from the start it had to be thus, and not otherwise, in the multiplication, the plurality of intersecting lines of thought, that one could, that one should speak of drawing today, in the *Now* of this "now" [*maintenant*]. As though it were precisely impossible to "take stock" ["*faire le point*"][7] (an expression Gilles Deleuze considered nothing less than "stupid") of this topic, and conversely, as Deleuze affirms, always necessary to "think of things as ensembles of lines to unravel, but also to overlap," because what matters in the drawing line is "not that the line goes between points, but that the point lies at the crossing of several lines."[8] This definition of line is not foreign to the one set forth in *The Pleasure in Drawing* by Nancy, who writes of the line that it "is the point itself . . . in the process of dividing space" (*P* 124/101), "a point that leaves itself behind, that ceases to be alone, that opens a relation [*rapport*]," according to Jean-Christophe Bailly[9]; thus, an infinity of points in itself that opens up a political dimension (I will return to this "indivisible and mobile point where a form and manner is born" and to its ability to open "new possibilities for other spacings"; *P* 124/101). But for now, let us merely note the line's "punctuality of existence" for Nancy, in other words its "being not only exposed but disposed to parting [*partance*] or dispatching" (*V* 297), and the fact that this multiplied punctuality is directly linked to the form of "free thinking" about the line, which is best rendered by "the free circulation of lines formed by thoughts and their intersectings" (*V* 297). Indeed, if in *The Pleasure in Drawing* Nancy offers a little "treatise" ["*traité*"] of sorts, he opens up this closed genre by inserting, at the head of each section, a series of free ideas, which he calls "*Carnets de croquis*" ["*Sketchbooks*"]. Recalling the style of the sketchbook – of which he says in parentheses that "Here one should explicate the role of the album

or sketchbook, drawing's handheld transcendental" (*P* 122/116
n. 47) – heterogeneous thoughts, sparks, and interruptions unreel
discontinuously and contiguously, forming a line nonetheless, but
a dotted one, leaving the question of drawing unresolved. Prior to
any other mode of consideration (aesthetic, philosophical, ethical,
political), it is thus the very form of the *line of thought* – one could
also say of the *drift of thought*, but all the while maintaining in this
drift something of the nature of the *drive*, which is no less than élan
and impulse[10] – that needs to be underlined, by borrowing from
the outset the Nancean logic of the "singular plural" in these three
works that conceive of the line of drawing in very close terms.

In *Lignes de chance* (*LC*), as well as in *On Line*, drawing is thus
appropriately considered to be "one of the important aspects of
contemporary creation" (Cousseau, *LC* foreword).[11] This does
not only concern drawing as a foundational practice in fine arts
instruction, but also a form of expression essential to the very
conception of the work of art, and this not only as the setting up
(preparation, draft, pentimento, etc.) of an artistic project, but,
more fundamentally, as the process of creation and of thought itself
("*dessin*," "drawing" and "*dessein*," "design/intention" share their
meaning in this regard). Indeed, the artists in the exhibit *Lignes de
chance* articulate it, each in her or his own way, each time differently: as Henry-Claude Cousseau puts it in the preface, drawing
is an "autonomous means of expression" (*LC*) irreducible to a
project or a sketch "with a view to . . ." What is more, "there is"
drawing; there is no drawing for Giuseppe Penone unless "the
action of drawing is the subject of the work, the means indispensable to the idea, to language, to the invention of the image"
(*LC*); or to quote him on another topic, a drawing is no longer
or not simply a question of style, of writing [*graphie*], or even of
"manner": it is that "which does not exhaust itself in the effect of
its technique, but which suggests a reflection upon the world and
offers an unexpected vision of reality" (*LC*). And this expectation
– this "adoration," Nancy would say,[12] underlining the *ad* of this
absolute address – is in fact the whole issue of drawing. As Bernard
Moninot[13] puts it, "drawing foresees the gesture capable of holding
together [*en coïncidence*] a thing's trait and a thought" (*LC*); it is

"the projection, the prolongation of the present, the anticipation of a thing that has yet to happen [*qu'il faut faire advenir*]" (*LC*). This very experience – or even experimentation or test, more so than experience – is what Marc Desgrandchamps accounts for when he says about drawing that it "keeps in mind certain moments of good fortune [*chance*], when the spirit of the trait attained identification with the trait of the spirit" (*LC*).

After writing profusely on painting among all the arts of the visible (but also on dance, cinema, music, and literature), it is no coincidence if Nancy then devotes his attention entirely to the art of *disegno* [drawing/design] in *The Pleasure in Drawing*. In sixteen short chapters and as many "*Sketchbooks*" (comprising quotations by writers and philosophers of art, often by way of hearsay accounts), this genuine treatise goes through the most salient aspects of the art, perhaps the first, the most "commencing" of all the arts. But if Nancy plays on the etymological collusion (false, for that matter, or made-up) that ties "*dessin*" to "*dessein*" in the Italian word "*disegno*," it is precisely to use it as a point of departure in order to separate and distinguish these two meanings. Closely interested in this homonymy, Jacques Derrida does so as well, in a conference significantly titled "*À dessein, le dessin*,"[14] in which he underscores, just like Nancy, that what is specific to drawing is its being "an aim without a target,"[15] a line jotted down or drawn, a "sketch [*jetée*], first draft [*premier jet*], initial sketch [*première pensée*]" (*P* 121/98) in excess of any project or intention. "What [drawing] intends to designate [*a dessein de désigner*]," Nancy remarks, "is exactly the *drawing of the nascent form whose form is nowhere given in advance*" (*P* 33/22). The ethics of drawing – and therefore the ethics of aesthetics as a whole, if distinguishing these two words that seem so necessarily bound to one another still makes sense[16] – is a process of "a 'repeated self-questioning' [*un 'se redemander'*]" (*P* 39/27), and like the pleasure that is the expression of its aisthesic experience and that incessantly wants to start over, to play itself out again "in an endlessly renewed act" (*P* 118/96). Moreover, drawing is characterized by the fact that it "demands liberty as *the power to begin again*, and consequently, [that its] Idea is Form beyond all form, or drawing whose line crosses all contours" (*P* 129/104–5). A "drawing whose line crosses [*passe*] all contours": how can one not interpret this trespassing [*outrepassement*] of the line [*trait*] – insurrection, unachievable extension, infinite disposition – that, in the thing [*chose, Ding*] of art, lifts and takes off, not letting itself be stopped or fixed in any finite form? Not only in its aesthetic (or, if you will, ethical) consequences, but also philosophical – since at stake here is that which is "*beyond being*" [*au-delà de l'étant*] (*P* 129/104) – and political, as art represents (but without analogy and without a model) the very mode of the "politics and beyond"[17] so insistently called for by Nancy.

If Nancy turns to drawing, it is due to deep elective affinities – philosophical, aesthetic/aisthesic, political – with this form that is always in formation, to borrow from Juan-Manuel Garrido's book title *La Formation des formes*[18] [*The Formation of Forms*], which finds itself *in statu formandi*, being a graphic energy always on the verge of being born, of emerging, or better yet, of *emanating* from the ground, extending itself toward a passage or a border – or of disappearing, of withdrawing/retiring (Nancy strongly insists on this *re-trait* [re-tiring, re-drawing, re-tracing] of the trait, and this very expression, present since his collaborative work on the political with Philippe Lacoue-Labarthe, is not irrelevant to his attraction to this art). This question of the *forma formans*, infinitely nascent, always emerging and springing up (but all at once exhausted, extenuated, vanishing), is what leads Nancy to privilege drawing over painting itself: "'To draw' is at once to give birth to form – to *give* birth in *letting* it be born – and thus to show it, to bring it to light [*mettre en évidence*] – or rather, and here again, to allow its evidence to offer and dispose itself" (*P* 33/22).

As Dominique Gauthier observes, drawings "are there to maintain [us] in a certain clarity, a transparency; do they already exist elsewhere, where does this pointed will for precision, this determined line come from?" (*LC*). Clarity, precision, pointedness: Nancy's thought perfectly adjusts itself here to this "object" (if still an object) or, as Gilgian Gelzer also puts it, "each drawing opens a new field of energy where thought unfolds and takes shape, where a sensation is materialized, an idea or a feeling realized" (*LC*). Neither prediction nor preparation, drawing offers itself as a snapshot [*instantané*], a *kairos* of the gesture, unique "but not isolated": it "is unfinished (in-finite) and it legitimately inscribes itself in an interminable (infinite) practice. Out of this incessant process, out of this incompleteness, an irresolute expectation is born" (*LC*), notes Philippe Boutibonnes, in terms very close to Nancy's when he evokes the "*finality without end*" (*P* 111) of art and that of drawing in particular: "Finality without end – the infinite renewal of the end, since it is nothing other than the inexhaustible profusion offered to us of forms, of lines of sense" (*P* back cover). This is undoubtedly why drawing, which could be defined as that which goes out in the open (English says it better: *drawing*, both coming and going at once, that which attracts toward itself and that which projects itself outside, making the limit between inside and outside imperceptible), can "follow the rules of perspective, the restitution of volumes, etc., but can also easily get rid of them" (*LC*), as Peter Soriano accurately views it. Being the form of the opening par excellence, drawing frees itself from grammar; its enunciation is not that of complete phrases but rather suspense always only pending, at the fine tip of language, of a language itself always still on the edge of sense: "Speech [*parole*] is thought expressed through the mouth. Drawing is thought expressed by the hand. [. . .] Drawing and speech are the purest extensions of thought" (Soriano, *LC*).

But drawing . . . what does it actually mean? It is clear: several of the artists' assertions in *Lignes de chance* echo the reflection Nancy undertakes in *The Pleasure in Drawing*. This is the case for instance, when François Bouillon evokes "a coming-and-going between [. . .] the subject and the object" (*LC*), or when Bernard Moninot speaks of "the tight bond between vision and forgetting," brushing "the edge that separates the perception of space and the thought of time" (*LC*). Drawing is also described by Moninot as the "ideal medium [*support*] of the idea that dwells in the interval between: sight and hearing, the visible and memory, the eye and the hand" (*LC*). It lodges itself, one might say, in these very gaps, and as such presents an exemplary form – always in movement and never completely stabilized, still vibrating when apparently fixed – of the *with*, a notion at the heart of Nancy's philosophy. For a drawing never occurs by itself, as Matisse wrote, whom Nancy, manifestly fond of this sentence, quotes and discusses twice over: "One must always follow the desire of the line, where it wishes to enter or where to die away." "Remember, a line cannot exist alone; [. . .] Do remember that a line does nothing; it is only in relation to another that it creates a volume."[19] A drawing is always "that which links one thing to another" (Moninot, *LC*). So much so that, as Philippe Boutibonnes underlines for his part:

> A drawing cannot be examined separately as an absolute given. Every aesthetic or ethical judgment regarding it must be suspended: a drawing is not more beautiful or ugly, neither better nor worse than those that precede or follow it. The repetitive and continuous gesture – that is to say, the activity – whose scansion is carried out by drawings, is alone the object of a sentence. [. . .] I am drawing. I shall never finish. (*LC*)

In this sense, drawing is the artistic gesture par excellence[20]: an act, a passage, not as acting out, but as passage *of* the act itself, its on–the–spot actualization. Drawing –and that is what attracts Nancy to it, too – is the thought of what is quickest; better yet, it is that which thinks between the lines. If we were to pick out a single trait among the "lines of sense" in Nancy's essay – itself a thought-drawing with, chiefly, the question of the "form-pleasure" (*P* 56/44) calling for a rethinking of the erotics of art ("The pleasure of desiring, not that of releasing a tension") and with it "eroticism itself" (*P* back cover) – it would be that drawing is "the opening of form" (*P* 9/1). Impetus, departure, lift, but also inexhaustible availability, that is to say, its own ability to be endlessly "opened up, opened out, initiated, incised" (*P* 10/2) by the trait (both mark and line, as well as trace, the trait is foremost the process and motion, the gesture by which the tracing out takes place). Trait that draws itself from nothing, for the sole pleasure of "a sense of gesture, movement, or becoming" (*P* 9/1). Drawing is no longer, in this perspective, a thing of will or intention (Picasso used to say to Brassaï: "To know what one wants to draw, one must start to do it"; in Desgrandchamps, *LC*), nor does it merely depend on expression or subjectivity in the usual sense of these terms: it is and remains a power [*puissance*] of being, a dynamic, potential force, before or beyond any form laid out on a medium (paper, screen or other: for drawing translates itself in every art, it is "melodic, rhythmic, filmic, poetic": *P* back cover). And this is exactly because drawing doesn't so much touch upon an idea of structure as it sets to work, through the drawing itself (without ever settling for the concept of "work" as such), "a structuring that is marked by its permanent exposure to and from itself"[21]; it is because drawing is this "'erring work of sense,'" impulse unbound from the unbinding, that it actualizes in or onto its very form a "politics of the 'infinite bond,'" an "'atheological politics,'" which is to be "understood as a politics of multiplication and de-multiplication of bonds, as the open space of a possibility of bonds in every sense"[22] (*V* 297). For, as Jean-Christophe Bailly aptly puts it, "it is in the very space of this disjunction that the necessity of bonding presents itself anew, that the opening of disenclosed [*décloses*] ties gapes – a kind of 'connecting infinitely'" (*V* 298).

Around the same time on the other side of the Atlantic, in a revelatory synergy of thought, the exhibit and the eponymous catalogue *On Line* also retraced "the continuous adventure of the line" (*V* 292) – from inaugural texts by Kandinsky (*On Line*[23] and *Point and Line to Plane*[24]) and Klee, to the research, conceptual and other (from the most formal and abstract "schematic limitation" to the most "unlimited expressivity," exploring a profusion of "forms of infinite flexibility," to draw on Kandinsky's words). Indeed, the line began increasingly to step outside, starting in the 1970s (but already much earlier, perhaps from time immemorial), to resolutely travel the world, giving rise to practices that deliberately extend beyond the paper medium, making the line "walk," out there, in the real world,[25] according to Klee's expression ("The primordial movement, the agent, is a point that sets itself in motion (genesis of form). A line comes into being. . . . In all these examples the principal and active line develops freely. It goes out for a walk, so to speak, aimlessly for the sake of the walk"[26]). "[L]ine left the plane of the page as a fully physical element – an existent within the world – to find a place on something that shared this quality of external space. Line was taken for a walk into the 'real' world – onto the floor, the walls of building, into the plains and mountains, close to the earth, high in the sky," comments Catherine de Zegher (*L* 99), who describes the trajectory of the drawing line making its way across the century in the following terms: "the idea of 'a line as a point in movement' as it was conceived in the early twentieth century by Kandinsky, Klee and others evolves in mid-century toward thinking of 'a point as a crossing of lines,' and beyond this, into the web of the present" (*L* 89).

The exhibit and the catalogue *On Line* seek, in this respect, a certain "line of thought" on drawing and on its breaking free from the medium. It is a matter of passing from "the line in the plane (surface tension)" to "the line broken free from that illusory surface into real space (line extension); and finally [to] its apparent return to the relational space of the real and the imaginary, but with each now transformed in the process (confluence). [. . .] Where thought had been linear and progressive, it has evolved into a kind of network, something more fluid, open, simultaneous, and undefined" (*L* 24). This layout [*tracé*] calls into question again all restrictive definitions of drawing, which according to Leonardo da Vinci's famous definition has "in itself neither matter nor substance" ("Definition of the Nature of Line," quoted in *L* 23), neither inside nor outside; the thought of the trait[27] – attraction, extraction, retraction, ex-tension – undoes any opposition that thinks it can limit – delineate – and determine it (especially the one that divides the entire tradition of history of art between drawing and color,[28] a question Nancy interestingly evokes in passing, in a note in *The Pleasure in Drawing*, reserving it for another work[29]). The reflection elaborated in *On Line* intersects with Nancy's thought in many aspects, then (even if his works on these arts are never cited in this book, unlike those by Deleuze or Badiou . . .), first of all in its way of positioning drawing as "an open-ended activity, drawing is characterized by a line that is always unfolding, always becoming" (*L* 23). And it is certainly remarkable that this emancipation of the line, this way of thinking of it in terms of "*Nasci*" ("'being born' or 'becoming'": *L* 65), which undertakes "[t]he fusing of opposites – inside and outside, subjective and objective, erotic and ascetic – " (*L* 65) and "undo[es] the binary [. . .], develop[s] the in-between, the relational" (*L* 56), also coincide, from the standpoint of perception/sensation, with "a sensation of boundlessness, a vertiginous ecstasy of dilation" (*L* 58). This expression strongly echoes Nancy's argumentation in *The Pleasure in Drawing*, which deals primarily with the question of desire in the line of drawing – desire "endlessly taken up again and revived," "un-satisfied," "that always transports itself further" (*P* 40/28); in its self-affection that sends it incessantly out of itself, to the experience of "pleasure or pain, in other words, the expansion or retraction of its being" (*P* 40/ 28), it does not reduce or exhaust itself. (Nancy makes this pleasure – ecstasy, more so than pleasure, actually – the very gesture of art: "the gesture of art in general, and of drawing in particular, does not aim for the repletion or discharge of a tension but rather the opening and revival or resurgence of an intensity. [. . .] What one calls 'art' is the knowledge of such a passion [*emportement*]": *P* 39–40/27–8). Moreover, in this play of lines, drawing is

> freed from both support and the task of representation, drawing has created a space for becoming that did not previously exist. If a line can articulate and alter the background – which is to say, the order of our social reality, potentially – then drawing allows a rare open space for the conscious formation and critical development of subjectivity and so for social change. (*L* 113)

Drawing is thus no longer the configuration of something; rather, it is the configuration of no-thing: "neither a 'construction' nor a 'composition' [. . .], but 'a configuration allowing for the work not to have an absolute fixity,'" in the words of artist Avis Newman (*L* 108). This entails, in turn, a radical rethinking of the ground/surface relation, "the line becoming ground and the ground becoming line, in an ongoing confusion" (*L* 117; how not to think, reading this proposal, of Nancy's work in *The Ground of the Image*?). The relevance of the question concerning the ground (inevitably linked to ground and foundation in perceptual and philosophical terms, as well as to the aesthetic articulation of ground/surface) is well known in the work of Nancy, constantly deconstructed through an exposure of the ground that involves another way of thinking about the relation of figure to ground. Indeed, figure (if this word still applies) in drawing or painting does not append itself to a ground, let alone apply itself to its surface or even simply detach itself from it. As Philip Armstrong notes, for Nancy it is instead a matter of conceiving it as:

a way of rendering the "original" ground other than – or to – itself, producing or creating this ground in the very process in which [the figure] detaches itself *on* the ground, just as this displacement simultaneously transforms the figure itself – the figure [. . .] at once figured and disfigured, opening toward a displacement internal to the very positing of the figure as such (figuration as simultaneous disfiguration, reconfiguration, transfiguration . . .) (*D* 34)

In this sense, Nancy's work is less a matter of retrieving the age-old question of ground/surface than of reopening it from the ground up, so to speak. In his text devoted to Rouan, whose practice he describes in terms that are very close to Nancy's, Armstrong rightly demonstrates what is at stake in this relation, in which ground and figure, depth and surface are "thus marked less by a distinction or separation in which two things now remain distinct and separate from one another but a detachment which is the condition of a *simultaneous* attachment, a detachment that functions in and through the figure's attachment *on* something else" (*D* 31). This detachment/attachment in relation to the ground (at play also in Nancy's reconfiguration of the mimesis/methexis issue, which in so many texts he turns "inside out") "opens the very between of the *entre-lacs*, opens the *en de l'entre* or the in of the in-between, like an interval that remains open to its inherent spacing" (*D* 28):

> This is the place of the *interstitium* as what stands or positions itself *between* and not within, the in of the in-between that constitutes an opening, a crack, a rip, or slit that joins in detaching itself, that articulates and folds what it simultaneously unbinds and unfolds, what glues itself together in the moment of its detachment on a surface, and that refolds that surface into its thickness and not the play between surface and depth. Nowhere does this constitute a form of self-reflexivity and self-reference. There is nothing here that constitutes a system of signs that turns back on itself. On the contrary, it is the initiating and inaugural measure in which space spaces. (*D* 38)

It is clear by now that the reconfiguration around drawing one finds in *On Line* also bears close affinities with Nancy's thought in *The Pleasure in Drawing*, in that the line of questioning conducted here not only impacts an aesthetic level,[30] but also entails philo-sophical and political consequences. That drawing has become this ever-nascent form, "a moving trace in time and space, stress-ing interreliance and transsubjectivity" (*L* 119) never constituted as such, making of line a site where a permanent genesis in the world and in art occurs; that drawing can be seen as the "mod-eling of the human milieu" (*L* 86), a way of thinking, through the intertwining of lines, about interactive forces, a "model of subjectivity-as-encounter" (*L* 86) affecting all that is interwoven, reticulated, in an infinite interconnectedness and interdependency, is of the utmost importance. It "impl[ies] an openness to the other and the possibility of relation in mutually shared realities" (*L* 89), if not *the* form of shared presence per se, a conviviality – to be precise: a co-viviality – of the relation or *rapport* which is the core of Nancy's thought of the "cum," the pulse of the *Trieb* or the inaugural event of "struction"[31] as he calls it lately, preceding any "construction" or "deconstruction." Art, or drawing, as the very form that "remakes us as much as we remake it. [For] [w]e are humans only in relation" (*L* 117). Drawing, thus, as what draws us to the world and pulls us apart from it, if "reality only takes form to the extent that it arises from an interdependent matrix of parts. Through this web of relation comes the realization that I am not merely grounded in this world, I *am* the world" (*L* 86). As early as 1927, in *The Non-Objective World*, Malevich called line "the element that generates form and, as such, the determinant of a way of perceiving the world" (*L* 47). I would like to end by echoing this remarkable convergence that on the subject of line and drawing unfolds on three planes at once – philosophical, aesthetic, and political. How drawing hovers between poetics and politics: this is indeed the line of thought that always needs to be pursued further, as I shall attempt to do in the last part of this essay.

("How drawing hovers between poetics and politics": Jean-Luc Nancy would perhaps not agree with such a view, judging this kind of phrasing both inflationary and vague to say the least. Clarification is called for as to the use of this word "*politique*," [politics/political] a word itself always in need of redrawing, of withdrawing/re-tracing. In a recent text titled "*Politique et/ou poli-tique*," Nancy returns exactly to the question of the political and its

"beyond," clarifying the expression "beyond politics" by offering
a sharper formulation:

> I try to work on a beyond that is not trespassing [*outrepassant*], neither
> extravagant nor extreme [*pas outré ni outrancier non plus*]. A beyond that
> in truth would come from below which would surpass politics, not
> toward a super-politics [*surpolitique*] but toward a resetting, or even
> a restriction of its concept. Henceforth detaching itself from politics
> itself. Or rather, detaching it from itself.[32]

I cannot do justice here, in this space of mine, to all the nuances
required by this question of the political, which traverses Nancy's
thought through and through, but one must at least insist upon this
necessary dehiscence of the political for him. For Nancy is attached
to this difference, adopted from Heidegger but still "unnoticed"
(*PP* 4), between "*politeia*," the Greek *polis*, and "politics," as conceived by modern political discourse (state, government, regulation,
organization, etc.), judging that it is this confusion of values "that
disturbs our thought on what we call 'political'" (*PP* 4). In order
for the word "*politique*" "to be neither 'all' nor 'nothing'" (*PP* 2)
and to find its proper place, one would have to start by posing and
elucidating the problem (which he qualifies as "crucial") of a word
"that understands itself as one of its parts" (*PP* 4), and distinguishing (always this gesture of the differentiating distinction – trait and
contour, line of the trait – which Nancy is so keen on) as rigorously
as possible between, on the one hand, the political sphere, and, on
the other, the "other spheres of existence 'in common' (which
is all of the existence, all but not as a whole)" (*PP* 5), and thus,
between "living-together" and "being-together,"[33] the one irreducibly incommensurable to the other. In other words, one would
have to untie and dispel this "internal distortion between two
values henceforth foreign to one another," albeit always "tied and
interdependent" (hence the source of confusion): "an existential
value and a societal value" (*PP* 9). Furthermore, Nancy specifies in
this text – and this intensifies the difference between politics and
what it must give access to under the names of "love," "thought,"
"gesture," or "art" – that politics can "satisfy" (it approximates a
demand, if not a need, and responds to finalities), but "not offer

joy" (*PP* 8). Only those spheres wherein there is *work*, that is to say "access and accomplishment" (*PP* 8), can offer this enjoyment [*jouissance*], for they are related to desire, and therefore *"unfinishable"* – which further explains the entire development in *The Pleasure in Drawing* around the erotics of *aesthesis*, exemplarily at work in drawing, where desire is "expectation or tension turned toward its own intensity, not toward an object of satisfaction" (*PP* 6). I now close this parenthesis that should, however, continue to delve deep into and open up everything that follows.)

One of the most important contributions in this work of Nancy's on art also concerns, then, the political, the being-together or the being-with of democracy. But make no mistake: at stake here is not a banal analogy between art – drawing, in this case – and finality, the intention [*dessein*] of the political. It is, rather, a matter of truly "thinking in drawing," seriously and rigorously, that is to say, by standing as close as possible to the "pulsation" of the nascent form and that which in it – form that is not a given, always nascent and yet to trace – can make one think about the modalities – though it is a modeling without model – of a making-sense [*faire-sens*] of the political (of politics, let us specify, considered in its existential and not only societal sense). "From here," says Nancy, "it becomes possible to understand that art, in all fields, cannot be separated from pleasure" (*P* 37/26): it is also "from here" – that is, a "there" nowhere localizable – that another way of tackling the question of the political could be disclosed, considered no longer in terms of "a need extended toward the aim of satisfaction or achievement" (*P* 36/26) but of the sole desire that "makes repeated demands on itself [*se redemande lui-même*]" (*P* 36/26) and whose "design is nothing other than an intensification and limitless differentiation or dissemination" (*P* 36–7/26). The last pages of *Vérité de la démocratie* [*The Truth of Democracy*][34] also called for a rethinking of this relation – of tension: neither bond, nor unbinding, nor articulation – between the aesthetic and the political; without referring to them directly, many passages in *The Pleasure in Drawing* further signal toward this space that has yet to be invented, no longer within the realm of ends, but of possibles. The experience of art would thus set to work a community of *aesthesis*, thought from the perspective of *sentir* [*sensing/feeling*], that is, *"sense* in the fullest extent of the term" (*P* 53/41). Such would be the image of the world to which drawing gives access, in making itself and in allowing for the coming of this thought of the quick: art, writes Nancy "is the impulse and pulse of being in the world, and all senses, sentiments, sensitivities, and sensualities are delineations of this impulse and pulse – taken up again in order to be more finely and intensely *drawn*, carried toward an infinite force [*puissance*] across what we call the 'arts'" (*P* 53/41).

In a brief essay entitled *Identité* [*Identity*], a reply to Nicolas Sarkozy's unfelicitous attempt to co-opt the so-called "national identity" issue, Nancy resorts several times to the figure of the line in terms very close to those of *The Pleasure in Drawing*, evoking for instance the identity of the "I" as "the form [which] is nowhere settled, it is not given, it is not given to [the 'I']: it is [the 'I'] that gives itself to [the form] or it is [the 'I'] that gives it its [form], which amounts to the same, and does so by identifying itself."[35] He also insists upon this "line, extended from the first absence to the last, a line of existence that comes back to you in particular, absolutely, exclusively," but which is "nowhere but at the end of your becoming" (*I* 35). There is no line, lineage or delineation, then, allowing the subject to grasp itself "from itself to itself, from the same to the same" (*I* 34). The same "double principle of fall and plasticity" (*I* 42) goes for both this other order of grandeur (the national, the social, the political, the community) and personal identity: "And democratic politics means one thing only: that to every possibility of identity (personal, collective, both together, this too is not given distinctly as such) *the space to trace, unfold, branch out its line or lines of identification be opened*" (*I* 36). I underline here this figure-more-than-figure of the line of drawing that relinquishes the question of identity, where the political is again strongly thought in terms of point and line:

> Identity is the point of fall – or of inscription, if one prefers – from which a line [*tracé*] departs. The point, by definition, is dimensionless. The line [*tracé*] can draw the furthest paths, the most twisted, entangled, and even smudged ones. But it is always traced from the point, traced from the same point. A point is a labyrinth, hence the secret of an identity. From the one to the other, permanent contact and perma-

nent dehiscence [. . .] [I]t is understood *a priori* that the infinitesimal nature of the point or the strictly unfigurable of the traced will never be reduced. (*I* 42–3)

Reading this and so many other passages, it is undeniable that the thought of the line in Nancy – where each and every trait is "a sending off, a pace, a given course, a more or less durable configuration lent to that which, in itself, has no figure but whose course, this drawing, reveals an unseen aspect" (*I* 59) – is political as well, and not only as a banal analogy or a "metaphor": this line is political inasmuch as it calls for self-deployment in space, and this space is that of the relation, of the "relation *to*," and hence political in the sense of the "beyond politics" previously evoked. It is obviously not a matter of subordinating these planes, the aesthetic and the political, to fasten them to one another, as one used to be able to do when speaking of "*art engagé*" in the name of profound and tenacious misunderstandings. Rather, it is about thinking this point of contact, of overturning, or opening, where they touch and trade places, as suggested in the title of Francis Alÿs's work: *The Green Line (Sometimes doing something poetic can become political and sometimes doing something political can become poetic)* (2007). And so, the line is political not only because "it is tempting to pair the freedom implied for line here to contemporary works in which a string or delicate line has great political, social, or aesthetic implications,"[36] but rather, as Jean-Christophe Bailly underlines, because of its pure ductility and address: "It is as such that the line opens itself to a political dimension" (*V* 293), for:

> The politics of the line in the light of drawing is that of the infinite in the act of the connecting [*rapport*], that of the possibility and of the necessity of the relation [*rapport*], that of a movement of points that go out to meet each other, not in the effusion of a convergence, but following the singular paths of a becoming always in the process of tracing itself and which, traced, is what is left to the viewer's eye as a sort of canvas on which one moves freely. (*V* 294)

Bailly adds – and this is close to Nancy's politics to come – that drawing, by remaining in withdrawal, "held back in gestation or wandering, operates at once, and even against itself, by the sole virtue of the line, the line that moves, attempts and links, like a movement in the direction of the relation and as that which embodies, taking off from surfaces and crossings, the enveloping tension of the relation" (*V* 294).

Drawing thus provides us with the most intimate image of a continued openness, or uninterrupted interruption, both made inaccessible yet tangible to us through art (a perfect drawing is just this appearing and disappearing form, engendering itself, creating itself in "the hesitant or cursive progress of what borders on the unknown," *V* 293). In *Dans quels mondes vivons-nous?*, Nancy examines the notion of "*struction*," as mentioned above, which according to him is even more primordial than any construction or destruction, and goes beyond any question of order or organization: "What is at stake beyond construction and destruction is the *struction* as such" (*M* 89). He states this positing that *struction*, being neither *con*struction nor *in*struction, is "the stack, the unassembled set. It is contiguity and co-presence, certainly, but without a principle of coordination" (*M* 89), an equally insightful proposition regarding the drawing-form; it is "the uncoordinated simultaneity of things or beings, the contingency of their co-belongings, the dispersion of profusions of aspects, species, forces, forms, tensions and intentions (instincts, impulses, projections [*projets*] élans). In this profusion, not a single order stands out above the others" (*M* 90). It is interesting to note that this description of *struction* as a "labile assemblage, disorganized, aggregated or amalgamated more than conjoined, collected, sorted or associated" (*M* 90) fits well both the extended drawing line pursued by Nancy in art and the "relation *to*" he relentlessly seeks to redefine in the political, calling for an altogether other mode of "sociation," deprived of any given association as such. Like the line of drawing, which relates, by "essence" (but there is, of course, no essence here, as we have seen) to the order of "contiguity, contact, tension, torsion, crossing, ordering" (*M* 92), so does this other political, this "beyond politics" where "[w]hat is given to us consists in nothing other than the juxtaposition and the simultaneity of a co-presence whose *co*- carries no particular value, other than that of contiguity or of juxtaposition in the limits according to which the universe itself is given" (*M* 91). In both cases, it is exactly this "un-limitation that bourgeons" (*M* 103) – un-limitation which is "that of the passage, of the transience mixed with eternity" (*M* 96), writes Nancy – in drawing and in the world, in the world henceforth without intention but always to be drawn ("it cannot be a question of setting limits to that which evidently ignores the limit": *M* 104), that gives us the most acute idea of what is at stake, or at play in the pulsating force of the drawing, the struction of the world – of the world as art.

Preliminary draft, sketch, birthing of forms that drawing itself would wish, exceeding all the forms of what is called "art," drawing is thus at once in "sub-work" ["*sous-oeuvre*"] and infinitely "more-than-the-work" ["*plus-que-l'oeuvre*"]; it exceeds all conditions, in tune with desire alone: with the impossible. And what if politics ceased, like drawing, to be a carbon copy of the forms of objects or of the world and, becoming passionate about its own movement and it alone, were "nothing other than a 'recreation' of the world" (*P* 117/95)?

Coda: Nancy drawing

What's in a line? Again this question, itself infinite: "Just as all lines in all drawings include the same infinity of points, so together they all respond with the same, endlessly modulated gesture, opening to infinitude" (*P* 114/ 93). There is no point, no end in sight, for even though the drawing is finite, its movement remains "infinite and *unfinishable*" (*P* 116/ 94). In "Éloquentes rayures," a text devoted to Jacques Derrida's stance on art, Nancy declares – and the words also apply to his own theoretical standpoints – that "art has no desire or disposition, not even an aptitude toward some discourse about it,"[37] noting that "No, he will not speak of or on art, and no, he will not make it speak" (17). One can think here of the inventive line drawn by Nancy in *Les Traces anémones*, in which he accompanies the work of Bernard Moninot, choosing not to describe, comment, analyze in any way its "object." Here he does not speak *of* art (he renounces discourse): he seeks rather to speak it. Nancy is led by a more adventurous line, maybe more radically than anywhere else in his multiple approaches of art, offering a series of very brief poems as ekphrasis that become themselves drawing lines, the trans-figuration of Moninot's lines into the poem's: "*Le vent fait dessiner la plante/comme une mère qui tiendrait/la main d'un tout-petit/ incapable d'écrire/et lui ferait tracer/ qui sait?/Qui sait quels signes doués/de quel sens*" [The wind makes the plant draw/like a mother who would hold/ the hand of a toddler/ unable to write/and would make him trace/who knows?/Who knows what signs endowed with/ with what sense]. Here, writing of "*fibrilles fils fissures*" [fibrils filaments fissures], of "*sillages d'errance et de danse/traînées gracieuses hasardeuses*" [furrows of drifting and dancing/graceful hazardous trails], of "*filets enlacés inlassables/ en négligés délassements*" [twining tireless tangles/in offhand diversions], of "*Trace soucieuse insouciante/trajectoire fractale fatale*"[38] [fretful care-free trace/ fractal fatal trajectory], Nancy traces lines of sense(s) that strive to render the very idea of drawing in its most sensible form. Drawn into drawing, he jumps the line, he crosses it, gets entangled with it: he draws. His writing moves beyond description, tracing out, in its very elliptic sketch, concise form, its syncope, suspense, and openness, a moving self-portrait. The bare essentials of the line are there – the path of passing through, movement, collision, edge, attachment, joining, sectioning. Incising: for that is what a line does.

How to write (of) the draught, how to extend it? This enigmatic series of poems is indeed an inventive "responsory." Here the line is both drawn and written. Better still: the drawn line coincides exactly with the line of thought. Is this the reason why thinking along Nancy's line on art always gives such pleasure – joy?

References

Bailly, Jean-Christophe. "La Venue, Jean-Luc Nancy," *Europe* 960: 290–9, Special Issue on Jean-Luc Nancy, ed. Ginette Michaud, 2009.

Barrau, Aurélien, and Nancy, Jean-Luc. *Dans quels mondes vivons-nous?* Paris: Galilée, 2011.

Butler, Cornelia H., and de Zegher, Catherine (eds). *On Line: Drawing through the Twentieth Century*. New York: Museum of Modern Art, 2010.

François Rouan. Découpe/Modèle 1965–2009. Paris: LIENART/Galerie Jean Fournier, 2011.

Garrido, Juan-Manuel. *La Formation des formes*. Paris: Galilée, 2008.

Jdey, Adnen (ed.). *Derrida et la question de l'art. Déconstructions de l'esthétique*. Nantes: Cécile Defaut, 2011.

Moninot, Bernard, and Bouillon, François. *Lignes de chance. Actualité du dessin contemporain*. Paris: École Nationale Supérieure des Beaux-arts de Paris, 2010.

Moninot, Bernard, and Nancy, Jean-Luc. *Les Traces anémones*. Paris: Maeght, 2008.

Nancy, Jean-Luc. *Vérité de la démocratie*. Paris: Galilée, 2008. *The Truth of Democracy*, trans. Michael Naas. New York: Fordham University Press, 2010.

Nancy, Jean-Luc. *Le Plaisir au dessin*. Paris: Galilée, 2009. *The Pleasure in Drawing*, trans. Philip Armstrong. New York: Fordham University Press, 2013.

Nancy, Jean-Luc. *L'Adoration. Déconstruction du christianisme 2*. Paris: Galilée, 2010.

6

Differing on Difference

Ian James

In January 2002, a conference dedicated to Nancy's work was held at the Collège International de Philosophie in the Rue Descartes in Paris. A number of prominent philosophical figures took part in this conference whose theme centered on the question of "sense" in Nancean thought.[1] These included Nancy himself, Alain Badiou, Catherine Malabou, and Werner Hamacher. The proceedings were brought to a conclusion with a discussion between Nancy and Jacques Derrida on the question of responsibility.[2] Along with his extended commentary in *On Touching – Jean-Luc Nancy* and his discussions of freedom, justice, and fraternity in *Rogues*, this concluding exchange represents one of Derrida's principal public responses to the philosophy of his close friend and occasional collaborator.

The discussion in question begins with the convenor Francis Guibal expressing his appreciation of the exchanges that have taken place between Derrida and Nancy, exchanges which "are not ones of identification, nor of mutual appreciation, but rather of crossing, it seems to me, and, as it were, of cross-fertilization."[3] In addressing the problem of the future and of our responsibility toward the arrival of the singular and the new, Derrida also explicitly addresses the question of "a possible difference between Jean-Luc and me, a difference which is [. . .] less one of position or philosophical argument than it is a difference in a way of doing, of manner, a difference of body, precisely, of flesh, of style, of gesture."[4] The difference between the two thinkers is, according to Derrida at least, a difference of gesture rather than a difference of philosophical position. It is also a difference which is somehow marked in a relation to the materiality of an embodied instance. This might be a difference in a relation to the body or flesh, that is to say, to the body which itself gestures, moves, and orientates itself within a meaningful world. Yet, for Derrida, the difference emerges, both here and elsewhere, far more as a difference of relation to the body of the philosophical tradition itself, to its material instantiation in terms, names, and concepts. So, where Nancy will embrace, "in a deconstructive, post-deconstructive" manner, "these great themes, these great concepts, these great problems that bear the names of *sense, world, creation, freedom, community*, etc.," Derrida has a desire to flee from these names of the tradition. It is as if he would "at the first contact, simply by *naming* such concepts, find myself, like a fly with its legs stuck, captive, paralyzed, held hostage, trapped by a programme."[5] Derrida's skepticism about the way in which Nancy reinvents or reworks "these great concepts" of the philosophical tradition is entirely consistent with his responses to Nancy elsewhere, for instance, his discussion of the term "fraternity" in *Rogues*, or, as will become clear, his equivocal reading of Nancy's use of the term "touch" in *On Touching*. If Nancy's readiness to name concepts or philosophical themes using traditional terms does indeed appear to be stuck to its metaphysical legacy like a fly glued to flypaper, then the post-deconstructive gesture of this discourse will inevitably be compromised by the calculations and programming of the tradition, and will, from the Derridean perspective, have no hope of being responsive to, or responsible for, the singular event and its alterity.

So Derrida's understanding of his difference with Nancy appears to be clear: the two share a deconstructive posture with regard to the tradition of metaphysical thinking, but Nancy has a different relation to the "body" of that tradition, its "flesh" so to speak; his practice of using the names of the tradition comes at the risk of a return to a non- or pre-deconstructive naivety that smuggles into the supposedly post-deconstructive space the very worst kind of logocentric prejudice. It is easy to see why Derrida will simply refuse to use all those key Nancean terms: sense, world, existence, community, body, flesh, and so on. It is also easy to see why some of the critical responses to Nancy, which can be broadly aligned with the Derridean perspective, tend to argue that the terminology he uses "flattens," or is unresponsive to, the "transcendence of the other."[6]

There is, however, a potential problem with the Derridean response to Nancy's philosophical gesture. This is less of a problem with Derrida's own very specific analyses (in *On Touching* and *Rogues* for instance) that are faultlessly careful, patient, and always generous in their own ways. The problem potentially lies with a more nonspecific or general Derridean response to Nancy, one which would take Derrida's own account of the difference between the two thinkers as an authority for a fairly straightforward, dismissive argument. Rather than affirm, as Derrida does, "I will not use these terms," this argument would more prescriptively assert: "Jean-Luc Nancy should not or cannot use these terms, for they are simply metaphysical." Such an argument, and to a certain extent Derrida's own affirmation that the two share philosophical positions but differ in the way they articulate them, runs the risk of not fully accounting for further, albeit subtle, differences that exist between the two thinkers. It also risks reducing the Derridean reading to a policing gesture, one that looks solely to secure deconstructive hygiene by normatively imposing the discursive strategies of Derrida himself. If other differences in philosophical argument can be brought to the fore, then the relation between Derrida and Nancy can be recast in a different light. Nancy may appear less of a Derridean who has been led astray by his attachment to a more traditional philosophical lexicon, and more of a thinker staking out a distinctive post-deconstructive position that needs to be judged as such.

Haptics as presence: technics as *différance*

Derrida's *On Touching* is his most extended engagement with Nancy's work. Published in 2000, *On Touching* is a major late work of Derridean deconstruction which ranges far beyond its central close reading of the Nancean corpus to give an extended analysis of a broader philosophical tradition in relation to which, he argues, that corpus can be situated. This tradition of European philosophy centers on the figure of "touch" or the haptic, and which would incorporate, amongst others, such diverse names as Maine de Biran, Ravaisson, Kant, Husserl, Merleau-Ponty, and Deleuze.[7] Just as a privileging of voice was highlighted in Derrida's early identification of a phonocentric tradition, and a privileging of word and concept in his use of the term *logocentrism*, so the figure of touch becomes the privileged motif of a "tactilist" tradition or a "haptocentric metaphysics." Once again it is the possibility of presence and its attendant philosophical baggage that is in question: "Touch, more than sight or hearing, gives nearness, proximity – it gives nearby [. . .]. In this regard, is it ever possible to dissociate the 'near,' the 'proximate' from the 'proper,' the 'propriate' [*propre*]? The proximate, the proper, and the present – the presence of the present? We can imagine all the consequences if this were impossible."[8]

What is at stake here is nothing less than the question of originary intuition and the manner in which, within phenomenology and elsewhere in the philosophical tradition, the notion of originary intuition is related to figures of touch and touching, which is then, in turn, thought as the ground of consciousness and the constitution of the meaningful world of sensible appearance. In this context, Derrida's analysis of the extensive use of the figure of touch throughout Nancy's philosophical writing is directly related to the question of whether his more general use of terms from the tradition allows for the persistence within his thought of an undeconstructed legacy of the metaphysics of presence. The key stakes of *On Touching* turn, therefore, on the issue of whether any thinking that organizes itself around the figure of touch can escape the legacy of hapto-centric metaphysics and the logic of presence that is programmed within it.

Derrida's response to Nancy is by no means unequivocal, however. For, as much as Nancy's use of the term "touch" bears the legacy of a haptocentric affirmation of presence, it is also made to resonate or become philosophically meaningful in a way that would escape, transcend, or perhaps more precisely, *transform* that legacy. So, far from simply arguing that Nancy is a metaphysical thinker despite himself, Derrida, through a series of subtle and extended close readings and philosophical digressions, seeks to uncover the ways in which Nancean thought is balanced between its possible recuperation into the tradition of haptocentric metaphysics and its articulation of a distinctive post-deconstructive gesture.

What separates Nancy's thought from a more straightforward reabsorption into the haptocentric logic of presence is, Derrida argues, his sustained engagement with the question of originary technicity, technics, or what is also termed "technical prosthetics." This is a question, of course, with which Derrida himself has engaged from the very beginning of his career. In *Of Grammatology*, the thinking of supplementarity, writing, and *archi-écriture* was closely bound up with that of technē and originary technicity (as will be explored further below). It is also a question that persistently runs throughout his discussions of Nancy in *On Touching*. In "Tangent I: Hand of Man, Hand of God," for instance, Derrida analyzes the motif of the "technē of bodies" such as it is developed in Nancy's 1992 work *Corpus*. In this context, and in an apparently marginal footnote, he refers back to *Of Grammatology* and to the reference he makes in that earlier work to the ethnologist and thinker of technics André Leroi-Gourhan. In particular, he highlights the continuing importance of Leroi-Gourhan's thought to Bernard Stiegler who, like Nancy, begins his philosophical career by taking Derridean deconstruction as a point of departure (in the first two volumes of his *Technics and Time* series).[9] What is at stake, Derrida notes, in his own and Stiegler's shared interest in Leroi-Gourhan is the relation of writing to the articulations of the human hand, and therefore to the question of the human itself, to human experience, consciousness, meaning, and so on. Through this seemingly marginal footnote, Derrida is highlighting the way in which Nancy's "technē of bodies" needs to be understood within a broader deconstructive and post-deconstructive interest in technics and embodiment that all three thinkers – Derrida, Stiegler, and Nancy – share (albeit in rather different ways). More specifically, the reference here to Leroi-Gourhan, to the human hand, and to writing, points toward the way in which originary technicity is understood by all three thinkers: as an interruption of presence. Just as any thinking of touch or haptics affirms the metaphysics of presence, so the intrusion of technics or originary technicity works to suspend it.

Derrida is very clear on this point: the body that touches, feels, hears, and sees, and in particular the "body proper" as thought by phenomenology, is a body that is originarily implicated in the interconnections of technical prosthetics. If, for Derrida, there is any originary intuition, it is also "the ageless intrusion of technics, which is to say of transplantation or prosthetics."[10] It is precisely this "ageless intrusion" of technics that interrupts the "tactilist" or haptic affirmation of the immediacy, continuity, and contiguity of contact within the thinking of touch. Interrupted also, then, is the propriety and self-identity of the "body proper," and with that, the presence of presence. Derrida attempts to think originary technics as that which "*suspends* contact in contact and divides it right within tactile experience in general, thus inscribing an anesthetic interruption into the heart of aesthetic phenomenality."[11] This in turn "would open up the spacing of a distance, a disadhering, a *différance* in the very 'inside' of haptics – and *aisthēsis* in general. Without this *différance*, there would be no contact *as such*; contact would not appear; but with this *différance*, contact never appears in its full purity, never in any immediate plenitude, either."[12]

Thus, the condition of possibility of originary intuition, touch, and contact, that is, technical prosthetics, is, at the very same time, its condition of impossibility. In *On Touching*, therefore, technics emerges as a key figure that quite explicitly reiterates the logic of *différance* that was elaborated in the earlier *Of Grammatology*. Technics, *différance*, supplementarity, and the splitting or dehiscence of presence all mutually imply each other just as haptics, continuity, proximity, propriety, and presence mutually affirm each other. However, in a typically Derridean moment of quasi-transcendental aporia, the latter is always inhabited by the former as both its condition of possibility and impossibility.

In this context, Derrida argues that Nancy's thought is held within a tension between two alternatives. On the one hand, he affirms his admiration for the way in which, from within the

language of the tactilist tradition, Nancy disassembles, in order
to think anew, the very foundations of the tradition itself via a
thinking of technics. On the other, he cannot help but caution
Nancy against his unapologetic use of certain terms and his lack
of concern with the possibility that he might find himself drawn
back into their traditional orbit or historical field of meaning. In
short, Nancy's extended use of the term "touch" is potentially
highly compromising; but since it cannot in any way be separated
from his thinking of technicity, his thought remains suspended
between a residual affirmation of haptocentric presence and a post-
deconstructive affirmation of "technical" *différance*.

Derrida does not seek to resolve this tension, nor the suspension
of Nancean thought between these two moments. Nevertheless,
toward the end of *On Touching*, he identifies a decisive difference
between their respective approaches and speaks of "two irreducibly different 'deconstructive' gestures" that mark their discourses.
Derrida has, throughout his writing, persistently repeated the
phrase "if there is any." Deconstruction, responsibility, justice,
etc. all might find themselves qualified by an "if there is any"
whenever they are invoked. Nancy, for his part, will say "there
is no '*the*' or 'there is not': 'touching,' 'essence,' 'the technical,'
etc."[13] For Derrida, Nancy is struggling or wrestling at the limits
of what discourse or meaning will allow. He is not deploying
terms in any straightforward manner, but speaking about instances
that place themselves outside of, or ex-scribe, that which they
seek to inscribe in writing: hence "there is no '. . .'" Derrida will
never cease to wonder here whether the "definite article is already
engaged or required by the discourse that disputes it," because he
will always, in a gesture as persistent as it is singular, remain with
the "if there is any."[14] At the conclusion of *On Touching*, therefore, Derrida reiterates his concern for questions of naming, and of
philosophical style or gesture. His equivocation regarding Nancy's
use of the term "touch" and the legacy of haptocentrism itself
remains suspended within this open-ended question of a difference
in deconstructive gesture.

It may not be surprising that Derrida's critical responses to Nancy
always return to the question of Nancy's relation to the body of
the logocentric tradition, or, more precisely, to the problem of

avoiding being glued to terms of that tradition, and therefore compromised by their programming of philosophical sense or meaning. This is consistent, for instance, with his earlier deconstructive analyses of other key figures with whom he clearly feels a great deal of sympathy, proximity or, indeed, friendship. His essay on Levinas in *Writing and Difference* might offer a good example of this.[15] In both cases, Derrida is concerned if the gesture of thought responds and does justice to alterity, or the Other, i.e. to that which escapes phenomenological reduction or ontological disclosure.[16]

However, it may be that the difference between Derrida and Nancy is not solely one of deconstructive gesture. As was indicated in the preceding discussion of *On Touching*, Derrida, Nancy, and Stiegler together share a fundamental concern for the way in which originary technicity interrupts or suspends presence, making technicity itself another figure for *différance*. Rather than a gestural difference, it may be that Nancy (and incidentally Stiegler also)[17] conceives of originary technicity in different terms, according to a different articulation of *différance*. A close comparison of Derrida's and Nancy's respective formulations relating to technicity in both *Of Grammatology* and *Corpus* may shed further light on this different articulation of *différance*.

Derrida: technicity as arche-writing and trace

In the third chapter of *Of Grammatology* ("Of Grammatology as a Positive Science"), Derrida poses the question of the origin of writing, of writing in both the limited sense of written language and in the broader sense of generalized inscription (or "arche-writing") and the question of the relation of arche-writing to writing:

> Where does writing begin? When does writing begin? Where and when does the trace, writing in general, common root of speech and writing, narrow itself into 'writing' in the colloquial sense? Where and when does one pass from one writing to another, from writing in general to writing in the narrow sense, from the trace to the *graphie*,

from one graphic system to another, and, in the field of graphic code, from one graphic discourse to another, etc.?

Where and how does it begin . . . ? A question of origin.[18]

As Derrida pursues this question throughout the third chapter, the figure of technics or technicity is taken up once again and begins to play an increasingly decisive role. It should be underlined here that the wide-ranging and complex analysis of the history of various conceptions of writing and its origin is beyond the scope of this discussion. What is worthy of note in this context, however, is the manner in which Derrida uncovers a "deep" unity between logocentrism and a "certain technicism" within specific moments of the historical trajectory he interrogates. This leads him to conclude speculatively: "The originary pre- or meta-phonetic writing that I am attempting to conceive here leads to nothing less than an 'overtaking' of speech by the machine."[19] Famously, a distinction emerges in this context between an instrumentalist and technicist conception of writing that is aligned with logo- and phonocentrism, and a conception of writing as originary technicity. In the case of the former, writing is conceived as a tool or instrument that we use to articulate an original purity of presence, voice, meaning, concept, etc. In the case of the latter, writing is conceived as a technical prosthesis, supplement, inscription, or trace that, as an originary instance, acts as a condition of possibility (and impossibility) for presence, voice, meaning, and concept.

In this context, then, the technicity of (arche-)writing and, indeed, all technical prosthetics is never of merely instrumental or utilitarian value, that is to say, it is never simply a means to fulfill ends that exist within their own pure sphere of autonomy or teleological purposiveness. Technicity and technical prosthetics, as an articulation of *différance*, are temporalizing and spatializing: they open up a meaningful temporal world by allowing for a generalized possibility of inscription and the experience of a sensible-intelligible world. With reference to the concept of the *grammè*, Derrida argues that the technicity of arche-writing is articulated in all kinds of inscription or iteration, from the genetic codes of early single-celled life (he refers to amoeba) to writing as we know it and beyond. With reference again to Leroi-Gourhan, he describes this generalized technicity of inscription, writing, and technical prosthetics as:

> an exteriorisation always already begun but always larger than the trace which, beginning with the programmes of so-called "instinctive" behaviour up to the constitution of electronic card indexes and reading machines, enlarges *différance* and the possibility of putting in reserve: it at once and in the same movement constitutes and effaces so-called conscious subjectivity, its logos, and its theological attributes.[20]

This decisive passage makes very clear the extent to which the originary technicity of arche-writing is, for Derrida, a generalized economy of life that far exceeds the human and the finite limits of human life or "so-called conscious subjectivity." As a fundamental opening, temporalization, and spatialization, the technicity of *différance* both precedes human life and consciousness and would continue to iterate and, as it were, to "differantiate" long after the disappearance of human life.[21] Most significantly for this discussion, and as has been signaled already at several points, this technicity has a quasi-transcendental status, that is to say, it is a condition of possibility and impossibility insofar as it interrupts or renders non-self-identical that which it makes possible.

The issue of the quasi-transcendental will be of key importance when it comes to comparing and contrasting Derrida's and Nancy's different articulations of technicity and *différance*. A final point to be noted in relation to Derrida's formulations in *Of Grammatology* relates to the question of the trace and to his understanding of temporality. It is quite clear from the quotation above that Derrida's conception of the *grammè*, of inscription or arche-writing, is resolutely materialist: the ideality of meaning and concept find themselves ruined insofar as the generalized economy of inscription and writing is their (quasi-transcendental) condition. This economy of inscription and iteration is itself thoroughly material. It is articulated in the genetic coding of DNA, the development of cellular life, phonetic writing systems, electronic card systems, and so on. And yet, Derrida also insists that the trace, or what he also calls *arche-trace*, is, *as* quasi-transcendental, *never made present as such*. If "the (pure) trace is difference" then it also, at the same time, "does not depend on any sensible plenitude, audible or visible, phonic or graphic. It is on the contrary the condition of such plenitude."[22] The trace therefore cannot be reduced to any sensible-material existence, thing or presentation, or as Derrida puts it earlier in his discussion: "The trace must be thought *before the entity*" [my emphasis].[23] It is never present or presented as such but belongs to an immemorial past that haunts every instance of presence or presentation, dividing it from itself. This logic of the trace will be very familiar to readers of Derrida. The key point to be noted here is that, despite his emphasis on materiality (DNA, phonetic writing, reading machines, etc.), the trace, given its status as a quasi-transcendental, is arguably a *dematerialized* instance since, by Derrida's own account, it necessarily precedes all material sensory experience, being its quasi-transcendental condition of possibility and impossibility. This "impresentable" character of the trace, together with the question of its de-, or im-materialization, will be of key importance in the consideration of Derrida's difference from Nancy.

Nancy – ecotechnics, embodiment and areality

Reading the section entitled "Technē of Bodies" in *Corpus* immediately confirms Derrida's concerns about the question of naming in Nancy's writing and his appropriation of terms from the philosophical (and theological) tradition. Alongside his use of the term "body" itself, he also uses the terms "creation," "production," "world," and "truth."[24] Such an appropriation or repetition of terms, occasionally but not always accompanied by quotation marks, would appear to more than justify the Derridean suspicion that Nancy's discourse may be smuggling metaphysical or logocentric contraband within its apparently post-deconstructive gesture. Yet this short section of *Corpus* also more than justifies the recognition Derrida gives (in *On Touching*) to the important role played by technicity in Nancean thought and to its deconstructive force. Furthermore, a close reading of this section also highlights Nancy's different conception of originary technicity.

Whereas in *Of Grammatology* Derrida develops this motif in relation to the question of (arche-)writing, the inscription of the trace,
and to a logic of the quasi-transcendental, in *Corpus*, following the
indication of the title itself, Nancy develops it in relation to the
body. This emphasis on the body is accompanied by an emphasis
on localization, situation, and place. This is more than just a difference of naming or discursive gesture. When Nancy uses terms
such as "creation" or "world," they make sense only in relation
to the very specific thinking of the body that emerges here. So,
for instance, Nancy talks of "Created bodies, that is to say arriving
bodies, and whose arrival each time spaces the *here*, the *there*."[25]
Creation here is a matter of the world presenting itself in multiple
and localized openings, *in* and *through* bodily experience and only
in the multiplicity of bodies. However, this is only so insofar as
"'Creation' is the technē of bodies." So, the philosophical sense
that Nancy gives to the traditional terms "body," "creation," and
"world" cannot be separated from technicity, or what he here calls
"ecotechnicity": "Our world is a world of "technics" [*la "technique"*], a world whose cosmos, nature, gods, whose entire system
in its intimate joining [*jointure*] is exposed as 'technics': a world of
the 'ecotechnical.'"[26]

Ecotechnicity, for Nancy, overturns the instrumentalist, technicist, or teleological conception of technical prosthetics in a manner
that recalls the formulations relating to writing in *Of Grammatology*.
Ecotechnicity, for Nancy, is not a network of tools or instruments
that bodies use to articulate specific ends that have their own
distinct sphere of meaning. Like the originary technicity of arche-
writing such as Derrida conceives it, ecotechnicity is primordially
disclosive of experience and of the possibility of a meaningful
world: "The ecotechnical functions with technical apparatuses to
which our every part is connected. But what it makes are our
bodies, bodies which it brings into the world and links to the
system, thereby creating our bodies as more visible."[27] It is not
bodies that use technical prosthetics for specific ends, but technical prosthetics that make bodies as such, connecting them to a
shared environment that is revealed as meaningful and as such. So,
like arche-writing, "The ecotechnical deconstructs the system of
ends."[28]

Originary technicity, here as in Derrida's work, interrupts the purity of presence and any system of meaning that would seek to affirm or establish firm foundations for the purity of meanings. And yet to speak of bodies interconnected with technical prosthetics in a way that primordially discloses a world of sensible appearances is very different from speaking of writing, of inscription, the graphie, the *gramme*, or the trace. Derrida might object to Nancy's formulations insofar as talk of bodies and technical objects appears to be already too laden with presence, already bound up with the thing or object that has already presented itself as such. For, as might be recalled here: "The trace must be thought before the entity," and therefore *before* any instant of presence or presentation. Yet, as Nancy makes clear, the ecotechnical, "far from turning bodies into technical objects [. . .] discloses them as such."[29] The ecotechnical precedes bodies and technical objects even as it is a generalized articulation of the bodily and the technical. It precedes their presence or presentation but does so in a manner that articulates a different logic from that of the Derridean trace and its quasi-transcendental operation. The difference hangs on Nancy's use of the rather obscure and difficult term "areal" [*aréale*] and the logic of trans-immanence that is articulated here. The ecotechnical discloses bodies and the world:

> through this *areal* connection which also creates a space for the withdrawal of any transcendental or immanent signification. The world of bodies has neither a transcendent nor an immanent sense. If we want to keep these words we have to say that one takes place within the other, but without being dialecticized – that one takes place *as* the other, and that places are this taking place.[30]

All of Nancy's difference with Derrida on the subject of difference can arguably be found within this short but decisive passage. Beyond the emphasis on bodies and their interconnection within the disclosure of an ecotechnical environment, what is perhaps most striking is the way in which a language of spatiality and of the localized opening of places is inseparable from a non–dialectical logic of transcendence and immanence. Or, more precisely, what is striking here is that the spacing or spatializing of space and the

coming of the world to presence occurs *as* a simultaneous tran-
scending of immanence and as an immanentizing of transcendence
without either term having any priority over, or dialectical relation
with, the other. This is what Nancy will call elsewhere the trans-
immanence of the sense of the world.

The difference between Derrida and Nancy, "if there is any,"
almost certainly hangs on the difference between their respective
logics: Derrida's logic of the quasi-transcendental and Nancy's
logic of the trans-immanent, each respectively informing their
different conceptions of originary technicity. It was noted earlier
that the Derridean trace, as a quasi-transcendental condition of
possibility and impossibility of presence, presentation, of "so-called
subjectivity," and so on, could never present itself as such, but
rather belonged always to an immemorial past haunting all presence. It was also suggested that the trace in Derrida could be
understood as a dematerialized instance since it "does not depend
on any sensible plenitude." If the temporality of the trace is the
temporality of delay, of divisibility, and spatial deferral in excess
of all presence, then, in Nancy, the *areal* is arguably an *a-spatiality*
that opens up prior to or in excess of all space. Areality, Nancy
writes, "provides the rule and the milieu of a proximity, at once
worldwide and local."[31] Areality, then, precedes sensible spatial
extension and opens or discloses it as such and, as is very clear,
is always engaged with bodies that are "made" within a generalized ecotechnical set of interconnections. But what, exactly, does
Nancy mean by areality?

In the short section of *Corpus* that gives this term as its title,
Nancy begins by noting: "Areality is an antique word signifying the
nature or specificity of an *aire* (area)."[32] As a figure or term, therefore, it has, first and foremost, a spatial sense and, in particular, it
foregrounds a localization of space. Nancy also notes: "By chance,
this word also serves to suggest a lack of reality, or rather a slight,
faint, suspended reality; the reality of a swerve localizing the body,
or a displacement within the body."[33] So "areality," for Nancy, is
a function of a spacing or localization of a body or bodies, but it
also, somehow, is a spacing that is different from or other than the
three-dimensional extension of space that we normally identify as
"reality." Nancy specifies his understanding of this term further,

adding it is "in effect a faint reality of ground, substance, matter or subject. But this faint reality makes the whole areal real, where the so-called architectonics of bodies is played out and articulated."[34] Areality, then, is a spacing or spatializing that is positioned prior to phenomenal space, to the spatial extension of appearances or worldly experience. Put simply, areality is the material spacing of the real from which bodies, locales, spaces, and places are made in the ecotechnical opening of worldly appearance. As Nancy himself puts it: "The real as areal [. . .] reunites the infinity of maximal existence [. . .] with the final absolute of an areal horizon."[35] The areal is that material space that infinitely exceeds the world of phenomenal appearance or presentation, but, at the same time, is nothing other than that world: it is an actual infinity within the finitude of existence upon which that finitude opens.

Some conclusions can perhaps now be drawn with regard to the stakes of the quasi-transcendental in Derrida and the trans-immanent in Nancy and with regard to the conception of originary technicity in each. Both arche-writing and ecotechnicity articulate instances that precede presence, sensible plenitude, and the experience or perception of spatial extension. These instances are given the names of the trace and of the areal respectively. The former is a possibility of inscription whose temporality is that of an immemorial past anterior to all sensible plenitude or presence, and is therefore, "impresentable" as such. The latter is an always localized but always also multiple spacing or spatializing in which an "architectonics" of bodies is played out in the ecotechnical creation of a world, but which is also in excess of any given world. In each case, a (albeit different) logic of spatialization and temporalization is being articulated (arche-writing, ecotechnicity). However, the difference between the trace that haunts the present but which is irreducible to sensible plenitude (being its prior condition) and the areal in which the architectonics of bodies are played out is perhaps precisely a difference in relation to the sensible itself. It is not, of course, that Derrida does not concern himself with the sensible. Rather, his deconstruction of presence affirms that the apparent plenitude of sensible experience has its condition of possibility and impossibility in something that is never purely or simply sensible, that is to say, the virtuality of the trace. Yet the areal as a spatial articulation of a bodily architectonic and as a production of bodies, things, and localized spaces is arguably less bound up with virtuality and more bound up with a certain concreteness or "concretude" of sense. It is always already bound up with that which is sensible in sense. It is not, however, it should be underlined, bound up with "sensible plenitude," for as Nancy noted, the areal connotes a lack of reality, substance, ground, etc. The areal is, as it were, the sensible void, abyss, or infinity, which remains no less sensible for all that.

It is arguable, therefore, that, far from being a simple gestural difference, a difference in relation to the body of the philosophical tradition, Nancy's different articulation of "*difference*" concerns the materiality or concreteness of the body in a more far-reaching manner. The ecotechnical, the areal, are all aimed at countering a certain de-materialization that the Derridean deconstruction of presence risks.[36] The difference between the quasi-transcendental and the trans-immanent in Derrida and Nancy may, therefore, be a difference that relates to divergent understandings of sensible presentation, virtuality, and the relation of embodiment to sense. Nancy has attempted to find a post-deconstructive thought in which the body, the sensible, and the localization of space and place can still have their place, and can still be thought outside of a logic of plenitude or purity of presence. Rather than a quasi-transcendental condition of possibility and impossibility, the trans-immanent in Nancy is first and foremost orientated toward a thinking of the production of bodies and space(s), the disclosure of shared worlds of sense. Trans-immanence is a material and spatial articulation that seeks to account for the ungrounded excess of the real over all phenomenal disclosure, but also to account for the material, sensible infinity of that real.

It may not, ultimately, be a question here of deciding for or against either Derrida or Nancy. Rather, understanding the complexity and specificity of the difference between the two thinkers may allow for a more productive reading of both. It should not be a question of remonstrating with Nancy for his continued use of traditional philosophical terms nor of finding Derrida wanting for his tendency to dwell within a logic of undecidability. More than anything, what emerges in the comparison of the two thinkers is the decisive role played in each by the thinking of originary technicity. What has been highlighted here is the way they come to conceive of this technicity differently. It is precisely this difference of conception that motivates or shapes their different gestures of philosophical style or technique. If, for Derrida, his divergence from Nancy is a difference between the "there is no . . ." and the "if there is any . . .," this may ultimately be because the originary technicity of arche-writing on the one hand and the ecotechnicity of bodies on the other demand a different discursive technique. "If there is any . . ." is a function of the quasi-transcendental and of undecidability (arche-writing). "There is no . . ." is a function of the trans-immanent and of areality (ecotechnics). In this way, the specific conception of technicity and the specific discursive technique mutually imply or dictate each other.

It should be clear from this that the legacy of Derrida's thought cannot be one in which philosophical discourses, and particularly those inspired by deconstruction itself, are simply policed or controlled for metaphysical contraband. Nancy's philosophical thought shows us that the deconstructive space can be one of creation, innovation and of the production of new, post-metaphysical forms of thinking. Reading Derrida's and Nancy's different articulations of difference may also show us that this potential for creation and innovation is far from exhausted.

References

Derrida, Jacques. *Of Grammatology*, trans. G. Spivak. Baltimore: Johns Hopkins University Press, 1998.

Derrida, Jacques. *Writing and Difference*, trans. Alan Bass. London: Routledge, 2001.

Derrida, Jacques. *On Touching – Jean-Luc Nancy*, trans. Christine Irizarry. Stanford: Stanford University Press, 2006.

Guibal, F. and Martin, J.-C. (eds). *Le Sens en tous sens: autour des travaux de Jean-Luc Nancy*. Paris: Galilée, 2004.

Nancy, Jean-Luc. *Corpus*, trans. R. Rand. New York: Fordham University Press, 2008.

7

(Mis)Reading in Dis-Enclosure

Isabelle Alfandary

Translated by Priyanka Deshmukh

Jean-Luc Nancy sets the tone as early as in the introduction, "Opening," to *Dis-Enclosure*, the text that does not intend to be a defense of Christianity, but aims, instead, to examine it since it would not be judicious to write it off:

> If it need be said, I am not advocating the public or promotional restoration of indulgences. I would wish, rather, that the Church abolish all it has preserved of these. However, it is a question of not resting content with judgments of "primitivism" and "clericalism," which put back into play and question paradigms of "rationality," "freedom," or "autonomy," at least as they have been imparted to us by the epic of humanity's emancipation. Perhaps we should also emancipate ourselves from a certain thinking of emancipation, which saw in it the cure for a *maladie honteuse*.[1]

For Nancy, it would involve a double movement that seems inherent in Christianity itself:

> This assertion, or series of assertions, implies the possibility not only of deconstructing Christianity – that is, leading it into the movement by which philosophy deports, complicates, and dismantles its

own closure – but of grasping in it (in it as it gets out of itself), from, it, the exceedent itself, the movement of a deconstruction: namely, the disjointing and dismantling [*désajointement*] of stones and the gaze directed toward the void (toward the *no-thing* [*chose-rien*]), their setting apart. (10)

In resorting to the use of the indefinite article ("the movement of *a* deconstruction"), the author, it would appear, is careful to avoid generalization. And yet, generalizations seem to be diffusely at work in the preceding paragraphs where Nancy tied, *passim*, the fate of Christianity to that of deconstruction in the West:

For the moment, one remark must suffice, but it is essential. Christianity designates nothing other, essentially (that is to say simply, infinitely simply: through an inaccessible simplicity), than the demand to open in this world an alterity or an unconditional alienation. However, "unconditional" means not undeconstructible. It must also denote the range, by right infinite, of the very movement of deconstruction and dis-enclosure. (10)

With regard to Christianity, Nancy retains a movement of opening, the requirement of a breach, the actualization of a separation in what he calls "this world," and he designates this movement "dis-enclosure." The thesis (if it is one), or premise, does not suggest an objective alliance between Christianity and deconstruction. Instead, it points to structural affinities between the terms. This identification is to be experienced (not without arousing a certain discontent) more than it can be read in the text's successive trials and errors, its confessions of uncertainty, its differing of argumentation, its abrupt beginnings, and its unexpected reversals.

The final subsection of the introduction, entitled "What Follows," opens with a resounding warning:

A simple warning for those who will not already have thrust aside this book in fury, pity, or discouragement. What follows here does not constitute the sustained and organized development one might expect. It is only an assembly, wholly provisional, of diverse texts that turn around the same object without approaching it frontally. It has

not yet seemed to me possible to undertake the more systematic treat-
ment of this object, but I thought it desirable to put to the test texts
that have remained little known to the public, even, for the most part,
once they were published. In fact, I do not feel particularly secure in
this undertaking: everywhere lurk traps. I do not foresee opposition
or attacks, or even eager endorsements, so much as I anticipate the
extremely narrow margin of maneuver that the operation (if it is one) I
am trying to discuss here has available to it. That margin is philosophi-
cally narrow, by definition, and socially narrow – caught in its fashion
between diverse tensions and complacencies. But so it goes. (12)

The anticipation of the introduction's reception justifies the
terms and motifs of the "simple warning." The least we could
say is that there is nothing simple about it. Rather, it places the
preceding passage, as well as those that follow, under the seal
of a complex articulation. The reader, to whom the warning
is aimed, is not just any reader: he or she is defined as one
who has not yielded to a violent impulse to reject the text.
Unique is the *captatio benevolentiae* that opens, or more precisely,
prolongs the "Opening." Surprisingly, Nancy appeals not to his
reader's perplexity, but to other passional sentiments: fury, pity,
discouragement. The warning affirms that the author does not
take for granted the minefield on which he treads in the pages of
the introduction. With one rhetorical gesture, he refrains from
dreading the reception that he no less embodies as the furious,
disappointed, discouraged reader, and then feigns impartiality to
both hostile and enthusiastic readers, in order to consider only that
which he calls the "narrow door" of an uncomfortable philosophical claim. The "thesis" of *Dis-Enclosure* – presented as precarious,
and withdrawn before it even takes the time to formulate itself – is
faced with the threat not only of being critiqued but also of being
condemned, while exposing its author beyond the limits of this
"simple" text. The book can be read as an instance of misreading
– a hermeneutic proposition carried out in the knowledge of a
cause that, as risky as it might be, does not stop its author. From
this point of view, the misreading is not a reading that can be
deemed a logical contradiction, nor a misinterpretation. Rather, it
is a mode of reading that is not blind to its problematic condition

– a reading against the tide, which is not unaware of itself as an act of reading subject to caution.

The reading of the introduction may arouse the reader's curiosity and raise a question: why does the philosopher embarrass himself at this inaugural stage with so many oratorical precautions, after having exposed himself in such an imprudent manner in the preceding pages? *Dis-Enclosure*, if it is to be believed, is born of an attempt, as dangerous as it is irresistible, to broach a subject obliquely – to formulate a thesis in a roundabout way ("without approaching it frontally"). The "operation" in question cannot be dissociated from a hermeneutic gesture that he just so happens to perform in the course of a series of more or less explicit readings where he invokes a few sparse but significant intertexts.

Through his warning, Nancy appears to disappoint his reader in advance. The reader finds himself doubly disappointed in effect: disappointed in relation to what comes before since that which follows will neither confirm nor reinforce it; and in relation to what follows, for the author himself is unsure whether it will turn out to be consistent with his subject. Thus, the opening – as elaborate as it is polemical, and as harsh as it is imprudent – will not keep its promise. It promises not to keep it. Such would be the sense of this ambiguous warning – a warning in the shape of a categorical refusal. What is offered to be read without disruption thus far is interrupted by a discursive movement of withdrawal that is unexpected, to say the least. To be sure, expectation is created, but no sooner does its horizon come into view than it is already retracted. The warning, however, is not a formal one: it places the essays that follow under the conditional regime of reserve, retreat; it insidiously affects the reading that Nancy suggests of deconstruction in its relationship to Christianity. Furthermore, the issue of deconstruction of Christianity somehow coincides with the circumstances of Jacques Derrida's passing, as Nancy says in a footnote that closes the introduction. Addressed to Derrida, the essays were meant to be a philosophical conversation between him and Derrida on the issue of the deconstruction of Christinianity:

> This essay was written shortly before Jacques Derrida's death. The discussion that I hoped to pursue with him on this theme, as on

the ensemble of themes of a "deconstruction" or a *dis-enclosure* of Christianity (or, indeed, of something else again, further back behind or before "Christianity" itself) will therefore not take place. I would simply like to say that Derrida was highly sensitive to the arguments in the texts published here under the titles "The Judeo-Christian" and "Of a Divine Wink," both of which were addressed to him. I have no doubt that Derrida would nonetheless have persisted in resisting me, as he resisted the themes of "fraternity" and "generosity" – to his mind they were too Christian. Nevertheless, the question cannot be limited to this opposition between us, for the stakes go well beyond those debates, and I believe he knew that, albeit despite himself. It is such a knowledge – if it is a knowledge at all – that we approach here: a knowledge of a very simple, even elementary, disposition toward the "outside the world" ["*hors du monde*"] in the very midst of the world, a disposition toward a transcendence *of* immanence. (176–7)

This footnote, serving as a tribute to the deceased friend and cloaked as an address to him who cannot answer, is far from innocent. A few of the collected essays had been written when Derrida was dying (e.g. "Consolation, Desolation"), while others were presented when he was alive, at times even in his presence (e.g. "The Judeo-Christian"). *Dis-Enclosure* as a *collection* belongs, nevertheless, to a different temporality: the essays were collected and prefaced *after* the philosopher's death. In the wake of Derrida's death, Nancy assembles the texts that are addressed to him. In that respect, Derrida becomes the addressee of an address to which he will never be able to respond. We could begin by questioning the form of the address delivered to the deceased person – a question on which Derrida himself pondered, as he does in *Memoires for Paul de Man*:

> What constrains us to think (without ever believing in it) a "true mourning" (if such there be) is the essence of the proper name. What in our sadness we call the life of Paul de Man is, in our memory, the moment when Paul de Man *himself* could answer to the name, Paul de Man, and answer *in* and *for* the name of Paul de Man. At the moment of death the proper name remains; through it we can name, call, invoke, designate, but we know, we can *think* (and this thought

cannot be reduced to mere memory, though it comes from a memory) that Paul de Man himself, the bearer of the name and the unique pole of all these acts, these references, will never again answer to it, never himself answer, never again except through what we mysteriously call our memory.[2]

Derrida's use of italics (*in* and *for* the name of), *with regard* to de Man, which has the effect of functioning as a typographical *mise en abyme* of the named subject insofar as he answers for his name and in his name in the act of speaking, and insofar as he acknowledges his death in order to attempt – in the same movement – to recover from it, differs from the effect that results from the use of the interpolated clause in the footnote ("albeit despite himself") deployed by Nancy. The comparison between the two posthumous modes of naming others is not without significance, if for no other reason than that Nancy – a careful reader of Derrida – cannot not have known the text of *Memoires for Paul de Man*, and more generally, of the issue of the Derridean farewell as it appears especially in the collection of eulogies, *The Work of Mourning*.[3] Indeed, Nancy's address is not so much a simple tribute as it is a unique rhetorical act. He "makes" Derrida speak for himself, literally reluctantly: "albeit despite himself." *Dis-Enclosure* is thus wholly or partially addressed to Jacques Derrida – regardless of his posthumous and postulated reluctance to a few theses that are outlined in it. What the interpolated clause does is nothing short of extracting a consent that is authorized by nothing, by nobody. Prejudging the secret or unmentionable thoughts of a living person could already be seen as an unforgivable act. Why, then, would the interlocutor and friend take the risk of assuming the thoughts of one who is departed? It is in the name of Derrida that Nancy occasionally speaks ["*prend la parole*," which in French means "to speak," as well as to literally "take speech away from the speaker"], and he does so at the risk of dishonoring the memory of a person who is deceased, insofar as he makes Derrida speak *in absentia* and insofar as he speaks in his name, under the cloak of the name "Jacques Derrida." In speaking *for* Jacques Derrida – instead of Jacques Derrida – he finds himself speaking *against* Derrida, *beyond* Derrida, in order to make him retract his speech, in order to misread him.

Such a device of address employed at the end of the introduction is neither common nor innocent. It opens and, like an infrapaginal reading pact, weighs down the collection, particularly the two chapters "The Judeo-Christian" and "On a Divine Wink." These two essays explicitly concern Derrida, and they enjoin him to answer. The enjoinment coincides exactly with the impossibility in which he finds himself to respond to this invitation. It is this challenge that we shall attempt to take up by making Derrida answer (if that is even possible) from a few positions and propositions that he may have had to defend, and by trying, in our turn, to misread him.

How can Nancy's absence of doubt concerning Derrida's answer – about a consent obtained past his reluctance, literally extracted from beyond and in the name of a higher stake which is in fact overlooked – be accounted for and interpreted? In a performative act whose strength and even violence should be measured (given the posthumous context), Nancy assumes nothing less than the answer of the friend whom he presumably knows better than the friend might know himself. With this act of interpretation as our starting point, we will think the notion of misreading in its unique relation to the posthumous address. Misreading would become the paradigm of reading, conceived as a replacement of a text written in the absence of its author. Radicalizing the act of reading, misreading could be conceived as a schema of reading. Misreading – let us note in passing – is an activity that is unknown to the French language, while its usage is certifiably common in English. What, then, is this "knowledge" ("It is such a knowledge [. . .] that we approach here") with which Derrida must reach an agreement, "albeit despite himself"?

In "The Judeo-Christian," the text based on his conference paper delivered in the presence of Derrida,[4] Nancy assigns the Judeo-Christian an eponymous identity that is, no doubt, fragile and problematic: "Today, then, for us, the Judeo-Christian will be James. And it will be, in a manner that remains to be discerned, a secret thread or a hyphen that could tie the historic James to that other James [Jacques] around whom, or on whose pretext, we have come together here; and who is another Judeo-Christian, or indeed another Judeo-Helleno-Christian" (46). Nancy's essay

constantly deals with two "Jameses" [*Jacques*], one being the author
of the Epistle in the New Testament, and "the other" being
Derrida, who is summoned in relation to his essay "Faith and
Knowledge." Nancy does not resist the pleasure of passing from
one James to the other,[5] from a Christian James to a Jewish, if not
"Judeo-Christian," James. Nancy wears out and wears down the
duplicity of James to such an extent that with each new instance,
a worry or an uncertainty that is as tenuous as it is transient grips
the reader who is forced to correct (himself) where necessary
since, in most cases, the James [*Jacques*] in question is that of the
Epistle. Nancy's essay does not toy any less with the possibility of
misunderstanding, or with the new effects of sense that misreading
entails. Written in this manner, the first name of the philosopher
constantly mirrors that of the apostle [*Saint Jacques*]. As obsolete
or hyperbolic as it might be, the possibility of such a misreading is
in force through the mechanism of playing on the confusion produced by first names.

As it happens, the first name "James" [*Jacques*] that the essay cites
over and over again – more than might be deemed reasonable –
and by which it obliquely calls out to Derrida, is not, in fact, his
birth name, not even the name given to him at circumcision as
Derrida has recounted.[6] It is the name taken by him at a turning
point in his editorial path, a name he gave himself as if at the
moment of philosophical baptism. "Jacques" – the *nom de plume*
that Derrida substitutes for "Jackie" – is not simply the Gallicized
version of his first name, but is also a biblical name: it is the name
of a patriarch, of an apostle – a first name that, by definition, is
"Judeo-Christian." "James," in fact, doubles as "Jacob." James
and Jacob are derived from the same Hebrew word that signifies
"heel." The biblical legend has it that Jacob was born holding
his brother Esau by the heel. Another substantiated etymological
root links Jacob to the verb "to supplant," alluding to the bowl
of lentil stew by means of which he took from Esau his rights as a
first-born. The first name James with which Nancy toys all along
the chapter (52) is therefore not exempt from the semantics of the
double and of duplicity.

This oscillation between the different first names – initially
discernible – ends up losing the reader gradually. When dealing

with the interpretation of Abraham's gesture of offering Isaac as
a sacrifice, both Jameses – the apostle and the French philosopher – find themselves caught in an exegetic competition for that
which is least anachronistic. Readers of Derrida who are aware of
the comment he made about the Abrahamic gesture in *The Gift
of Death*[7] must suspend their judgment until the subsequent sentence in Nancy's text, which contradicts their nonetheless plausible
reading hypothesis. Nancy is talking about the other James (that
of the Epistle) in relation to another reader of the Christic Word
whose performative interpretations marked and informed tradition:
Paul. "Contrary to Paul (Romans 4), James maintains that Abraham
is justified by his work, designated as the offering of Isaac" (53).
Although Nancy (deliberately or otherwise) does not deal with it,
let us note in passing that the Pauline reading of this point of exege-
sis[8] is in accordance with Derrida's reading of the episode of the
sacrifice of Isaac in the chapter "Pardon for not meaning (to say)"
[*"Pardon de ne pas vouloir dire,"* in *The Gift of Death*]. Strictly from
this point of view, Derrida breaks away from the James [*Jacques*] of
the Epistle in order to move closer to Paul with whom he has in
common – by birth – the religion of the Covenant.

However, the Judeo-Christian in question, among others, is
(or "will be," as Nancy puts it) Derrida – the author whose name
is tied to "deconstruction," a notion, if it is one, or else a word,
Nancy had attempted to define two pages earlier, in the midst of a
parenthesis, in a double, if not redoubled, definition:

> (A parenthesis for two axioms. 1. A deconstruction is always a penetra-
> tion; it is neither a destruction, nor a return to the archaic, nor, again,
> a suspension of adherence: a deconstruction is an intentionality of the
> to-come [*l'à-venir*], enclosed in the space through which the con-
> struction is articulated part by part. 2. Deconstruction thus belongs to
> a construction as its law or its proper schema: it does not come to it
> from elsewhere.) (44)

Through the "Judeo-Christian," Nancy reads deconstruction as
an effect of construction – as always already inscribed in the hyphen
of a substantive, the terms of which, when bound together, invite
one to think about their difference. What "Judeo-Christian" opens

onto – what it invites one to do – is a conjunction that cannot be separated from a disjunction: it is a conjunctive disjunction. The sense of Judeo-Christian, as Nancy understands it, is to be found in the hyphen that he also calls "the possibility of the *cum* considered in itself" (44). Beyond the figure of speech and quotation marks, the Judeo-Christian historically took the shape of Christ's person. Christ is, by definition, the first Judeo-Christian of the tradition, the very incarnation of the concept. The hyphen is at work in the heart of the figure of Christ, all the way to his martyrdom. Jesus is the figure through which one religion joins the other to become another:

> Thus a deconstruction comes to pass even before construction, or during construction and at its very heart. The deconstruction does not annul the construction, and I have no intention to reject, in James's name, the subsequent study of Christian construction – I don't want to take out the gesture of "returning to the sources" and of "purification" of the origin, so obsessive in Christianity, monotheism, and the West. But this deconstruction – which will not be a retrocessive gesture, aimed at some sort of morning light – henceforth belongs to the principle and plan of construction. Deconstruction lies in its cement: it is in the hyphen, indeed it is *of* that hyphen. (58)

At the turning point of the argumentation, an inextricable double-entendre, "in James's name," offers itself up to a reading. In this instance, it is impossible to assign a specific face to "James": it can be understood as both the prophet and the philosopher. Furthermore, it seems that it is exactly in this location that two reading options – far from excluding each other – are superposed. The interpolated clause ("and I have no intention to reject, in James's name, the subsequent study of Christian construction") echoes as a reiteration of a claim already encountered in the warning. What Nancy seeks to highlight is the intrinsic consistency of Christianity with deconstruction. This formulation implies – past its ambiguities – confessing to what extent "James's name" could have stood in the way of such a questioning. The all-too paradoxical invocation "in James's name" is the speech act of disregard – as if the possibility of "James" to refer to Derrida could have, in the manner of a prohibition of the superego, prevented a hypothesis from being formulated or explored. *Dis-Enclosure* can also be read between the lines as the effect of a lifting of inhibition in the wake of the demise of a quasi-paternal figure.

Thus, Judeo-Christianity is to be understood as a deconstruction (of Judaism) – a deconstruction that does not entirely exclude the possibility of its destruction in the form of its sublation [*relève*] not exempt from negativity. In his reading of the Epistle of James, Nancy suggests instead that he does not defend the thesis according to which deconstruction might be Christian since Christianity can be understood as always already being caught up in the movement of (its) deconstruction. What emerges as a hesitation – as a grammatical oscillation that the two axiomatic definitions provided in the introduction already manifested – constitutes the turning point of the argumentation, as well as its blind spot: the more or less imperceptible shift from *a* deconstruction ("a deconstruction is always a penetration") to deconstruction ("Deconstruction thus belongs to a construction as its law": 44). The legitimacy of such a shift from the definite to the indefinite – and of the conditions of the possibility of this generalization – does not go without saying. If one were to assume that deconstruction as a force is at work in any particular deconstruction, the reader of *Dis-Enclosure* would then be led to reflect on the point of knowing whether the deconstruction of Christianity is one deconstruction among others or deconstruction itself. The question – as irrepressible as it might be – threatens to prove itself specious: can there exist deconstructions? Is deconstruction not entirely at stake in any deconstruction? The determiner – whichever it may be – is a trap. Nonetheless, Nancy juxtaposes the two terms without commenting on them.

He insists that de-construction be read as being articulated around a hyphen that renders its constructive dimension salient. Deconstruction is not a destruction, but the law of any single construction. It is defined as the condition of possibility of all edifice – the rule of articulation of all of its parts and the jointing of all of its stones. What holds the elements together is precisely that which separates them, opposes them, disunites them. The hyphen is the typographical marker of an articulation that is originally not meant to – and cannot – hide itself away in the mindless sublation of the

primary struggle between its constituents. The metaphor of cement
– which precedes that of the hyphen, and with which the hyphen
confuses (if not fuses) itself – is justified by the tropism of construction. The slight grammatical forcing to which Nancy turns, and
by which the definite article is substituted by a partitive ("*of* that
hyphen"), could also be read, beyond the material and paradigmatic quality thus brought to light, as an indication of an inevitable
future. The hyphen does more than reunite or join: it cements,
fuses, and confuses. It loses itself as an instance of mediation – as
a site of discernible articulation, or of an in-betweenness. What is
lost in the disappearance of the definite article ("the hyphen") is
the possibility of identifying a space halfway between the terms –
the site of *différance*. The hyphen between the words, perhaps even
inside the words (de-construction), eventually winds up erasing
itself – like the cement between the stones – whereas their respective existence is indispensable to them.

Hence, the cement of de-construction is penetrating, and turns
out to be more negative than one would think. The hyphen
indicates a horizontality that could conceal a sublation [*relève*]
that implies a verticality. Under such circumstances, how can the
hyphen be thought of as mere coexistence rather than as absorbent
negativity? In cementing the stones, the hyphen does not leave
them intact but worms its way between them. It would be difficult
to wager on the innocence or the innocuousness of a hyphen. We
cannot categorically rule out that there appears to be a figure of a
sublation [*relève*] (a Christic figure of dialectics), although Nancy
claims to be fiercely wary of this term.[9] In "Judeo-Christian," the
second term makes the first run the risk of an overtaking – of a
future that could turn out to be more destructive than expected.
Might it not be that Christianity alone is part of – and a sublation
of – "Judeo-Christianity"? As the unique equation of Judaism
whose to-come [*à-venir*] is unpredictable and unexpected, might it
not be that "Judeo-Christian" signs the operation of the sublation
of Judaism commonly known as Christianity?

Despite its horizontality, or, in fact, because of its horizontality,
the hyphen holds together the parts or the stones of an edifice.
The first name of another apostle that Nancy does not mention
lurks in the shadows of the chapter like a homophonous specter,

as if it were breaking in: Peter. The irrepressible invocation of an intertext seems to follow: the word of Christ that ties the apostle to the fate of the Church and ob-liges him: "And I tell you that you are Peter [*Pierre*], and on this rock I will build my church, and the gates of Hades will not overcome it. I will give you the keys of the kingdom of heaven; whatever you bind on earth will be bound in heaven, and whatever you loose on earth will be loosed in heaven."[10] Peter and the apostles (among whom James) are instituted by Jesus to serve as foundations – as the "living" stones of his Church. The metaphor of masonry relates to that of the Church being conceived as a common house, as well as to that of its underlying petrification. Construction is not an ordinary semanteme because any construction potentially gestures toward the Church.

Far from being incidental, the place that Derrida's death holds in *Dis-Enclosure* resonates with the hyphen in that it cements the chapters together: it is the *basso continuo* – the law of thematic composition of the work. It holds together the different parts of the book and gives it its invisible architecture, as a work of silent mourning. The essay "Consolation, Desolation," which is strangely placed at the heart of the book, is the eulogy that Nancy extended to Derrida in *Magazine Littéraire.*[11] *Dis-Enclosure* could be read as a borderline "mourning diary" insofar as mourning entails ambiguities: it is a tribute to a deceased friend, a track record of deconstruction, and perhaps even a settlement of scores with the departed one who, because of his defection – albeit involuntary – is held responsible for leaving the field of deconstruction excessively empty, desolate, and open. At the end of "Consolation, Desolation," when Nancy evokes the "unbearable" law of mortality, he quotes Derrida in a manner that remotely echoes the gesture of the introduction: "Who then would live, ultimately, without practicing, albeit without knowing it, what I am here designating with *a citation extracted by force and placed out of context:* 'a hymn, an encomium, a prayer,' turned toward the other of the present life within life itself, 'an imploration for surrection, for resurrection,' such that it is this itself, this imploration, that is the resurrection?" (103; my italics). The misreading at work in *Dis-Enclosure* consists not in the application of a force that is extrinsic to reading, but rather of a force *within* reading itself. The "out of context" citation of the philosopher, who himself theorized the principle of the iterability of the sign, will not surprise the reader. However, this citation, in its being caught up in the movement of reiteration, escapes, by definition, the non-reiterable context of its first inscription; and with originary intentionality, it is said to have been "extracted by force." Why call it "by force?" Why dramatize such a violent act committed in the very place of elegiac speech? Why the need to appeal to force, and to recall the cruelly obvious "out of context" that beckons toward death? The force that is exercised is related to the Derridean body of work [*corpus*] – a body of work that is severed from the body of its author. The corporeality of the text does not consist in the only catachresis of the corpus, but finds itself revived here in the identification of the act of citation as "extraction." To the Derridean body of work, there no longer corresponds – there does not correspond, there most likely never has corresponded – a body that could answer for his name, for his author's authority. The death of the author is, Derrida maintained, only a particular case of the state of deficiency in which every author finds himself in relation to his text. On that issue, Bennington has written:

> My proper name outlives me. After my death, it will still be possible to name me and speak of me. Like every sign, including "I," the proper name involves the necessary possibility of functioning in my absence, of detaching itself from its bearer: and according to the logic we have already seen at work, one must be able to take this absence to a certain absolute, which we call death. So we shall say that even while I am alive, my name marks my death. It already bears the death of its bearer. It is already the name of the dead person, the anticipated memory of a departure.[12]

It is this possibility of "naming me and speaking of me after my death" that Nancy explores. He "ventures" upon this very possibility from which stems the principle of every signature, insofar as it summons a "countersignature," which, as Bennington mentions, is to be understood in every sense of the term, including the polemical force of the preposition "counter." In *Dis-Enclosure*, Nancy *touches* on Derrida's signature: he grazes it, caresses it, just as much as he contradicts and forces it. In the chapters dedicated to him, he reads *against* Derrida, staying as closely as possible to him, to the point of allowing the intimacy that bound him to Derrida to turn the Derridean text *virtually* against itself. It is as if, for Nancy, reading Derrida faithfully (in the name of the fidelity to the friend and to the (ad)venture of deconstruction) implies reading against him and exposing the Derridean text to unforeseen contexts – to a high-risk to-come [*à-venir*]. The misreading could be understood as the ultimate and sublime form of fidelity – one that is ready to run every risk up to and including injustice. In the two instances that were pointed out, the mentioning of Derrida's name serves an end that exceeds it, be it a real text (as in the case of the citation), or an implied subtext – a reading between the lines.

Surprisingly enough, Bennington appears to be curiously reserved in his gloss of the Derridean thesis of the signature. Despite what he suggests, "I" is not an ordinary sign as far as the outliving of the name is concerned. If its future is not perceptibly different, it is indisput-ably more radical than that of all of the other signs. More than any other sign, "I" is not only likely to detach itself, but does, in fact, detach itself from its author as well as from its noun [*nom*] in the pro-nominal operation. In order for Derrida to become "I" to himself – for him to utter this sign in his place, to manifest himself through it, to exist in and by means of it – it was necessary for him (as for any subject of an enunciation) to give up being called "Jacques Derrida" in his own discourse. It belongs to the structure of the sign to be detachable. In the case of the subject pronoun, it is always already detached from its bearer. "I" makes sense, and gestures only to, and from, the one who has disappeared from his proper name.

In fact, death is only a particular case of the absence of the author from the text that he signed and *de facto* abandoned as a result of his signature. In appending this mark, the author indeed definitively resigns from his writing. The author's signature that can be read on the cover, or at the bottom of the publishing contract, signals his taking leave from his position as the subject of enunciation or marks his regressing to a place of an outsider – his self-exclusion. The text, which is his, can only belong to him on the strict condi-tion that he take leave from it. In order to exist, a text requires the defect, the defection, or the default, of the author's personhood.

The text contains death in its structure, in that it postulates absence to itself as its constitutive device. From this stems the idea that the experience of writing conveys to its author the schema of death.

Yet the dying with which "The Judeo-Christian" concludes is part of a whole different logic. The unction with which James closes his epistle has nothing to do with signature. In the case of signs, where the author is absent, death is the paradigmatic modality of absence. Unction, though, is the very rule of living that places the living being in a struggle with presence. Presence is not immediately conceived as stolen away, but, on the contrary, as a striving toward a limit-experience. The difference here lies in the status of presence, in its orientation with regard to the time line. In writing, it is always already lost: it is the object of mourning of the self as withdrawn, impoverished, whereas in faith, it is the experience of the Other predicated on the modality of hope, ceaselessly revived, always on the verge of being touched and missed. If writing has in common with death the quality of being "inappropriable," it radically differs from it in terms of the "proximity of presence" (60) that it ignores:

> This is to say that unction signs not what will later be called a life eternal beyond death but the entry into death as into a finite *parousia* that is infinitely differed or deferred. This is the entry into incommensurable inadequation. In this sense, every dying one is a messiah, and every messiah is a dying one. The dying one is no longer a mortal as distinct from the immortals. The dying one is the living one in the act of a presence that is incommensurable. All unction is thus extreme, and the extreme is always what is nigh: one never ceases drawing close to it, almost touching it. Death is tied to sin: that is, tied to the deficiency of a life that does not *practice* faith – that cannot practice it without failing or fainting – at the incommensurable height of dying. Yet despite this, faith gives; it gives dying precisely in its incommensurability ("to give death," "the gift of death," he says): a gift that is not a matter of receiving in order to keep, any more than is love, or poverty, or even veridicity (which are, ultimately, the same thing as dying). (59)

The unction signs but not in the sense of writing. The author does not enter death because for him, death is not part of a unique to-come [*à-venir*], but is metonymically communicated to him only as absence, of which death is one modality among others, and marked in the structure of the sign. If absence is the law of the sign, presence is, paradoxically, a category that is virtually irrelevant in the realm of writing. If death "puts the existent in the presence of existing itself" (60), it is posited as a law of Christianity, as truth of Christian life: "He [i.e. Man] becomes the dying one in a dying that doubles or lines the whole time of his life" (59). Christianity's thinking of death as knowledge of the limit of presence – un-knowledge of presence that it touches on – consists in a splitting up (that is as paradoxical as it is arithmetic) of the time of life devoted to dying.

In the passage quoted above, a Derridean intertext is invoked by Nancy *passim*, and as freely as ever: a simple wink that is unburdened, and that does not lead to any gloss on the rather explicit identity of the author of "he says" (59). "The Gift of Death," as Derrida (reader of the episode of the sacrifice of Isaac) conceives it, is in no way assimilable, nor even comparable to the gift of death that Nancy talks about at this precise point in his argumentation. More than relevance, it is the sense of the invocation that begs to be questioned. The Derridean intertext seems to return, almost despite itself, in the form of an echo, to the formulation that appears under his pen, unless Nancy's formulation ("it gives dying precisely") is itself derived from the thinking of a third party whose memory the philosopher honors as he recalls it. Of course, Abraham (in Jacques Derrida's reading) cannot practice his faith without running the risk of failing when he delivers the fatal blow. Nor can Nancy faithfully read Derrida's text without the risk of betraying him. However, the faith that propels him and holds Abraham back in an almost simultaneous movement is independent of the question of sin.

In *Archive Fever*, Derrida had, in a gesture that is reminiscent of the implicit stake of *Dis-Enclosure*, questioned the kinship, or filiation or affinity, between Judaism and psychoanalysis. He did not take up this question in his own name, but through Sigmund Freud. In the pages that Derrida devotes to this question, he seems to have anticipated a response to the Nancean theory when he evokes "Freud's secret, of his dissimulated or unavowable thought according to which psychoanalysis would be Judaism without God,"[13] unless the text of *Dis-Enclosure* is read as a posthumous appeal from Nancy to the Derrida of these few pages of *Archive Fever*, of which Nancy makes no mention.

The author of *Dis-Enclosure* does not go so far as to maintain that deconstruction *is – could be –* Christian. Such a thesis would be unacceptable, if not absurd. However, an implicit thesis, which I would be tempted to call hypo-thesis, and which certain rhetorical difficulties seem to betray since it is neither able nor willing to be entirely articulated, nonetheless ties Christianity to deconstruction. And yet, the idea according to which deconstruction might be the very source of Christianity is more than just an implied suggestion. This idea seems to be formulated cautiously but clearly. As for its correlate, it floats like a specter over the introduction and "The Judeo-Christian." If psychoanalysis could be said to be Jewish, would deconstruction then be Christian? Could the faith that Nancy evokes in the final words of the essay be part of a (Christian) faith without God? How to interpret the performative community to which the first person plural pronoun ("us") pertains: "That is what places that curious day still before us, ever before us, ahead of us, like a day that would be neither Jewish, nor Christian, nor Muslim – but rather like a trace or hyphen drawn to set space between every union, to untie every religion from itself" (60)

Nancy thus finds himself face-to-face with Derrida, in a similar position in which Yerushalmi found himself face-to-face with Freud. Derrida and Freud, both deceased, are invoked to respond to a virtually unutterable intuition whose formulation itself is problematic: the theoretical possibility is perplexing and the idea makes the authors shudder slightly. Nancy and Yerushalmi both obtain a response to their suggestion in a text that precedes their respective questions, as if after-the-fact. In both cases, it seems that the "phantom of the patriarch" of psychoanalysis, like that of deconstruction, responds to their disciples in the future perfect:

> First of all, it seems that in private, and I stress this point, in a *private letter*, Freud had already given, in the essentials, the very response that Yerushalmi seems to be waiting for or pretends to be waiting for, by promising to keep it to himself, as if he wanted to have for himself in

secret, here, for his very own self, Josef Hayim Yerushalmi, the principle of an equally private response which Freud had *already* given (sixty
five years earlier!) to Enrico Morselli. As if he wanted to share with
Freud, all alone, a secret that Freud had already confided to someone
else, before Yerushalmi was even born: "In 1926," Yerushalmi writes,
"you wrote privately to Enrico Morselli that you were not sure that
his notion that psychoanalysis is a direct product of the Jewish mind is
correct, but that if it is, you 'wouldn't be ashamed.'"[14]

What, then, would be Derrida's response to Nancy's unformu-
lated question – to the undisclosable equation of *Dis-Enclosure*?
It seems to be written in black and white a few pages earlier in
Derrida's own text. The categorical refusal that he addresses (as if
in anticipation of *Dis-Enclosure*, and not without leaving room for
doubt) consists in the originary and eminently problematic nature
of the archive as the founding moment:

> [A] science, a philosophy, a theory, a theorem, are or should be *intrin-
> sically* independent of the singular archive of their history. We know
> well that these things (science, philosophy, theory, etc.) have a history,
> a rich and complex history that carries them and produces them in a
> thousand ways. We know well that in diverse and complicated ways,
> proper names and signatures count. But the structure of the theo-
> retical, philosophical, scientific statement, and even when it concerns
> history, does not have, should not in principle have, an intrinsic and
> essential need for the archive, and for what binds the archive in all its
> forms to some proper name or to some body proper, to some (famil-
> ial or national) filiation to covenants, to secrets. It has no such need,
> in any case, in its relationship or in its claim to truth – in the classi-
> cal sense of the term. But as soon as one speaks of a Jewish science,
> whatever one's understanding of this word (and I will come back to
> this in an instant), the archive becomes a founding moment for science
> as such: not only the history and the memory of singular events, of
> exemplary proper names, languages and filiations, but the deposition
> in an *arkheion* (which can be an ark or a temple), the consignation
> in a place of relative exteriority, whether it has to do with writings,
> documents, or ritualized marks on the body proper (for example,
> phylacteries or circumcision). At issue here is nothing less than taking

seriously the question whether a science can depend on something like a circumcision.[15]

Derrida does not seek to deny the existence of the historical relations between Judaism and psychoanalysis. Deconstruction, one may object, is not a science and, probably, neither is psychoanalysis – at least not a science like any other, despite Freud's attempt to establish it as such. Deconstruction is not even a full-fledged philosophy. It is no less a movement that should be understood, not in the restrictive sense of its being a philosophical school of thought, but in the sense of a force at work in the texts. No more Christian than Jewish, deconstruction is born of and inhabited by a complex of traditions that amount to as many contradictory archives as the term "Judeo-Christian" might be able to cover, but with which they cannot be identified. But it is not possible, nor is it even "serious," to maintain that deconstruction can be a Christian science (or Jewish, for that matter) or be part of any assignable historical origin. Deconstruction, as a science of interpretation of texts whose methodological literalism might call to mind the work of the Talmudic tradition, might have been said – in an equally unsustainable way – to be of Jewish inspiration, if not of Jewish origin. But these statements do not avail, for deconstruction is like language: it does not belong. If it crosses the archive – if it brushes it, intensifies it, passes through it – it cannot, under any circumstances, nor in any other capacity, rely on it, nor lay claim to it, let alone help itself to it.

Nancy is wary of taking the plunge and qualifying deconstruction as Christian, despite the subtle "Deconstruction of Christianity" that seems to invite a reversal in the antimetabole "Christianity of deconstruction." The thesis of the hyphen developed in "The Judeo-Christian" gestures to the archive and tends not to establish deconstruction in Christianity, but allows (itself) the thinking of deconstruction within its organic relationship ("proper name," "body proper," as Derrida puts it) to Christianity. The hyphen certainly renders secret the exact nature of the relationship, the sense of the relationship. The genitive ("of") in the expression "Deconstruction of Christianity" seems to operate in a similar way, without its being possible to disentangle the objective genitive from the subjective genitive.

How, then, to read *Dis-Enclosure*? Given the philosophical reading pact that the book offers, can one do anything other than misread, if not mid-read [*mi-lire*], it? It is the very nature of the thesis, the possibility of a hypo-thesis, of a secret thesis, that I would like to question, as a conclusion. Perhaps Nancy gives the key to reading *Dis-Enclosure* in the chapter "On a Divine Wink" in which he comments on a comment made by Derrida:

> We will return to this question. The *Wink* is a sign of awaiting, or of putting expectation in the position of a sign. It is suspended between hope and disappointment. We must await its interpretation, but that waiting is, in itself, already a mobilization, and its mobility or motility is more important than its final interpretation. The most current model of the *Wink* (model in the sense of example or modalization) is given in the *clin d'oeil*. A wink is always to be translated, but at the same time, it has already gone beyond its translation by its gesture. It has jumped in one bound, in the twinkling of an eye, beyond the sense it has prompted us to await. (106)

The thesis of *Dis-Enclosure* remains suspended (or put off, deferred), unable to be situated or articulated on a thetical mode – vague, yet impossible to find. "The privilege of *Wink* consists, in short, in the fact that its sense is spent in the passage immediately stolen away, in the hint suddenly hidden of a sense that vanishes, and whose truth consists in vanishing" (108). The hypo-thesis of *Dis-Enclosure* (if we follow Nancy here and trust him in order to read it) would not be the existence of a secret thesis, but indeed, the vanishing of the thesis. The site of the thesis would deliberately be left empty in favor of an uninterrupted blinking (batting of eyelids). The text resumes its course, from chapter to chapter, from a suspension that is not exempt from philosophical suspense. It does not deviate from the dividing line on which it writes itself. The motif of the *Wink* that Nancy raises to the rank of a philosopheme strangely substantiates the experience of reading *Dis-Enclosure* in the manner of a meta-commentary or a metalepsis. The essays collected under this title fall in between a blink that suspends, hints at, and addresses a third party at the very moment when it becomes blind to itself, at the very place of what Nancy calls a "*clin*" (a "slant": 112). In the

Wink, witnessing is conditioned by a suspension of the possibility of exercising one's gaze – the renunciation of the faculty to stare at one's interlocutor. Blinking consists in losing sight in order to see, to signal to others at the moment when the subject of the *Wink* is no longer in the position to exercise an intentional sense. The sign (gesture) that is made goes through a momentary blindness of the self, the disappearance of others. The reading that can be considered as much a commentary as a simple deciphering (and not only a translation, as Nancy mentions) stems from a blinking that assumes that the text vanishes as a result of a batting of eyelashes. No reading can take place without one's losing sight of the text.

Reading from the point of view of the *Wink* necessarily consists in reading wrongly – misreading. "There is always excess, lack, or curvature of sense: *winken* is, in fact, first and foremost to curve or bow, to angle, vacillate, wobble, list" (106). Besides, misreading is never distant from dis-reading [*dé-lire*], from an etymological derailment: "The fact is, a *Wink* departs from the established order of communication and signification by opening up a zone of allusion and suggestion, a free space for invitation, address, seduction, or waywardness. But that departure beckons toward the ultimate sense of sense, or the truth of sense. Here, sovereignly, sense excludes itself from sense: such is the wink's monition" (107). The author's definition of "monition" reflexively and retrospectively alludes to the warning in the introduction: "A simple warning for those who will not already have thrust aside this book in fury, pity, or discouragement. What follows here does not constitute the sustained and organized development one might expect" (12). Through these "Opening" words, Nancy was – in a sovereign gesture – interrupting the movement of the initial thought and suspending *sine die* and in a singularly derogatory way the demands of discursive argumentation. It is of the incredible violence of this gesture that the possibility of a reading (as misreading) and the exercising of a sovereignty is born: "Where there is exception, there is sovereignty" (106). By means of this performative act of warning, Nancy was not only deviating from the modalities of philosophical speech, but was also creating the implicit conditions of a reading pact that is agreed upon unilaterally. The violence of the "warning" is the result of its being absolute: "In order to be absolute, power must absolutize itself, that is, absolve itself from any tie or responsibility other than that of being answerable for itself and self-authorizing" (109). The text of *Dis-Enclosure winkt* at this particular point: it conveys to its reader a "sign of complicity" that, to begin with, is unintelligible:

> Nothing is more specifically characteristic of sovereign majesty than the frown, the wink, the expression said to be "imperceptible," the reply to which is called a "sign of complicity" [*signe d'intelligence*], in the sense that, in that complicity, connivance precedes and exceeds understanding, in the sense that complicity has already understood whatever it is that has not been openly offered up to the understanding, but is expected. The *Wink* opens an expectation at the same time as an impatience to which the decision to understand without waiting, in the twinkling of an eye, responds. (107)

The hypo-thesis of the book stems from this formulated principle in that it is never strictly offered up to "understanding," that it therefore cannot be openly disputable, as it is inarticulate. However, the hypo-thesis can implicitly be "expected" ("one might expect," as the warning states). The writing of the *Wink* postulates misreading because the *Wink*, in its very structure, determines a reading (in advance) of a claim that is always deferred, always deformed. From this point of view, the *Wink* is part of a logic that we might dare to describe as perverse ("Ambivalence is constitutive of sovereignty," Nancy writes: 109). The thesis of *Dis-Enclosure* derives from a glaring subtext, the reason for which is difficult to identify: no sooner is it pointed out than it slips away and turns against its imprudent commentator even though he or she is overcome with an intimate conviction that is unassignable, but persistent: "The *Wink* triggers; it acts and it activates a play of forces on the sly or in counterpoint to the sense" (110).

Any reading, insofar as it considers itself the to-come [*à-venir*] of a text, exposes and alienates it. Aware of this risk, Nancy sets out knowingly, while at the same time being deliberately, if not sovereignly, ignorant of the outcome that offers itself to him, and to what the to-come has in store for him. From this point of view, *Dis-Enclosure* is a text that is part of deconstruction in more ways than one: not only does it deal with deconstruction, but also actualizes it in that it presents itself as a text *under* deconstruction, subject to a movement of writing that takes the shape of an open to-come, and which, page after page, does not necessarily know in advance what it seeks to achieve, nor which steep, slippery paths it might take, possibly leading nowhere. In a note to the chapter "On a Divine *Wink*," addressed to Derrida, and which opens with a gloss on a Derridean gloss on Heidegger, Nancy writes, in the manner of a confession: "If I take a very different, even an opposite direction, this is less a question of differing interpretations than of an interpretation, such as Courtine's, as opposed to the extrapolation and free use of the texts upon which I venture" (184). Throughout the work, the author of *Dis-Enclosure* ceaselessly qualifies, interrupts, amends, comments on, and authorizes his method.

The structural responsibility (which Nietzsche called orphan) of any text, and even more so, of any work, exposes it to every violence, extraction, decontextualization, "free use," and "extrapolation." Reading involves the application of a force inseparable from a violence because reading designates an act by which a reader literally authorizes himself to respond in his proper name, in lieu of the proper name of the missing author. The least of the ironies is that Nancy concluded his eulogy on the notion of exactitude for which he is thankful to Derrida for having credited him.[16] It is the unique nature of the act of reading that Nancy seeks to bring to light when he addresses a final salutation – an ambiguous goodbye – to the friend and the work. Reading is never doing justice.

References

Bennington, G., and Derrida, J. *Jacques Derrida*. Chicago and London: The University of Chicago Press, 1993.

Derrida, Jacques. *Archive Fever*, trans. Eric Prenowitz. Chicago and London: The University of Chicago Press, 1996.

Derrida, Jacques. *Chaque fois unique, la fin du monde*. Paris: Galilée, 2001.

Derrida, Jacques. "Faith and Knowledge." *Acts of Religion*. New York and London: Routledge, 2002.

Derrida, Jacques. *The Gift of Death*, trans. David Wills. Chicago and London: The University of Chicago Press, 2008.

Derrida, Jacques. *Memoires for Paul de Man*, trans. E. Cadava, J. Culler, P. Kamuf, and C. Lindsay. New York: Columbia University Press, 1986.

Nancy, Jean-Luc. *Dis-Enclosure: The Deconstruction of Christianity*, trans. B. Bergo, G. Malenfant, and M. B. Smith. New York: Fordham University Press, 2008.

8

Sovereignty Without Subject

Irving Goh

Sovereignty is at its height more than ever today, according to Agamben. Rather than an exceptional occurrence, the "state of exception," Agamben argues, has become a norm of governance everywhere since the twentieth century. There is, however, another line of thought, no less aligned to a continental mode of philosophizing, but more or less faithful to the "deconstructive" trajectory of Derrida and of Nancy in this case, which argues that sovereignty, like any other concept or thing, deconstructs itself. This line of thought would be inclined to announce the reduced force of sovereignty. To be sure, it will not say that sovereignty has been dissolved, or that it has vanished into nothingness. Instead, it would say, as Geoffrey Bennington does, that it is failing,[1] or, in Wendy Brown's rhetoric, that sovereignty is waning.[2] Certainly, one could follow Bennington in applying a "deconstructive" reading to Rousseau's writings on sovereignty, and underscore sovereignty's "auto-deconstruction" the moment it defers to another political body, for example the government, to carry out its legislative commands. Bennington would also call this moment sovereignty's stubbornness, if not stupidity [*une bêtise*].[3] This is because, even at that moment, the sovereign figure continues to believe in representing himself or herself as absolutely

singular or singularly whole, as if without any need for a supple-
mental body to disseminate his or her word of law. This is not to
mention, Bennington adds, that the deferral to the government to
execute the sovereign's decision constitutes the technical dilution
of sovereignty: it is, as Bennington puts it, the beginning of the
"execution" – in both senses of commencement *and* demise – of
sovereignty.[4] One can also follow Brown no less in lifting the veil
on the spectacle of sovereign force by certain nation-states today
in their wall-building projects, and call their bluff by showing how
the latter only dissimulate the states' lack of control over the illicit
flow of capital, people, and information across the borders where
the walls are built.[5]

Yet, as Derrida reminds us in *États d'âme de la psychanalyse:
l'impossible au-delà de la souveraine cruauté*,[6] as long as there is cruelty,
not just cruelty to others but also cruelty to oneself, and as long
as there is the drive for power [*la pulsion de pouvoir*], there is
always the trace of sovereignty. We have seen this trace unfailingly
reiterate itself explicitly and forcefully lately in the brutal police
evictions of the Occupy movements in Oakland, at the University
of California campuses in Berkeley and Davis, and at Zuccotti Park
in New York City (where the eviction was planned and decided
on in sovereign secrecy by its mayor), despite the fact that, in
large part, the participants of the movement were only engaged
in peaceful sit-ins at those places. In those cases, not only is state
sovereignty rearing its head in a display of undeniable force, but
also restating, as Derrida has told us too in *Voyous*,[7] its hegemonic
monopoly on the use of violent force. Given that such sovereign
readiness to unleash cruelty onto others still exists today, we cannot
rest content with just stating the apparent failing or waning of sovereignty. In other words, we cannot, for example, with respect to
Brown's focus on states walling themselves in, just point to how
the monolithic presence of sovereignty might seem to be dissolving behind the walls. We must also keep in mind, at the same
time, the lesson drawn from Foucault's analysis of surveillance
structures: the apparent retreat of powers of surveillance does not
necessarily mean the weakening of sovereign powers.[8] On the contrary, it might even signal their dissemination or reinforcement in
more insidious ways since it can suggest that they no longer need

to be present in order for the work of surveillance to be done. It is possibly the case that these powers are now free to step away, as the consciousness of surveillance has completely penetrated every individual, even to the point where it has even translated itself into a surveillance consciousness that induces individuals to also conduct surveillance on other individuals. Going back to the case of sovereignty, its disappearance therefore can also mean that sovereignty has freed itself of all work, in which case, its disappearance is but its consolidation as a true Master in Lacanian terms. That is to say, sovereignty now no longer needs to know how the safeguarding of its sovereign territory, including the work of surveillance, is done. That work is after all being accomplished, not by itself, but by subjects subordinated to it.

To reiterate, it would be sheer philosophical complacency if we brought too much optimism to the announcement of the failing or waning of sovereignty, and suggested that sovereignty is on its way out. I certainly am not doubting or abandoning "deconstructive" insights by which sovereignty is unveiled to be always emptying itself out right at its moment of installation. In fact, I would even follow Nancy's argument of sovereignty as essentially empty. Yet Nancy would even be cautious to warn us that the empty space of sovereignty would always allow another figure with sovereign ambitions to usurp and occupy it.[9] Articulating the "auto-deconstruction" of sovereignty is not enough, therefore. To a sovereignty that has shown itself to be still cruel, either by deciding on the use of violent force on others or by allowing others to practice cruelty on other others, we must respond with a philosophical resistance that goes beyond stating sovereignty's failings. On this resistance, one could even look to Schmitt, whose thesis on sovereignty as that which decides on the exception has undeniably inflected our contemporary perception and understanding of sovereignty. According to Schmitt, "whether the extreme exception can be banished from the world is not a juristic question"; rather, he goes on, "whether one has confidence and hope that it can be eliminated depends on philosophical, especially on philosophical-historical or metaphysical, convictions."[10] In a move that seems to take on Schmitt's challenge, but which certainly goes further than Schmitt as well, Nancy would suggest that we can even be "sovereign otherwise": "Sovereignty has probably lost the sense that it had, and has reduced itself to a kind of 'black hole' of the political. But that does not mean that the sense of being-in-common, insofar as sense itself is in common, cannot render itself sovereign otherwise [*à se faire autrement souverain*]."[11] As I read it, we can have a practice of sovereignty that renounces the singular decision on the exception and/or the monopoly of violent force that suspends existing laws while implementing new ones without democratic consultation or deliberation.

The aim of this essay is to inquire into how one can indeed sidestep Schmittian sovereignty and be "sovereign otherwise." Now, for Nancy, implicated in Schmittian sovereignty is also the modern concept of the *subject*, i.e. the post-Cartesian "fiction" of a self that not only believes himself to be auto-sufficient in his (pre)supposed holistic self-representation, but also presumes the prerogative to found himself as a point of authority, from which he claims a right to decide that his worldview is the only one worthy to be disseminated to the rest of the world.[12] Such a *subject* is also known as *subjectum*, and Schmittian sovereignty is very much predicated on this *subject-subjectum*. In that case, and this is the hypothesis of this chapter, if one seeks to put in place a non-Schmittian sovereignty, perhaps one should first address the question that Nancy posed earlier in 1986 – the question of who comes after the *subject*.[13] In other words, to be "sovereign otherwise," one must perhaps do away with, or else, to use Nancy's rhetoric, "de-suppose," the *subject*.[14] To be sure, "de-supposing" the *subject* here is not meant to return to the thought of sovereignty according to Bodin, who has argued that sovereignty has no place for the *subject*.[15] Predating Descartes's philosophy, to which the beginnings of the *subject-subjectum* are attributed, Bodin's *subject*, in more precise terms, is actually the *subjectus*, which is always subordinated or subjected to another being of higher status or authority. Bodin's sovereign prince undoubtedly has these *subjects* (*subjectus*) under him, but he can never abdicate, or defer, any sovereign decision or function to any of these *subjects-subjectus*. It would be an oversight, however, to say that the modern sense of the *subject* as *subjectum* is absent in Bodin. Schmitt is right to point out that the *subject-subjectum* nevertheless belies Bodin's sovereign prince, as the latter reserves for himself the right to decide on issues such as laws and the pardoning of his *subjects-subjectus*. To be "sovereign otherwise," or to think a sovereignty *without subject*, is certainly *not* to resurrect Bodin's notion of sovereignty, under which the *subject-subjectus* submits all sovereignty to a *subject-subjectum* to come. Nancy's "sovereign otherwise" neither presupposes nor entails a condition whereby one is *subject* to another, ordered by some form of hierarchy whose foundation is only mystical. For Nancy, a turn to the *subject* only closes the question of (an *other*) sovereignty, negating the possibility of being "sovereign otherwise." As he states in the introduction to *Rejouer le politique*, written with Lacoue-Labarthe, sovereignty as an open question, which would include opening sovereignty to a thought of being "sovereign otherwise" of a Schmittian sovereignty, is closed off when sovereignty is reattributed [*réimputer, réassigner*] to the *subject*.[16]

Before suggesting how one can be "sovereign otherwise" *without subject*, or think of a "non-subjective sovereignty,"[17] a little more on Nancy's notion of being "sovereign otherwise" is in order. As seen earlier, Nancy's thought of being "sovereign otherwise" is not so much motivated by the question of cruelty, as is the case with Derrida in thinking the impossible but necessary sovereignty that asserts itself without sovereign cruelty.[18] Instead, for Nancy, to be "sovereign otherwise" is more a question of "being-in-common," which is, simply put, a matter of acknowledging existence in its very fact, i.e. existing always already *with* others.[19] It is not simply a question of acknowledging the existence of others who will have come before, alongside, or after oneself, though. Rather, it concerns the further re-cognition that the relation with others is never fixed or singular. There is, instead, an infinite multiplicity of relations through which one is free to develop further an existing relation, or better, renew it each time; *and* one is equally free to undo that relation and construct new ones with other others.[20] In any case, it is imperative to underscore that in "being-in-common," there is no single *subject*, if not, more simply, *no subject* ordering, determining, totalizing, and essentializing or substantializing any of those relations. As Nancy states, "being-in-common does not signify a substance or subject of superior degree taking charge of the limits of disparate individualities [*individualités séparées*]."[21] Put another way, "being-in-common" is the fact of existing in its bare or even naked form, where relations are stripped of all notions of essence, substance, foundation, hierarchy, and even of a "social contract."[22] "Being-in-common" in this regard is based on, or drawn upon, *nothing (rien)*; and there is *nothing* to which it works toward or projects itself. Or, as Nancy would say, "being-in-common" is *nothing (rien)*, where *nothing* here does not point so much to the meaning of void or emptiness as to the Latin *res* (from which the French *rien* for *nothing* is derived), which signifies *thing*. "Being-in-common" as *nothing* is just the *thing*, and that is precisely the sovereignty of "being-in-common," which, as Nancy would want it, is close to Bataille's declaration that "sovereignty is NOTHING." As sovereignty that is *nothing* other than the fact of bare or naked existence, i.e. a sovereignty of relations whereby relations freely disseminate, disperse, or dissipate, rather than relations of sovereignty such as those between the *subject-subjectum* and the *subject-subjectus* – that is how "being-in-common" is "sovereign otherwise" without predicating itself on the *subject*.[23]

In freeing sovereignty from any predication on the *subject*, do we need another conceptual figure to sustain the thought of sovereignty as *nothing*, a thought of sovereignty that resists the "appropriative violence of the subject"?[24] I would say yes, given that the *subject* tends to return in philosophical discourses, either in its post- or hyper-Cartesian form, despite contemporary French thought's endeavor not only to critique the *subject* by exposing all the problems associated with it, but also to be done with this figure of thought.[25] To counter this return, I would like to suggest supplementing the thought of being "sovereign otherwise" with what I have been calling the *reject* (which would also be my response to Nancy's question of *who comes after the subject*). As I have stated elsewhere, I understand the *reject* through three turns.[26] The first turn concerns the *reject* as a passive figure targeted to be denigrated, abandoned, or even banished, and this is how the *reject* is conventionally understood. I recognize that the *reject*, however, can also actively counteract the forces that are suppressing or repressing it. It can even *first* reject those around itself with a force so overwhelming that it is subsequently rendered a *reject*. These active aspects of the *reject* constitute its second turn. In addition to these two turns, I would also like to think that the *reject* turns the force of rejection on itself, and this is where the third turn of the *reject* as *auto-reject* comes in. To be sure, this is not a self-nihilistic gesture: it is not a self-deprecating or self-negating measure that sends the *reject* sinking into a hopeless or abject abyss. Instead, auto-rejection is put in place only to prevent hypostasizing oneself on a particular disposition or thought. In other words, auto-rejection allows the *auto-reject* to think itself anew constantly or differently at each instant. The more critical dimension of auto-rejection, however, is its potentially ethical force, particularly when auto-rejection involves not occupying a place whereby one asserts oneself or one's perspective (as a *subject* is wont to do), but allows the coming to presence of others. One should be precise to add too that the *reject* as *auto-reject* does not insist on the latter: it does not demand the other to come before him or her, as if it has, like the monarchical *subject*, the sovereign prerogative to make that demand. Instead, it leaves the other free to decide if it desires to present itself or not. It is with this figure of the *reject*, in all its three turns that are always turning on one another, that I would argue one can maintain the thought of a sovereignty *without subject*, or of being "sovereign otherwise," and I will now proceed to explicate how the *reject* can do that.

Let me begin with the passive *reject*. Perhaps there is no better figure than this *reject* to begin thinking being "sovereign otherwise," especially if "sovereign otherwise" is also some sort of impossible sovereignty.[27] Indeed, throughout the history of sovereignty, it is unthinkable, or almost impossible, to accord sovereignty to a figure such as a passive *reject*. As Derrida has noted, all sovereign figures so far must assume, without exception, an assertive carno-phallogocentric subjectivity.[28] In other words, if we want to be "sovereign otherwise," or to put in place an impossible but necessary sovereignty *without subject*, perhaps we have to proceed with a figure incommensurable to that naturalized image of a sovereign. As I see it, the passive *reject* could be that figure, and that *reject* may be Bodin's *subjectus*. Or, in more contemporaneous terms, it may be embodied by the largely silent, fugitive stateless people, refugees, and clandestine/illegal immigrants or *sans papiers*, whose existential conditions consist in them essentially

not having "rights to have rights" (Arendt). The fact of their existence as such, unfortunately, is largely ignored by state institutions,
leaving very little done to address the injustices suffered by these
rejects. What those institutions typically demand is that these *rejects*
become "citizen subjects" (Balibar) first before any act to correct
the wrong inflicted upon them will be implemented. Too often,
what follows from such a demand is deferred justice, if not, worse,
the largely unjustified paranoia of how *rejects* can threaten national
security and sociocultural integration. That paranoia will typically
make it impossible for those *rejects* to gain "citizen subject" status,
in which case, justice will never be served. However, if one recognizes these *rejects* as sovereign, that is to say, "sovereign otherwise"
than "legitimate" political or citizen *subjects* that are granted the
privilege to assume power and authority, but sovereign *just* – and
I mean *just* in both juridical and temporal senses – in their fact of
existence that is essentially "in-common" with everyone else, then
a more timely justice can be accorded them. In this case, there is
no condition requiring *rejects* to become-(citizen-)*subjects* before
the wrong done to them is addressed. Instead, these *rejects*, as *rejects*,
are acknowledged to exist as sovereignly as any other legitimate
political or citizen *subject*, existing in "being-in-common" with the
latter, and hence must be equally accorded justice to ensure that
their existence will not be endangered.[29]

Waiting for existing political institutions to radically transform
their ways of thought and practice, e.g. waiting for them to re-cog-
nize passive *rejects* as sovereign, is regrettably utopian, if not even
naive. Too often, these transformations, when (finally) in place,
have involved long-drawn out or even bureaucratic processes such
that justice might even have been deferred to a point where it no
longer matters. There are times, therefore, when the *reject* must
actively engender change. The potentiality of the active *reject*, particularly with regard to effectuating a rupture within an ostensibly
indivisible sovereignty and through which one moves toward a
shared sovereignty, has also been intimated by Derrida. Of course,
Derrida does not mobilize the term *reject*. Derrida's term is the
voyou, which he has in mind "rogue" as its translation.[30] *Voyou*, in
the French context, is a delinquent, a figure that roams the streets.
However, the *voyou* does not simply roam the streets in an idle

fashion. At times, it does so in ways that disturb the peace of the neighborhood, which results not only in its being largely regarded with scorn and suspicion by the residents there but also in its being under much police surveillance. In that respect, I would say that the *voyou* is no less a *reject* in the eyes of civil society. According to Derrida, this *voyou* nonetheless bears a political potentiality. It presents a critical challenge to democratic hospitality because, while the latter seeks to welcome *anyone* in its space, it still sees the need, if not has the wish, to reject from that same space the *voyou*, which can very well be a legitimate "citizen subject," in order to maintain what it envisions as some sort of democratic propriety, integrity, or security of the space. In other words, the *voyou* pushes democracy to its limits by testing democracy's commitment to put into practice its principle of opening itself to *anyone*, including *rejects* such as *voyous*. The greater political potentiality of the *voyou*, however, as Derrida argues, is its challenge to the state's monopoly of violent force. This is especially so when there is more than one *voyou*, or when the *voyou* becomes numerous, or a multitude, to use the term that Hardt and Negri have made current.[31] In that case, the *voyous* present a force – and Derrida, following Flaubert, calls this counter-sovereign force *voyoucratie* – that the state finds disturbing to its authority and to the sanctity of the space that it governs. Fearing that the *voyous* might increase in force and mass beyond its control, the state typically deploys preemptive measures to break up the gathering of *voyous*, measures that tend to take on the form of violent police action. It is precisely at this point, when the state mobilizes violent police action, that the very existence of the *voyous* exposes the fact that the monopoly of hegemonic violence lies in the state, and this is where Derrida argues that the critique of the state's monopoly of hegemonic violence can begin with the *voyou*.

We have seen the "politics of the streets" of *voyous* in force and even almost on a global scale recently, as made manifest by the Occupy movement in late 2011. The participants of that movement adopted the disposition undoubtedly of *voyous* as they staged peaceful sit-ins in major cities around the world. Of course, they did more than merely or idly occupy the streets, for they strategically occupied those in close proximity to key financial districts, creating disturbance, distraction, and at times, interruptions to the smooth economic running of the cities. Like Derrida's *voyou*, these *voyous* were also no less *rejects*, given their slogan of "we are the 99 percent" i.e. those who were denied the riches that the wealthy 1 percent enjoy due to the unequal distribution of wealth. No longer willing to be passive subjects of housing foreclosures, unemployment, and sheer poverty, which have only been the consequences of irresponsible banking practices and financial speculations, these *rejects* chose to actively reject the economic status quo. In their manifestation as a mass or multitude of *voyous*, they certainly did not fail to expose the state's monopoly on the use of violent force, as it was only a matter of time before police actions, as mentioned earlier, were mobilized to preempt any insurrectional *voyoucratie* in Oakland, at the University of California campuses in Berkeley and Davis, and at Zuccotti Park in New York City. It is beyond the scope of this essay to examine whether or not the movement was an effective counter-sovereign force in breaking the indivisibility of state sovereignty, especially its hold on hegemonic force. What is more interesting, or rather more pertinent, to the concern of this chapter is whether the *voyous* or active *rejects* of the Occupy movement were an expression of being "sovereign otherwise," if not that *other* sovereignty that is "the revolt of the people"[32] or "being-in-common" in Nancy's terms.

Now, one could be really precise to say that "being-in-common," which is, to reiterate, the sovereign fact and right of existence of every singular body, precedes and exceeds all political movements, including Occupy. Put another way, "being-in-common" is already there before and beyond all political endeavors that seek to construct and ensure forms of coexistence. However, there are nonetheless economic, political, and social structures that suppress or deny the fact of "being-in-common" – the empire of global capital networks being one such structure, which decimates other forms of economic practices, and which the Occupy movement opposed in large part. In other words, we still need to rearticulate and reaffirm "being-in-common" wherever it is under the threat of erasure. The Occupy movement seemed to serve that purpose, especially in light of what several contemporary theorists, such as Žižek, Hardt and Negri, and Butler, have found the movement to express: the sense of a "common."[33] One must ask, though, if that "common" really serves as a reaffirmation of "being-in-common." It would seem to be the case in the movement's initial phases, as the gesture of occupying a certain street or public space took on the appearance, as Butler has argued in several public lectures soon after the inauguration of Occupy, of the exercise of "the right to appear" of any body, unrestricted by categories such as class distinctions, gender norms, employment statuses, etc. One could argue that that instance of "the right to appear" resonates with Nancy's "being-in-common," which also affirms the coming-to-presence of every singular being in the world; and in that regard, the *voyous* of the Occupy movement at that moment even presented the potentiality of being "sovereign otherwise." However, I would argue that any sense of being "sovereign otherwise," of "being-in-common," and also of the "common," soon dissipated after the movement's initial stages. This became evident when the *voyous* decided to claim or appropriate public places to the extent that it became difficult or even impossible for others to gain access to these places. In other words, these places were no longer *public* spaces, no longer places where any body can freely be present as "being-in-common" with other bodies there; instead, they became limited spaces in the sense of being more like territories of the *voyous*. Such territorialization consequently began to infringe upon the peace and safety of neighboring locales, leading the residents there to render the *voyous* a public nuisance, which did not assist the *voyous* in garnering greater collective support for their causes.[34] And if these *voyous* were losing a certain sense of a "common" with the rest of the world when they became a nuisance to those around them, fissures were also emerging among the *voyous*: a rift began to separate the *voyous* of the Occupy movement and the more "original" homeless and poor *voyous*, the former charging the latter of causing disorder within the encampment sites, even though the Occupy movement in part was to speak for them.[35] At this point, there is surely hardly any sense of a "common," not to even mention the sense of "being-in-common" according to Nancy.

A multitude wherein one group rejects another is certainly not the "revolt of the people" according to Nancy. A phenomenon that was potentially rearticulating and reaffirming "being-in-common" then lost its chance of being "sovereign otherwise" of Schmittian sovereignty. What became evident instead was a certain becoming-*subject* of the *voyous* of the Occupy movement, which was no doubt set in motion the moment these *voyous* decided to reorder the city so as to (re)claim for themselves certain spaces that would be outside the control of the city's existing political economy. As Nancy reminds us, the *subject* is there whenever there is some sort of ordering or reordering.[36] The question of the *subject* among those *voyous* was only reinforced when they insisted on *occupying* those spaces, that is to say, grounding their subjectivity there, territorializing those spaces as if they were the foundations of their existences, if not their seat of power. The becoming-*subject* of the *voyous* no doubt encouraged them to exercise power over others, which became evident at moments when they (ab)used their political self-organization, or their "frequent assemblies and participatory decision-making structures,"[37] as a platform to denigrate the "original" poor and homeless *voyous* in order to exclude them from the movement.[38] And yet, becoming-*subject* also had a negative effect on the movement's *voyous* themselves. Their becoming-*subjects*, sovereign in their own terms, only confirmed the state's suspicion of their imminent *voyoucratie*, which resulted, as mentioned already, in the state's mobilization of violent police force against them. As I see it, becoming-*subject* turned out to be a trap for the *voyous* themselves, giving them more explicit presence through their self-representation, drawing them to anchor themselves within a certain spatial ground as their foundation, and therefore making it easier for the state to identify, contain, and eradicate them within manageable limits. In short, it is the process of becoming-*subject* that gave the movement its vulnerability, paving the way toward its undoing.

How does one sidestep this becoming-*subject* then, such that one does not presume oneself to be more sovereign than others and therefore possessing some kind of prerogative to negate others, or such that one assumes a more subtle, mobile, and therefore more effective strategy in counteracting the state's monopoly and use of violent force? How, in other words, can active *rejects* such as the *voyous* of the Occupy movement maintain the possibility of being a "revolt of the people" that is "sovereign otherwise" and

not allow the "appropriative violence of the subject" to close off
that horizon? As I would argue, this is where the turn of the *auto-
reject* becomes critical, i.e. auto-rejection is the key to prevent any
inclination to become-*subject*. The question that remains is how to
put in place an auto-rejection, or how one becomes an *auto-reject*.
One possible way of thinking auto-rejection, perhaps, is to take
Nancy's notion of *resistance* as a point of departure. According to
Nancy, resistance is not confrontation, the latter being "a relation between wills to dominate [. . .], a relation of conquering
and destructive hostility, pure and simple,"[39] a relation that the
voyous of the Occupy movement evidently had not only with
the state but also with the "original" poor and homeless *voyous*.
Resistance, in Nancy's terms, is not about such wills to power,
which are but wills to be sovereign *subjects* that subordinate others
or present a front against other sovereign entities. Rather, what is
more important in resistance is the freedom to express "a force of
affect" that is "essentially heteronomous." For Nancy, this resistance is "inherent in being-with."[40] It is perhaps at this point where
one can elicit a sense of auto-rejection since Nancy would go
further to say that "being-with [. . .] resists *itself*."[41] To be precise,
there is nothing nihilistic here. Auto-rejection in this case of resistance involves, instead, the refusal of any sense of foundation:
"being-with" "refuses to be fulfilled under any form of hypostasis,
configuration, institution, or legislation"; or else, it is "its resistance
to its own gathering [*rassemblement*]."[42]

One ought to be more precise and say that "being-in-common,"
in "its resistance to its own gathering," does not mean any retreat
into solitariness or renunciation of any community-to-come
(which is also a community without *subject*). Certainly, being "sovereign otherwise" in this manner might appear at first glance to
refuse all forms of sociality. However, it does so only to remind us
that there is no model or foundation for any "social tie," or social
contract, or even "people."[43] The latter is "nowhere founded and
nowhere destined."[44] That is to say, if implicated in the "people"
is always some form of relation or tie, that tie is never a "presup-
posed knot,"[45] as if destined to be ordered in a certain way and
never to change once that order is in place. As Nancy says, one
must "not make a knot of that tie."[46] Instead, that tie must be

something that is always in progress, always a question of "how
to think this tie as always in formation, each time."[47] Always in
the process of forming (itself), this would also mean that the tie is
no less in the process of de-forming (itself) so that other ties can
always be possible. It is in this regard that the tie constituting the
relation is – and we hear once again the echo of Bataille's "sovereignty is NOTHING" here – "nothing, no *res*, nothing but a
placing-into-relation that presupposes at the same time proximity
and separation, attachment and detachment."[48] In other words, it
is only through affirming both the freedom of entering into a tie,
and of untying oneself from it, that we have an "infinite tying," an
"incessant tying up of singularities."[49]

Such resistance or auto-rejection is what the *voyous* of the
Occupy movement were unfortunately incapable of. They have
shown themselves to be keener, instead, to consolidate into some
sort of stable entity or substance, if not an alternative political
model. In other words, these *voyous* were not prepared to give up
their sense of political gathering that seemed to have the potential
of a sovereign *voyoucratie*, a sense that they have accumulated over
the days of encampment. Being "sovereign otherwise," however,
as suggested above, requires one to give up any such imminent
sovereign subjectivity.[50] There is indeed some sort of paradox here:
as Nancy argues, to be "sovereign otherwise," which is also a "true
sovereignty" according to him, one must put in place a thought of
"abandoned sovereignty."[51] "Abandoned sovereignty" is not just
the abandonment of all ambitions of being a sovereign monarch
who lords over others, but also the freeing of thought from thinking that the existence of a particular being at a particular time in a
particular form is sovereign once and for all. Instead, "abandoned
sovereignty" is the abandoning of oneself to the next sovereign
moment of existence, the form of which is never decided or imagined by oneself in advance, and one could say that this is the other
sense of being "sovereign otherwise," i.e. sovereignly existing differently at each time. Nancy acknowledges that there is an excess
of thought in the thinking of "abandoned sovereignty" in order
to be "sovereign otherwise," but it is through this excess that one
could follow through the Bataillean trajectory of maintaining sovereignty as NOTHING, rather than a thing. As I see it, following

from the notions of resistance and "abandoned sovereignty," what this could have meant for the *voyous* of the Occupy movement would be for them to have learned how to *walk away* from any form of sovereign gathering or collective, from any "decision-making structures" that were not only giving the *voyous* a certain fixed identity but also the subsequent tendency to exclude or reject others (e.g. the "original" poor and homeless *voyous*) who did not strictly share the same political affiliations and objectives. *Walking away* could also have meant resisting any insistence on occupying the public spaces when state counterrevolutionary measures were becoming imminent. To be sure, *walking away* here, or auto-rejection in general, does not mean an abdication of one's cause in the face of danger. Neither does it mean a denial or even a repression of violence since implicated in the *auto-reject* is always the active *reject* (the turns of the passive, active, and *auto-* rejects are not mutually exclusive, but turn on one another all the time), which is no less critical to counteract oppressive and repressive forces, but *not* to target and exclude others. In the face of state reactionary measures then, one *walks away* only to safeguard the lives of oneself and others, preserving life in this regard so as to come up with other better and more effective strategies that will not only sidestep state violence but also continue to serve one's cause at a later time. In resistance or auto-rejection, one does not insist on *occupying* therefore, which only risks sacrificing life, and therefore the cause too, in a single instance. *Walking away*, put another way, or rather in Blanchot's term, is a question of a "right to disappear" from any totalizing structure that holds life captive.[52]

If the notion of decision is never far from the question of sovereignty, especially Schmittian sovereignty, since what characterizes it is the decision on the exception, one could perhaps say that resistance or auto-rejection, as discussed above, is, at most, a minimum decision at the heart of being "sovereign otherwise." In other words, being at most a minimum decision, it never gets so far as to decide on any exception. Instead, it is all but a matter of recalling and reaffirming the fact of the freedom of oneself and of others to exist. From there, it takes care to ensure that any subsequent action does not endanger that freedom, which includes refraining from one's course of action, or even retracting it, if following it through would mean compromising another's freedom of existence. Admittedly, such a move might give the *reject* a semblance of a *subject*. Let it be clear though that thinking the *reject* does not entail annihilating the *subject*; otherwise, it would also be guilty of negating the freedom of existence of another, thus making it an inadequate figure of thought for being "sovereign otherwise." To reiterate, thinking the *reject* counteracts the *subject* only by not making it a supposition, whereby the *subject*'s point of view, or its way of thinking, becomes a fixed, guiding principle in one's interaction with the world. In other words, if taking into consideration the freedom of existence of others involves a minimal decision or even calculation, then the *reject* must not deny that minimal subjective move. But in fact, to be precise, the minimal decision in question is not the decision per se on the freedom of existing. That decision, according to Nancy in *The Experience of Freedom*, precedes and exceeds any conscious, subjective act or calculation: it is "nothing subjective," or else, it is an "ontological archi-decision."[53] It is only with such a decision – a decision *without subject* as Nancy would put it – that we have "an authentic freedom."[54] For Nancy, this freedom is also more sovereign than sovereignty,[55] deciding on itself without any dependence on the Schmittian sovereign suspension of existing laws or the declaration of an exception: "there is neither law nor exception for [this] decision."[56] The minimum decision to *walk away* in resistance or auto-rejection then does *not* in effect consist in (subjectively) deciding on the freedom of oneself and others to exist. It only decides in recalling and reaffirming that "ontological archi-decision" of "an authentic freedom" to exist, or, in short, that "access to letting-be."[57] At the same time, then, it keeps in mind that that decision never pushes things toward nihilistic or fatal ends but always allows things to begin.[58] Any decision that results in the contrary, i.e. in "the refusal of existence," only constitutes, according to Nancy in *The Experience of Freedom*, "evil."[59]

In more recent texts such as *L'Équivalence des catastrophes (après Fukushima)*, or in the interview in *La Possibilité d'un monde*, Nancy would also suggest that, in respect of "authentic freedom," the best or most we can do is to be attentive to, or to be in esteem

of, that freedom inhering in oneself as well as in others, which is
tantamount to "an adoration turned towards singularity as such."[60]
That is to say, in the encounter between one and the other,
there is a respectful approach, or a mutual respect for one and
the other's freedom of existence in ways by which one's freedom
does not come at the price of the other's. That is why a more
veritable or authentic "revolt of the people," i.e. a revolt that reaffirms "being-in-common" or the freedom of existence shared by
everyone, cannot insist on grounding their gathering upon some
fixed identity of foundation, rejecting others who do not share
in the latter; it also cannot insist on staying their ground in order
to fight to the end, in the face of fatal countermeasures against
them. It has to resist or abandon all these tendencies, or *walk
away* from them, so that others can retain the freedom to exist or
let-be without needing to align themselves to this "people," or so
that this "people" can also live on and pursue other life-affirming
strategies that also possibly avoid collateral damage that only put
nonparticipating others at risk. In that regard, the freedom of existing should be the horizon of being "sovereign otherwise." I have
said earlier that auto-rejection does not necessarily imply an abandonment of the original political cause, but Nancy would in fact
go further to say in several places that politics must perhaps surpass
itself, if not auto-reject itself too.[61] That is perhaps where the heart
of being "sovereign otherwise" lies – a sovereignty prepared not
just to adopt a "non-sovereign politics"[62] but also to abandon all
political contours, prepared thence only to respond rigorously to
the question of "authentic freedom."

References

Bennington, Geoffrey. "The Fall of Sovereignty," *Epoché* 10(2) (2006):
    395–406.
Bennington, Geoffrey. "Sovereign Stupidity and Autoimmunity," in
    Pheng Cheah and Suzanne Guerlac (eds), *Derrida and the Time of the
    Political*. Durham and London: Duke University Press, 2009, 97–113.
Bodin, Jean. *On Sovereignty: Four Chapters from the Six Books of the*

Commonwealth, ed. and trans. Julian H. Franklin. Cambridge and New York: Cambridge University Press, 1992.

Brown, Wendy. *Walled States, Waning Sovereignty*. New York: Zone Books, 2010.

Derrida, Jacques. "'Eating Well,' or the Calculation of the Subject: An Interview with Jacques Derrida," trans. Peter Connor and Avital Ronnell, in Eduardo Cadava, Peter Connor, and Jean-Luc Nancy (eds), *Who Comes After the Subject?* New York and London: Routledge, 1991, 96–119.

Derrida, Jacques. "Psychoanalysis Searches the States of Its Soul: The Impossible Beyond of a Sovereign Cruelty," in *Without Alibi*, ed., trans., and intro. Peggy Kamuf. Stanford: Stanford University Press, 2002, 238–80.

Derrida, Jacques. *Rogues: Two Essays on Reason*, trans. Pascale-Anne Brault and Michael Naas. Stanford: Stanford University Press, 2005.

Hardt, Michael, and Negri, Antonio. "The Fight for 'Real Democracy' at the Heart of Occupy Wall Street: The Encampment in Lower Manhattan Speaks to a Failure of Representation," *Foreign Affairs*, October 11, 2011. www.foreignaffairs.com/articles/136399/michael-hardt-and-antonio-negri/the-fight-for-real-democracy-at-the-heart-of-occupy-wall-street.

Nancy, Jean-Luc, Philippe Lacoue-Labarthe, et al. *Rejouer le politique*. Paris: Galilée, 1981.

Nancy, Jean-Luc. *The Inoperative Community*, ed. and trans. Peter Connor. Minneapolis and London: University of Minnesota Press, 1991.

Nancy, Jean-Luc. "Un sujet?" in *Homme et sujet: la subjectivité en question dans les sciences humaines*, conférences du Centre d'Études Pluridisciplinaires sur la Subjectivité, collected and edited by Dominique Weil, Paris: L'Harmattan, 1992, 47–114.

Nancy, Jean-Luc. *The Experience of Freedom*, trans. Bridget McDonald and foreword by Peter Fenves. Stanford: Stanford University Press, 1993.

Nancy, Jean-Luc. *The Sense of the World*, trans. with foreword by Jeffrey S. Librett. Minneapolis and London: University of Minnesota Press, 1997.

Nancy, Jean-Luc. "War, Right, Sovereignty – Technē" in *Being Singular Plural*, trans. Robert D. Richardson and Anne E. O'Byrne. Stanford: Stanford University Press, 2000, 101–44.

Nancy, Jean-Luc. *La Communauté désoeuvrée*, expanded and revised edn. Paris: Christian Bourgois, 2004.

Nancy, Jean-Luc. "Church, State, Resistance," trans. Véronique Voruz, in Hent de Vries and Lawrence E. Sullivan (eds), *Political Theologies: Public Religions in a Post-Secular World*. New York: Fordham University Press, 2006, 102–12.

Nancy, Jean-Luc. *The Creation of the World* or *Globalization*, trans. and intro. François Raffoul and David Pettigrew. Albany: SUNY Press, 2007.

Nancy, Jean-Luc. *L'Équivalence des catastrophes (après Fukushima)*. Paris: Galilée, 2012.

Nancy, Jean-Luc. "Hors colloque," in *Figures du dehors: autour de Jean-Luc Nancy*. Paris: Cécile Defaut, 2012, 519–38.

Nancy, Jean-Luc. *Le Poids d'une pensée, l'approche*. Strasbourg: Phocide, 2008.

Rousseau, Jean-Jacques. *Du contrat social ou principes du droit politique et autres écrits autours du contrat social*, foreword, commentary, and notes by Gérard Mairet, Paris: Poche, 2011.

Schmitt, Carl. *Political Theology: Four Chapters on the Concept of Sovereignty* [1922/1934], trans. and intro. George Schwab, foreword Tracy B. Strong. Chicago and London: University of Chicago Press, 1985.

9

Dialogue Beneath the Ribs[*]

Jean-Luc Nancy

Translated by Irving Goh[1]

(T1 and T2 designate Transplantee and Transplant respectively)[2]

T1: Are you there, Transplant?

T2: Yes, of course I'm here. Why do you ask?

T1: Because I do not hear you . . . You are so silent that I wonder if you are there.

T2: Really? But if I were absolutely silent, you would not be able to ask me anything. You wouldn't be there either.

T1: That's true. I forgot. I forget about you, in fact. I do hear you, sometimes, at night; or else when I experience a strong emotion.

T2: Like what?

T1: Do not provoke me! You know well what I'm talking about. But it is true that most often, I do not hear you, I do not feel you.

---

[*] Translator's note: Nancy composed this piece for the Third Clermont Conference on "Medicine and Psychoanalysis" in 2011, twenty years after his heart transplant. Nancy sent us this piece after we requested a piece that might reflect on his heart transplant. This request in turn was made after having received an email from Nancy (to Irving Goh), dated March 9, 2012, saying, "you know, it will soon be 21 years since I had my transplant [*vous savez, il y a bientôt 21 ans que je vis avec ma greffe*]."

T2: Of course, I am your heart. I only take care of the machine that allows you to feel, act, and think.

T1: My heart, which has come from elsewhere. And I acknowledge that it makes no difference. My former heart did not make itself known any more than you. Nonetheless, when I feel you, I worry. I say to myself: it is tired; it is worn out.

T2: And you're not wrong. In twenty years, you have worn me out. You impose upon me a frenzied rhythm, twice that of a long-distance runner . . .

T1: But I impose nothing on you. I can't help it. But I did not expect to be led, drums beating, like a *chamade* . . .

T2: What is a *chamade*?

T1: It was a trumpet-call or the beating of drums to signal an emergency, often the urgency to capitulate or to surrender to the enemy. It signifies a call – from the Italian *ciamare*.

T2: Your old heart did not pound like a *chamade*?

T1: Oh yes. And sometimes it was hardly beating . . . I felt it was letting go. It had the right to do so, and I did not blame it. And then you came . . .

T2: That is, they came to get me, without me asking for it!

T1: I know. But something searched you out: the monitoring and information system, the science that controls the living and the dead, with its measurements and calculations, like a helicopter ready for takeoff . . . *I* did not ask for anything . . .

T2: Really?

T1: Really. Nothing. I knew the other heart could stop . . . I did not know, of course, what that would entail, but I didn't really care. In fact, I was rather afraid of you.

T2: How so?

T1: Should you arrive, they would have to make a huge opening in my chest, which they did, in fact. Presently, my sternum keeps the steel wires that have been tightened around my chest to close it up. I did not like that idea. I could only visualize the void in my chest – impossible for me to imagine a new heart. In fact, I still don't.

T2: You are right. There is nothing to imagine. I am faceless.

T1: Sometimes on the coronary angiographic screen, I see your tousled face, and the long coronary claws or roots that nourish your muscle. The other day there was one that was stifled, blocked. They inserted a stent there.

T2: Yes, that was quite good. I felt my blood circulating again. It's like the pacemaker that they have placed beside me: it relieves me when necessary; it puts me back in step, giving me back my rhythm.

T1: I do not feel all of this. But, my heart, I do feel it – the entire machinery, without considering all the chemical gruel . . .

T2: I know; I certainly feel the anticoagulants passing through me, as well as the immuno-depressors that protect me – for your body would reject me if it were allowed to have its own way.

T1: Yes, but it knows nothing. That poor thing – it believes it is a self-sufficient machine. Of course, as you said, it is machined, and it functions like a machine. But it is nonetheless the doctors who keep the system running . . .

T2: Them, and you, and me: the living!

T1: Yes, it is life that maintains itself, transmits itself, and reboots itself. Twenty years – think about that. You would not have lived for twenty more years otherwise!

T2: Life takes care of itself, but it threatens itself, too. Life makes life difficult for itself. Remember when candida colonized the catheter of the pacemaker, right in the middle of a ventricle? We had a narrow escape!

T1: Yes, but it was nice to know that those organisms like inert bodies – the bits of metal or plastic that one introduces into the living. For they are without immunity: they reject nothing. I can imagine the candida hanging comfortably in a cluster on the catheter . . .

T2: But what labor to remove them! And the time it took, and all those by-products! And it was necessary to switch to an epicardial pacing; but it suits me well.

T1: If the doctors did not succeed, we would not have been here years ago.

T2: Do you really think the number of years matter? You had lasted fifty years, and me thirty. What about it? Perhaps it was enough for each of us.

T1: Yes, certainly. There is nothing interesting in lasting. What is interesting is to reboot, to be revived, to start again. Then again, at some moment, one would have begun again . . . to leave, and that is again a way to start again, to go beyond, to go much further.

T2: In any case, we will leave together!

T1: We'll see, we'll see . . . Perhaps another transplant awaits its chance? Or else an all-new nice little electric heart?

T2: Stop it! It's fine as it is. We have worked well, lived well. Let's salute each other!

T1: Yes, I'll stop. I'll stop playacting. For you're not an other. That cannot be. I act as if you were an other in me, but you're not that. Quite simply, you are my heart!

T2: Why then do you speak to me as if I were a person? Why do you call me "Transplant" as if it were a proper noun, like you were calling me "Griffon," or else as if it were a kind of title, like the French "Greffier" as a clerk is sometimes addressed? Is this all only a game?

T1: Yes, it's a game, for you are not someone. You are myself in me, myself considered a pump and pulse of life, neither more nor less than that which you replaced twenty years ago. And yet you are an intruder, for you do not fulfill your office without being armed with chemical, electronic, and mechanical auxiliaries. You are yourself a complete system of maintenance, surveillance, and control, not only of your own organ and its vessels, but also of the rest of the body through which are diffused all the substances for controlling and balancing it, all the flows and the alluvia that slowly reconfigure my kidneys, my lungs, my muscles, composing in me another fellow who, however, is not an other. An other who is twenty years younger and has some additional years of wear and tear. An other who is not only seventy years old but more and less at the same time, and this "same time" constitutes the complicated, confused, and agitated time of my most proper existence . . .

T2: You get the picture. As you say it yourself: this other that I am, it's you. And do you think that this is so different from what happens to every one of us? Do you not believe that each is always in and to himself or herself an intruder? One who comes from elsewhere and goes to who knows where? One who is always more and less than one? One who is traversed by flows, molecules, thrusts, repulsions, divagations, and outbursts? One who bears the polymorphic marks of instruments and substances, of observations and interventions, of information and phantasms of all those who conspire in the strange scheme to prolong and propagate the life of the living without any moderation – for where would the limit come from?

Notes

Prelude: The Silhouette of Jean-Luc Nancy

1 Translator's note: See Jean-Luc Nancy's "Être abandonné," in *L'Impératif catégorique* (Paris: Flammarion, 1983, 151).

2 Translator's note: See *L'Impératif catégorique*, 141, 145, 148. Translations mine.

3 Translator's note: In this paragraph, Agamben is referring to a section in Aristotle's *De Anima* where the sense-organ for touch is in question. According to Aristotle, while sight is determined by our eyes, or hearing by our ears, we cannot precisely say which bodily organ determines our sense of touch. In other words, the medium of touch always eludes us. And so, Aristotle writes, "the tangible object is different from visible things and sound-sources, for these we perceive because the medium has an effect on us, whereas with the tangible things we are not affected by the medium but at the same time as the medium" (*De Anima*, trans. and intro. Hugh Lawson-Tancred, London: Penguin, 1986), 186.

4 Translator's note: In Aristotle's text, we read: "we perceive both the rough and the smooth through other things, just as with the audible and the visible objects and the smell-source. But while we perceive this last group at a remove, we perceive the first two nearby and so

miss this [i.e. the medium or sense-organ for touch]" (*De Anima,* 185).

5 Translator's note: See *De Anima,* 185.

Introduction: Time in Nancy

1 Jacques Derrida, *On Touching – Jean-Luc Nancy,* trans. Christine Irizarry, (Stanford: Stanford University Press, 2005), x, trans. modified.

2 We note here that Nancy has written, in one of his essays on art, that "it takes time for there to be anything," or that "it takes time for things to present themselves as they are" ("The Soun-Gui Experience," trans. Simon Sparks, *Multiple Arts: The Muses II,* Stanford: Stanford University Press, 2006), 211.

3 "The Soun-Gui Experience," 211.

4 "Espace contre temps," in *Le Poids d'une pensée, l'approche,* Strasbourg: Phocide, 2008, 85. Translations from this text are ours.

5 See "The Soun-Gui Experience," 201–2.

6 Nancy makes the distinction between passing and happening in relation to time again in the essay "The Soun-Gui Experience." There, he writes:

> "It passes by" [*ça passe*] refers to the thing in time: it comes and goes; it is still to come, or it is past [*passé*]; it steps outside time or disappears into it, all the while leaving time intact, like a vast, soft, empty shell. With things that come and go, we have no experience of time. "It happens" [*ça se passe*] refers to time itself. It refers to time within the thing itself [. . .]. Time does not pass. It is always here. No, time *is* passage. It is the "it happens." (213)

A little later, Nancy also adds that time is "what never stops happening" (214).

7 "*Espace contre temps,*" 87. According to Nancy in "The Soun-Gui Experience," "the [chronologic] present is a spacing in which presence is concealed or no longer supported, no longer given, posed, deposed, available as an object, as a thing. The present runs contrary to presence; it ruins it, supplants it, in the very moment by which it supports it" (202).

8 "*Espace contre temps*," 85, 86. In a way too, Nancy turns his back on the philosophy of time in this essay, as long as this philosophy is predicated on chronological time. According to Nancy, such a philosophy is essentially concerned with grasping every unit of chronological time that passes by, which only betrays its "avidity for mastery" of time-flow ("*Espace contre temps*," 87). This avidity, or the rush or frenzy to keep up with the chronological flow of time, however, not only renders the thought of time "extemporaneous," barely touching on time or the present, but also "deforms the face of thought" ("Espace contre temps, 86). This is the philosophy of time that Nancy refuses.

9 "Espace contre temps," 87.

10 "Espace contre temps," 87.

11 "Espace contre temps," 87. In the earlier "Finite History," Nancy also says that the coming of presents is "the very operation of space," but will go on to add that "this spacing," which "spaces time itself, spacing it from its continual present," nonetheless "is a temporal operation" (in *Birth to Presence*, trans. Brian Holmes et al., Stanford: Stanford University Press, 1993, 150, trans. modified).

12 "Espace contre temps," 88.

13 *L'Équivalence des catastrophes (après Fukushima)* (Paris: Galilée, 2012), 62. Translations from this text are ours.

14 *L'Équivalence des catastrophes*, 38.

15 *L'Équivalence des catastrophes*, 64.

16 *L'Équivalence des catastrophes*, 63.

17 *L'Équivalence des catastrophes*, 64–5.

18 *À la recherche du temps perdu*, Quarto Gallimard edn, 2280, translation ours. One notes, however, that for Nancy in the essay "Espace contre temps," Proust's gesture remains spatial: "Lost time, thinks Proust: and hereby writing, the spatial gesture, spacious, spacing par excellence, [is] made to work in the monumental work: art as memorial – instead of eternity" ("Espace contre temps," 86).

19 *L'Équivalence des catastrophes*, 65.

20 Nancy makes a distinction between esteem [*estime*] and estimation [*estimation*]. In Nancy's words: "estimation – or evaluation – belongs to the series of calculations of general equivalence, which is either that of money, or that of its substitutes, which the equivalence of forces, capacities, individuals, risks, speed, etc. Esteem, on the

contrary, addresses itself to the singular and to the singular manner of coming to presence – flower, face or timbre" (*L'Équivalence des catastrophes*, 66).

21 *L'Équivalence des catastrophes*, 67. To reiterate, the present also needs time to come to presence. As Nancy writes in "The Soun-Gui Experience," "the time of the present as it presents itself, always not yet and always already there" is "of time flowing like the slow thaw of the block of ice, its imperceptible yet unrelenting deformation that takes hold from the moment that the ice comes into contact with a space that is not ice [. . .]" (211).

22 *La Possibilité d'un monde, entretiens avec Pierre-Philippe Jandin*, Paris: Petits Platons, 2012, 119. Translations from this text are ours.

23 *La Possibilité d'un monde*, 117.

24 *La Possibilité d'un monde*, 118.

25 *La Possibilité d'un monde*, 118.

26 On the relation between time and syncope, Nancy writes in "Espace contre temps": "Come-and-gone: coming-and-going of the present: beating: syncope" (88). Syncope as a musical time-lag or syncopation can also be found in Catherine Clément's *La Philosophie de la syncope*.

27 With the discussion on listening, rhythm, and cadence, it would indeed be fruitful to turn to *Listening* (trans. Charlotte Mandell, New York: Fordham University Press, 2007), where Nancy will speak of "sonorous time" in contrast to chronological time.

28 *Déclosion* has indeed been translated recently as "dis-enclosure." However, we keep to a simpler "dis-closure" as its translation since it still points to the notion of opening or reopening what has been closed, which *déclosion* seeks to convey, and also because it preserves the question of secrecy that is not foreign to Nancy. The question of secrecy is there even in the question of time. In the essay "The Soun-Gui Experience," Nancy writes that time involves "the secret of presence" (214).

29 "The Soun-Gui Experience," 217.

30 It is also via the medium of air that the *aria* is able to have resonance.

31 "The Technique of the Present: On On Kawara," *Multiple Arts: The Muses II*, 200.

32 "The Soun-Gui Experience," 212.

33 "The Soun-Gui Experience," 213.

34 "The Soun-Gui Experience," 211.

35 "The Soun-Gui Experience," 217.

36 "The Soun-Gui Experience," 211.

37 "The Soun-Gui Experience," 215.

38 "Finite History," 165, trans. modified. In the same passage, Nancy also says, "'Now' neither signifies nor represents the present": "the present, as we know it throughout our entire tradition, is not presentable. The present of 'now,' which is the present of what comes, is never present" (165, trans. modified).

39 "The Soun-Gui Experience," 215.

40 "Finite History," 150, trans. modified. One also does not forget that Nancy insists that "in the spacing of the present," there is always "coming-*and*-going" ("Espace contre temps," 87, italics added).

41 "The Soun-Gui Experience," 207.

42 "Finite History," 156, trans. modified.

43 "*Espace contre temps*," 87.

44 *The Experience of Freedom*, trans. Bridget McDonald and foreword by Peter Fenves (Stanford: Stanford University Press, 1993), 68, trans. modified.

45 See especially the essay "The Surprise of the Event" in *Being Singular Plural*, trans. Robert D. Richardson and Anne E. O'Byrne (Stanford: Stanford University Press, 2000), 159–76.

46 As Nancy says in *La Possibilité d'un monde*, before the ephemeral "we are in [a state of being in] 'attention to' [*l'attention à*]" (117).

47 A similar revisiting of such older French form can be found in Luce Irigaray's *J'aime à toi*, where the *à*, in Irigaray's terms, is critical in putting a distance between "me" and "you," ensuring that, in love, or even in spite of it, neither gets fused or assimilated to the other in a subordinating sense, where one loses one's difference.

48 The philosophical force of *à*, in Nancy's thought, is such that it is the preposition ineluctable from his ontology: instead of a *Being* that is fixed, stable, and identical to itself, Nancy argues for a notion of *being-to* [*être-à*], where the preposition shifts the emphasis toward the always transitive fact of exist-ing, i.e. exist-ing that is existing from one moment to the next, existing at a different time and present, and therefore existing differently too not only in relation to oneself at a particular time but also to different others at one time and another. For more on the preposition force or force of the preposition in Nancy's thought, see the forthcoming *diacritics* special issues on "The

Pre-Positional Senses of Jean-Luc Nancy," co-edited by Irving Goh and Timothy Murray.

49 *La Possibilité d'un monde*, 129.

50 "Finite History," 163, trans. modified.

51 "Finite History," 156, trans. modified.

52 See especially "De la struction" in Aurélien Barrau and Jean-Luc Nancy, *Dans quels mondes vivons-nous?* (Paris: Galilée, 2011), 89–90. Translations from this text are ours.

53 "De la struction," 96.

54 "De la struction," 95–6.

55 "Abandoned Being," trans. Brian Holmes, in *The Birth to Presence*, 41.

56 These terms refer to Nancy's reading of On Kawara's installation pieces. See "The Technique of the Present: On On Kawara," 193, 194.

Chapter 2 Nancy's Inoperative Community

1 Jean-Luc Nancy, *La communauté désoeuvrée*, 1983/1986 (2nd edn, Christian Bourgois, Paris) (translated as *The Inoperative Community*, ed. Peter Connor, University of Minnesota Press, 1991); Maurice Blanchot, *La communauté inavouable*, Paris: Editions de Minuit, 1983 (translated as *The Unavowable Community* by Pierre Joris, Station Hill Press, 2006).

2 The same year a more orthodox Freudian psychoanalyst and political theorist, Eugène Enriquez, had published *De la horde à l'Etat. Essai de psychanalyse du lien social,* to which Blanchot will refer immediately.

3 It probably stems from the debates inside the *Centre de Recherches Philosophiques sur le Politique,* created at the École Normale Supérieure in 1980 by Nancy and Philippe Lacoue-Labarthe, which included Jacques Derrida, Jean-François Lyotard, and occasional collaborations from Claude Lefort, Jacques Rancière, Etienne Balibar, and so on.

4 We can also notice that Fredric Jameson's *The Political Unconscious* was published in 1981, Louis Dumont's *Essais sur l'individualisme* in 1985, and the journal *Il Centauro* founded by Esposito, Cacciari, Tronti, Marramao, etc., was published from 1981 to 1986, etc.

5 Hegel's *Phenomenology of Spirit* calls it an *action of everyone and anyone*

[*Ein Tun Aller und Jeder*]: in Hegel himself, it will become represented as a state construction, but in Marx as a revolutionary transformation of the world. See my essay "*Zur Sache selbst.* Du commun et de l'universel dans la *Phénoménologie* de Hegel," in *Citoyen Sujet et autres essais d'anthropologie philosophique*, (Paris: Presses Universitaires de France, 2011).

6 I leave aside provisionally Rancière's own trajectory during the same years (from *Aux Bords du politique*, collecting essays from 1986 to 1990, to *Disagreement*, or *La Mésentente*, 1995, which obviously are part of the conversation. In 2000, I published an essay, "Citizenship without Community," in which I attempted a paradoxical combination of Nancy and Rancière to explore possibilities of dissolving the institutional equation of Citizenship and Nationhood (reprinted in *We, the People of Europe?*, Princeton University Press, 2004).

7 An idea derived from Kantorowicz's *The King's Two Bodies* (1957, but translated into French only in 1989). The "Centre de Recherches Philosophiques sur le Politique" also carried on discussions on Arendt's concept of totalitarianism (I particularly remember a controversy between Derrida and Lyotard about her concept of "radical evil" and her reading of Kant).

8 Although Sartre had not written: "communism is the unsurpassable horizon of our time," in his *Question de méthode*, later to become the long introduction to the *Critique of Dialectical Reason* (1960).

9 Let us note in passing that this was *also* Althusser's critique (see *For Marx*, 1965 and *Reading Capital*, 1965).

10 *La Communauté désoeuvrée*, 75.

11 A sociological and historicist version would be the narrative of the "decomposition of the primitive or premodern communities" and its possible "reconstitution" in communism as the end of history.

12 This idea of a "beyond" of politics is a constant in Nancy's thought, who returned to it in a conversation with Philip Armstrong and Jason E. Smith, published in French as *Politique et au-delà* (Paris: Galilée, 2011).

13 This "communication" is crucially distinguished from every form of Hegelian *recognition*, therefore every *identification process*, however "mediated" through conflict, deprived of every form of *specularity* (another interesting crossing with the Althusserian language, especially since the category of "interpellation" is used incidentally).

14 See in particular his later essay (first written as a preface for an Italian translation of Blanchot): *La Communauté affrontée* (Editions Galilée, 2001).

15 "L'Inconvenance majeure," in *L'Entretien infini* (translated as "Insurrection, the Madness of Writing", *The Infinite Conversation*, translation and foreword by Suzanne Hanson (University of Minnesota Press, 1993), 217–29.

16 This was precisely the "answer" that Nancy himself wanted to give to his own "sophistic" question, posed to an assembly of French philosophers: "who comes after the subject?" (see E. Cadava, P. Connor, J.L. Nancy, *Who Comes after the Subject?*, Routledge, 1991).

17 I am tempted to add myself: they *say* that they embrace (as in Schiller's *Ode to Joy* with Beethoven's music: "Seid umschlungen, Millionen . . ." Or they find equivalents: this is the obscene eroticism of military parades, which could be understood as a form of "kiss" . . .

18 This is reflected in the last paragraph in a typical "supplementary" remark that "this is a *political question*," which I consider to be the starting point of Blanchot's reaction to the "short-circuit" of communism and *communauté des amants* as analogous instantiations of the negative community.

19 See my essay on *Blanchot l'insoumis,* now in Étienne Balibar, *Citoyen Sujet et autres essais d'anthropologie philosophique* (Paris: Presses Universitaires de France, 2011).

20 This negative ontology will be fully developed later by Nancy in his great book *Being Singular Plural* (*Etre Singulier Pluriel*, Galilée, 1996, entirely based on the untranslatable "nous autres", which ought to be rendered at the same time as "ourselves" and "we, the others").

21 This is where one must be surprised that Nancy seems to avoid a discussion of Freud's understanding of the relationship between love and the death drive in the production of identification processes: the reference to Freud will return in Blanchot's footnote as in Derrida's margins, but another kind of bifurcation seems to be at stake here.

22 As Hegel had explained in the section of his *Phenomenology of Spirit* dedicated to "the revealed religion," immediately preceding "absolute knowledge", which is in fact nothing other than the abolition of representation in historicity.

23 See Jean-Luc Nancy, 'L'Insacrifiable,' *Une pensée finie* (Paris: Galilée, 1990), 65–106.

24 In his most recent *grand oeuvre*, called "Deconstruction of Christianity", Nancy has included another essay on Blanchot, where he questions in return his paradoxical way of addressing the symbol of resurrection: as "resurrection of death" itself (see Jean-Luc Nancy, *La Déclosion (Déconstruction du Christianisme, 1)* (Galilée, 2005), 135–46: "*la surrection qui dresse la mort dans la mort comme une mort vivante*").

25 Occasionally the *bodies* – but perhaps also only the *dying bodies*, as in the romantic myth of the "common death" or the "dying in common" of the lovers where "subjectivity" triumphs by losing itself.

26 This is also the point of his well-known controversy with the Lacanian heritage. See *L'"il y a" du rapport sexuel* (Galilée, 2001).

Chapter 3 "Literary Communism"

1 Jean-Luc Nancy, *La Communauté affrontée* (Paris: Galilée, 2001), 31–2.

2 Nancy, *La Communauté affrontée*, 26.

3 Nevertheless, Nancy's own writings from the period I am referring to – particularly on community and "the community of those who have no community" – had a direct influence on the phenomena known as the "return to religion" in North American circles of Continental Philosophy. In an interview that appears in *Le Magazine littéraire* in 2003, Nancy describes the "return to religion" as a "new political correctness (and thus indecency)," referring specifically to its resurgence in academic philosophy in the United States, but also to the writings of Agamben, Esposito, and others. For a fuller discussion of both Nancy's (and Derrida's) troubled relationship with this theme, see my "Decrypting 'the Christian Thinking of the Flesh, tacitly, the Caress, in a word, the Christian Body' in *Le Toucher*," *Sophia* 47(3) (2008): 293–310.

4 Nancy, *La Communauté affrontée*, 31–2.

5 For the sake of historical accuracy, it is important to notice that democracy is not even entertained as a possibility, given the weakened and corrupt forms of western democracies at precisely this moment. This is something that Nancy and Blanchot both underline in their more recent replies to various attacks on the writings of the

prewar years by Bataille, Blanchot, and other French intellectuals. See Nancy, *La Communauté affrontée*, 16.

6 Quoted in Denis Hollier, *Le Collège de Sociologie: 1937–1939* (Paris: Gallimard, 1955), 55ff.

7 Here, we must note that Nancy never says "literature is writing," but rather, always, offers the alternative, "literature, or writing," that is, if we accept the "coincidence" of these two terms according to the modern invention of the myth of writing, but also with regard to the power accorded to this new myth to essentially "interrupt," if not to suspend, all the previous mythical foundations of community. Therefore, as Nancy writes, "a name we have given to this voice of interruption [of the myth of community]: literature (or writing, if we adopt the acceptation of this word that coincides with literature)." See Jean-Luc Nancy, *The Inoperative Community*, trans. Peter Connor (Minneapolis: University of Minnesota Press, 1991), 63.

8 Hollier (ed.), *College of Sociology*, trans. Betsy Wing (Minneapolis: University of Minnesota Press, 1988), xxvi. According to Hollier, the rejection of literature is a common denominator of the three texts that appear in the July issue of *La Nouvelle Revue* (1937), and especially in the collective manifesto of the College of Sociology initialed by Roger Callois, "For a College of Sociology." In "The Sorcerer's Apprentice," Bataille denounced artistic activity as a product of the dissociation of the complete man (*l'homme integral*). In a letter, he had already told Kojeve that the man of unemployed, purposeless negativity was unable to find in the work of art an answer to the question that he himself is.

9 Bataille, *Absence of Myth: Writings on Surrealism*, trans. Michael Richardson (London: Verso, 1994), 109.

10 This is from a review of Monnerot's book, *Les Faits sociaux ne sont pas des choses* that appears in the first issue of *Critique* (June, 1946). This theme will dominate most of Bataille's writings in the immediate postwar period and follows from the research undertaken by the College of Sociology collective between 1937 and 1939, of which Monnerot was a member.

11 Bataille, *Absence of Myth*, 111.

12 Bataille, *Absence of Myth*, 111.

13 Nancy, *The Inoperative Community*, 64.

14 Nancy, *The Inoperative Community*, 72.

15 Maurice Blanchot, *The Unavowable Community*, trans. Pierre Joris (New York: Station Hill, 1988), 15.

16 Nancy, *The Inoperative Community*, 80.

17 Nancy, *Dis-Enclosure: The Deconstruction of Christianity*, trans. Bettina Bergo et al. (New York: Fordham University Press, 2008), 90.

18 Although Nancy's own logic is sometimes quite tortuous around this question of origins, especially concerning the original myth of writing, I will only note here that he often uses the terms "myth" and "mythology" negatively, as lies or diversions, even while he speaks of a bias that precedes us unconsciously from "the very depths of community."

19 Nancy, *La Communauté affrontée*, 39.

20 Nancy, *La Communauté affrontée*, 39.

21 Blanchot, *The Unavowable Community*, 15.

22 Blanchot, *The Unavowable Community*, 7–8.

23 Blanchot, *The Unavowable Community*, 5.

24 Blanchot, *The Unavowable Community*, 15.

25 Quoted in Blanchot, *The Unavowable Community*, 18.

26 Blanchot, *The Unavowable Community*, 15. See also Nancy, *The Inoperative Community*, 29.

27 Nancy, *The Inoperative Community*, 29. My emphasis.

28 Blanchot, quoted in Patrick ffrench, *After Bataille: Sacrifice, Exposure, Community* (Oxford: Legenda, 2007), 132. For an alternative and, in many respects, parallel discussion of this episode, the reader should refer to chapter 3 of this excellent study on Bataille.

29 Blanchot, *The Unavowable Community*, 9.

30 Blanchot, *The Unavowable Community*, 9.

31 The Christian community, at least in its Pauline formulation, is established (or founded) on the death of Christ *qua* particular, and it is from this relationship that every Christian receives a new identity as "a brother or sister in Christ." Of course, this gives the Christian community an occult character, and the non-believer would never be able to fathom the deeply personal and real grief expressed by certain Christian communities, including many that exist today, in the ritual observance of the crucifixion.

32 Bataille, *Absence of Myth*, 111.

33 Blanchot, *The Unavowable Community*, 6.

34 Blanchot, *The Unavowable Community*, 7.

35 Blanchot, *The Unavowable Community*, 6.
36 Quoted in Blanchot, *The Unavowable Community*, 7.
37 Blanchot, *The Unavowable Community*, 7. What is commonly referred to as the "Guyana massacre" took place in 1978, five years before Blanchot's comments.
38 Nancy, *The Inoperative Community*, 29.
39 Nancy, *The Inoperative Community*, 63. Upon invoking this word, Nancy interrupts himself in the voice of another as if to interrupt the invocation of a new myth, which would be a danger he also wants to avoid: "Certainly, there is a work only if there is a 'revelation' (you might interrupt me here: 'What are we to make of the use of this word 'revelation'? Does it not go along with 'myth,' as it does moreover with 'image'? But this is the space of absolute unsuitability: each one of these words also bespeaks its own interruption)."
40 Nancy, *La Communauté affrontée*, 32.
41 Nancy, *The Inoperative Community*, 73. In this context it is important to recall that Lacoue-Labarthe, in the same moment and even in his collaboration with Nancy, never employed the concept of community or sought to give it any political use since, for him, the term would always refer to the social environment of fascism. See Nancy, *La Communauté affrontée*, 32n.
42 In a 2011 interview with Philip Armstrong and Jason Smith, published as *Politique et au-delà*, Nancy expresses a similar anxiety concerning Alain Badiou's definition of politics as "*destinée collective de l'humanité*," which recalls a similar statement made by Napolean to Goethe: "*Le destin, c'est la politique.*" In reply to both statements, Nancy recalls the following line from a 1993 interview with Derrida: "*Le 'politique' lui-même est un philosopheme – et finalement très obscure.*" Nancy, *Politique et au-delà*, interview with Philip Armstrong and Jason Smith (Paris: Galilée, 2011), 50–2.
43 The theme of an excessive trait that is "proper to man" is properly Derrida's and concerns the following series covered in his last writings: sovereignty–stupidity–freedom. See Jacques Derrida, *The Beast and the Sovereign*, Vol. 1, trans. Geoffrey Bennington (Chicago: University of Chicago Press, 2009).
44 Blanchot, *The Unavowable Community*, 5.
45 Blanchot, *The Unavowable Community*, 2.

Chapter 4 Monograms: Then and "Now"

1   *Monogrammes I, Digraphe 20* (1979), 131–7; *Monogrammes II, Digraphe
    21* (1979), 133–8; *Monogrammes III, Digraphe 22–3* (1980), 221–9;
    Monogrammes IV, Digraphe 24 (1980), 131–40; *Monogrammes V,
    Digraphe* 25 (1980), 199–208. Due to the short length of these texts,
    page numbers will not be provided in citations. All translations are by
    Georges Van Den Abbeele.

2   *Monogrammes VI, Futur Antérieur 10* (1992: 2); *Monogrammes VII,
    Futur Antérieur 11* (1992: 3); *Monogrammes VIII, Futur Antérieur
    12–13* (1992: 4–5); *Monogrammes IX, Futur Antérieur 14* (1992: 6);
    Monogrammes X, Futur Antérieur 15 (1993: 1); *Monogrammes XI, Futur
    Antérieur 16* (1993: 2), 141–4; *Monogrammes XII, Futur Antérieur
    17* (1993: 3); *Monogrammes XIII, Futur Antérieur 18* (1993: 4);
    Monogrammes XIV, Futur Antérieur 19–20 (1993: 5–6). All translations
    are by Georges Van Den Abbeele.

3   In February 2013, after this piece was completed (and as if to punc-
    tuate the inevitable achronicity of any chronicled remarks), Nancy
    did nonetheless relaunch the series of *monogrammes,* publishing as
    of this date, October 2013, three more installments in the journal
    L'Impossible: Monogrammes 15, 16, and 17 respectively in *L'Impossible*
    10 (February 2013), 12 (April 2013), and 13 (Summer 2013).

4   *Chroniques philosophiques* (Paris: Galilée, 2004); Franson Manjali, trans.,
    Philosophical Chronicles (New York: Fordham University Press, 2008).

5   The website address is http://multitudes.samizdat.net/_Nancy-Jean-
    Luc_

6   See my "Singular Remarks," *Paragraph* 16(2) (1993): 180–6; special
    issue on Jean-Luc Nancy, edited by Peggy Kamuf.

7   The French word *actualité,* as used by Nancy, presents a number of
    challenges in translation. *Actualité* in common French designates what
    is current, recent, or happening now, as in the plural form, *actualités,*
    which is the French term for news or current events. It thus has an
    overridingly temporal significance. At the same time, *actualité* is the
    technical French translation for German *Wirklichkeit* (English, "actu-
    ality"), in the Hegelian philosophical sense, to describe the unity of
    essence and appearance. The *actual* is thus to be distinguished from
    the real or mere existence (*Dasein*) insofar as its essence is objectively
    revealed, or "actualized," by self-conscious thought, leading to his

famous dictum that "the actual is the rational and the rational is the actual." Nancy in his *Monogrammes* moves between the differing though not entirely contradictory meanings of the term, which I am thus sometimes obliged to translate as "current" situation, current events, currentness, timeliness, etc., and sometimes as "actual." In many cases, I am stuck using the neologistic expression "actuality" to refer to what is in fact both "current" and *wirklich*. Clearly, a sustained analysis of the "actual" in Nancy remains to be done, but that is beyond the scope of the present work.

8 "The real question is philosophical: all duplicity set aside, to *take on the figure* of the philosopher [*faire figure de philosophe*], *to pass oneself* off as a philosopher [*se donner pour philosophe*], that is to give (produce, present, take) philosophy as that which can take on a *figure*, and as a figure which henceforth can *speak*, and which in speaking, can *announce* a given truth whose announcement is, precisely, sanctioned by the voice and the figure of a philosopher – this comes down to a misunderstanding of philosophy. It is to misunderstand, in effect, with a dizzying ignorance and carelessness, that which makes for the very question of philosophy, at least since Kant and Hegel (since the *double bind* of metaphysics in Kant and Hegel): the possibility, or rather the (im)possibility that it *presents itself,* that it takes on a *figure*" (*Monogrammes I).*

9 The question of the monogram as "out-line," contour, or de-lineation, demands a critical comparison with what Jacques Derrida calls the "parergon," in *The Truth in Painting*, trans. Geoff Bennington and Ian McLeod (Chicago: University of Chicago Press, 1987).

10 See my "Lost Horizons and Uncommon Grounds: For a Poetics of Finitude in the Work of Jean-Luc Nancy," in Darren Sheppard, Simon Sparks, and Colin Thomas (eds), *On Jean-Luc Nancy: The Sense of Philosophy* (London: Routledge, 1997), 12–18.

11 The text appears in the collective volume, *Sur l'ex-Yougoslavie, Actes de la journée du 6 mars 1993* (Paris: Collège International de Philosophie, 1993).

12 Here again, the reference to Jean-François Lyotard's *The Postmodern Condition*, trans. Geoff Bennington and Brian Massumi (Minneapolis: University of Minnesota Press, 1979) imposes itself, most notably in Lyotard's discussion of the role of performance as the pervasive criterion of legitimation under postmodern conditions.

13 "As soon as one attempts to find, to produce and, in the first place, to posit and to thematize the non-given conjunction of power and meaning (what we shall call 'democracy'), politics at once gets defined as that which has still not taken place but rather demands its place at the point where the disjunction between power and meaning reigns. It is, therefore, not so much utopia that is first of all political, but, rather, it is politics that is always utopian." "In Place of Utopia," trans. Patricia Viera and Michael Marder, in Patricia Viera and Michael Marder (eds), *Existential Utopia: New Perspectives on Utopian Thought* (New York: Continuum, 2012), 8; the text was first published in French as "Au lieu de l'utopie," in *Les Utopies et leurs représentations: colloque franco-japonais, Tokyo, 2000* (Paris: Le Quartier, 2002). On the proposed notion of "exonomy," Nancy writes:

> we will not oppose autonomy with heteronomy, with which it forms a pair. Being heteronomous toward another subject that is itself autonomous changes nothing, regardless of whether this other autonomous thing is named god, the market, technics, or life. But, in order to open a new path, we could try out the word *exonomy*. The word would evoke a law that would not be the law of the same or of the other, but one that would be unappropriable by either the same or the other. Just as *exogamy* goes outside of kinship, *exonomy* moves out of the binary familiarity of the self and the other. (*Philosophical Chronicles*, 9–10)

14 Immanuel Kant, *Critique of Pure Reason*, trans. and ed. Paul Guyer and Alan Wood (Cambridge: Cambridge Univerity Press, 1999), 272.

15 Karl Wilhelm Friedrich von Schlegel, *Athenaeum Fragmenten,* in Jean-Luc Nancy and Philippe Lacoue-Labarthe, *L'Absolu littéraire* (Paris: Seuil, 1978).

16 The exact citation reads as follows: "die Eule der Minerva beginnt erst mit der einbrechenden Dämmerung ihren Flug [The owl of Minerva begins its flight only when twilight falls]," Georg Wilhelm Friedrich Hegel, "Vorrede," *Grundlinien der Philosophie des Rechts* (Leipzig: Felix Meiner, 1911), 17 (my translation).

17 One might compare Montaigne's lonely castle and redoubt, on the one hand, and Descartes's sense of beneficent isolation in the

very heart of urban Amsterdam, on the other ("amidst a great and populous nation, extremely industrious and more concerned with their own business than curious about other people's, while I do not lack any conveniences of the most frequented cities, I have been able to live a life as solitary and retired as though I were in the most remote deserts," René Descartes, *Discourse on Method,* trans. John Cottingham, Robert Stoothof, and Dugald Murdoch, in *Philosophical Writings of Descartes* (Cambridge: Cambridge University Press, 1985), I, 126. I treat these and other examples in my forthcoming *The "Retreat" of French Thought.*

18 Heidegger glosses this line to read: "the schemata of the pure concepts of the understanding 'determine' time," which follows from his inference that "time is the schema–image and not just the form of intuition which stands over and against the pure concepts of the understanding." Martin Heidegger, *Kant and the Problem of Metaphysics,* trans. Richard Taft (Bloomington: Indiana University Press, 1997), 73–4; also see Nancy's invaluable commentary on Heidegger's reading of Kant in *The Ground of the Image,* admirably translated by Jeff Fort (New York: Fordham University Press, 2005), 80–99.

19 "Each single one of the memories and expectations in which the libido is bound to the [lost] object is brought up and hyper-cathected, and detachment of the libido is accomplished in respect of it." Sigmund Freud, "Mourning and Melancholia," trans. Richard Strachey, *The Standard Edition of the Complete Psychological Works of Sigmund Freud* (London: Norton, 1976), XIV, 244.

20 Among other instances: "From his present vantage point, he could confirm that he had been living not just in a fairy tale but in a paradise, in which his love for his mother coincided with his love of Nature" (30); "With her light-brown hair and gray eyes and rosy skin, his mother was like an American bird – the rose-breasted grosbeak, for instance" (21); Mary McCarthy, *Birds of America* (New York: Harcourt Brace Jovanovich, 1965).

21 William Shakespeare, *Hamlet* (I, ii, 65).

22 On the question of the "future of philosophy," Nancy writes:

> philosophizing always turns itself towards the 'to-come' (*avenir*) of philosophy. But this coming is not exactly a future. A future is

predictable, calculable, appreciable or imaginable. A 'coming' is incalculable and inappreciable. In a sense, philosophy is always, in essence, 'to-come.' It is not ever given, never already done or befallen. It always begins, as the essential beginning of an inchoate thinking that knows itself as such. (B. C. Hutchens, *Jean-Luc Nancy and the Future of Philosophy*, Montreal: McGill/Queens University Press, 2005), 162)

23 On this "foresight" of the schema, see Nancy's remarks in *The Ground of the Image* on Heidegger's deployment of the word, *Vorbild*, in connection with his reading of Kant: "the *Vorbild* (fore-image) or the model of a 'being that is yet to be created or produced.'. . . a model of the fore-vision of the unity that anticipates itself in the precession of its own succession: time as a series of time, which forms the first of the schemata" (p. 95).

24 Jean-Luc Nancy, *La Déclosion (Déconstruction du christianisme, I)* (Paris: Galilée, 2005), 17.

25 Nancy, *La Déclosion (Déconstruction du christianisme, I)*, 23.

26 Nancy, *La Déclosion (Déconstruction du christianisme, I)*, 23.

27 *Philosophical Chronicles*. All citations below are from the first lecture, 1–3.

Chapter 5 Extended Drawing

1 Jean-Luc Nancy, *Le Plaisir au dessin* (Paris: Galilée), coll. "Écritures/ Figures," 2009. (Featuring drawings by Valerio Adami, Pierre Alechinsky, Jean Le Gac, Ernest Pignon-Ernest, François Rouan, Gérard Titus-Carmel, Vladimir Veličković.) Hereafter *P*. Author's emphasis in all citations unless otherwise noted. This is the revised and expanded version of the text, first published in the catalogue of the eponymous exhibit (Paris: Hazan, 2007), which Jean-Luc Nancy co-curated for the Musée des beaux-arts de Lyon in 2007–8. Nancy will again curate an exhibit, this time on color, for the Musée des beaux-arts de Lyon. I am most grateful to Philip Armstrong for sharing a draft of his translation of Jean-Luc Nancy's *Le Plaisir au dessin* (*The Pleasure in Drawing*, New York, Fordham University Press, 2013).

2 Translator's note: As provided by the author, citations of *The Pleasure*

in Drawing in the present text, preceded by those of the French text, follow Philip Armstrong's translation. For all other citations, translations are my own unless otherwise noted.

3 My title takes after that of the recent exhibit *Extended Drawing: Sol Le Witt, Robert Mangold, Bruce Nauman and Richard Serra*, September 18, 2011–January 15, 2012, Bonnefantenmuseum, Maastricht.

4 In Cornelia H. Butler and Catherine de Zegher (eds), *On Line: Drawing through the Twentieth Century* (New York: The Museum of Modern Art, 2010), 6. Hereafter *L*.

5 Catalogue of the eponymous exhibit, March 9–28 2010, Fondation d'entreprise Ricard, Paris: École nationale supérieure des beaux-arts, Beaux-arts de Paris les éditions, 2010, n. p. Hereafter *LC*.

6 It is a reworking of the last chapter of *Le Plaisir au dessin* (pp. 120–30), under the title "The Desire of the Line."

7 Translator's note: While "to take stock" conveys the sense of "evaluating" or "assessing" in the French expression "*faire le point,*" it loses the language of points and lines that the author is sketching out here. A related expression in English would be to "take point," as in becoming the lead scout in a military operation. But the logic of multiple, plural lines of intersecting thoughts opposes a squad's going in only one direction, that is, its drawing a single line led by a point.

8 Gilles Deleuze, *Pourparlers* (Paris: Minuit, 1997), 219; quoted in de Zegher, *L* 89.

9 "La Venue, Jean-Luc Nancy," *Europe* 960 (Paris): 290–0, Special Issue on "*Jean-Luc Nancy,*" ed. Ginette Michaud, April 2009, 293. Hereafter *V*.

10 See J.-L. Nancy, "Freud – pour ainsi dire," in *L'Adoration (Déconstruction du christianisme, 2)*, (Paris: Galilée), coll. "La philosophie en effet," 2010, 144–7. Nancy in this text defines the Freudian drive [*pulsion*] in terms that are also those of drawing: "impulse [*poussée*], élan, pulse, fieriness, passion [*emportement*] [. . .], a forcing of sense, even, before and according to all signification" (147).

11 A first version of this section appeared in French under the title "Désir du dessin" ["Desire of Drawing"], *Spirale* 239, Special Issue on "*Jean-Luc Nancy, lignes de sens – philosophie, art, politique,*" ed. Ginette Michaud (Winter 2012): 53–4.

12 See J.-L. Nancy, *L'Adoration*, 22–5, 31–2.

13 Moninot is an artist with whom Nancy made *Les Traces anémones*

[*The Traces Anemones*] (Paris: Maeght Éditeur, 2008), a very small artist's book (11 x 8.5 cm), for which Nancy penned a series of very short poems to accompany a project of the artist's on the "'threads of the virgin'," these "strange attachments of veils woven from invisible lines carried in space as the winds blow" (*LC*).

14 The paper's title means literally "Deliberately Drawing," playing on the homonyms "*dessein*" and "*dessin*." It is related to the exhibit *Mémoires d'aveugle* (see *Memoirs of the Blind. The Self-Portrait and Other Ruins*, trans. Pascale-Anne Brault and Michael Naas, Chicago, University of Chicago Press, 1993). Unpublished, the paper was delivered by Jacques Derrida at the invitation of artist François Martin in his seminar on drawing, which took place at the École Supérieure d'art du Havre on May 16, 1991 (Jacques-Derrida Archives, Institut Mémoires de l'édition contemporaine (IMEC), Abbaye d'Ardenne, box 01, new reference DRR162, 46 p.). François Martin recently confirmed to me in an email (July 8 2012) that the title was his own, and covered a cycle of conferences which he organized and in which Derrida took part, as well as an exhibition curated by Martin (École Supérieure d'art du Havre, 13 May–7 June 1991). As the title was inscribed on the copy deposited in the IMEC archive, we have decided to keep it as the title of Derrida's conference as well. An edition of this text was published in 2013 (*À dessein, le dessin*, followed by *Derrida, à l'improviste*, by G. Michaud (Le Havre: Franciscopolis Éditions) and will appear in the book collecting Derrida's writings on the arts [*Penser à ne pas voir. Écrits sur les arts du visible (1979–2004)*, ed. Javier Bassas, Joana Masó, and Ginette Michaud (Paris: Éditions de La Différence), 2013; forthcoming, trans. Laurent Milesi, The University of Chicago Press].

15 ["*visée sans cible*": Translator's note: the English expression loses the French homophony between "*sensible*" and "*sans cible*."] I pick up this expression from Bernard Moninot who uses it in his text "*Penser en dessin. Notes, aphorismes et repentirs*" ["Thinking in Drawing. Notes, Aphorisms, and Pentimenti"]: "[. . .] drawing starts well before the first trait, the gesture in suspension is already drawing: an aim without a target" (*LC*). Derrida and Nancy would subscribe to this proposition.

16 Or, inversely, "separated," adds Nancy according to this chiasmatic figure he often privileges: "If we retain the term, aesthetics is in itself

an ethics in that it gives itself the supreme rule not to be satisfied with anything, and to measure its pleasure by the desire not to be satisfied" (*P* 128/104). In other words, even the Idea of the Good does not make for a good enough measure here.

17 See J.-L. Nancy, *Politique et au-delà. Entretien avec Philip Armstrong et Jason E. Smith* [*Politics and Beyond. A Conversation with Philip Armstrong and Jason E. Smith*] (Paris: Galilée), coll. "La philosophie en effet," 2011. See also "*Politique tout court et très au-delà. Entretien avec Jean-Luc Nancy*" ["Just Politics, and Quite Beyond"] (with Ginette Michaud), *Spirale* 33–6.

18 Juan-Manuel Garrido, *La Formation des formes*, Paris: Galilée, coll. "La philosophie en effet," 2008.

19 *Matisse on Art*, rev. edn, ed. Jack D. Flam (Berkeley and Los Angeles: University of California Press), 1995, 48; cited by Nancy in *P* 51, 122–4, and *LC*.

20 On this gesture of art, see J.-L. Nancy, "Art Today," trans. Charlotte Mandell, *Journal of Visual Culture* 9(1) (April 2010): 91–9, Special Issue on "Regarding Jean-Luc Nancy," ed. Louis Kaplan and John Paul Ricco, especially 96–7. See also my comment on Nancy's text in the same issue: "Outlining Art: On Jean-Luc Nancy's *Trop* and *Le Plaisir au dessin*," 77–90.

21 Philip Armstrong, "'Between Distress and Denouement,'" in *François Rouan. Découpe/Modèle, 1965–2009* (Paris: LIENART éditions/ Galerie Jean Fournier), 2011, 25. Hereafter *D*.

22 In this passage, Jean-Christophe Bailly cites Nancy's *Le Sens du monde* (Paris: Galilée, coll. "La philosophie en effet"), 1993, 181.

23 Kandinsky's propositions are, as we know, an obligatory point of passage for any reflection on line. "From these two graphic entities – point and line – derive the entire resources of a whole realm of art, graphics./The point is now able to increase its size *ad infinitum* and becomes the spot. Its subsequent and ultimate potential is that of changing its configuration, whereby it passes from the purely mathematical form of a bigger or smaller circle to forms of infinite flexibility and diversity, far removed from the diagrammatic./The fate of line is more complex and requires a special description./ The transference of line to a free environment produces a number of extremely important results. Its outer expediency turns into an inner one. Its practical meaning becomes abstract. As a result, the

line discloses an inner sound of artistic significance./A fundamental
turning point is attained. Its fruit is the birth of the language of art./
Line experiences many fates. Each creates a particular, specific world,
from schematic limitation to unlimited expressivity. These words lib-
erate line more and more from the instrument, leading to complete
freedom of expression" (Vassily Kandinsky, "Little Articles on Big
Questions: On Line," 1919, reprinted and translated in *Kandinsky:
Complete Writings on Art* (ed. Kenneth C. Lindsay and Peter Vergo
(Cambridge, MA: Da Capo Press, 1994), 121; quoted by de Zegher,
L 22).

24 As de Zegher notes, "Klee was deeply concerned with the process
by which a point becomes a line, a line becomes a plane, and a plane
becomes a body," as was his friend Kandinsky who, in *Point and
Line to Plane*, 1926, writes: "When *a force coming from without* moves
the point in any direction, [a] line results [whose] initial direction
remains unchanged and the line has the tendency to run in a straight
course to infinity./This is the *straight line* whose tension *represents
the most concise form of the potentiality for endless movement* " trans.
Howard Dearstyne and Hilla Rebay, ed. Rebay (New York: Dover,
1979), 57–8; quoted by de Zegher, *L* 38. Nancy quotes this text by
Kandinsky in *The Pleasure in Drawing*, reassesssing its far-reaching
impact:

> Following Kandinsky, we should also add line and point and
> plane, given his proposal for an aesthetic transversality of draw-
> ing's elements. (However, what Kandinsky believed reducible
> to a single graphic notion must, on the contrary, be thought as
> an irreducible plurality. There are as many "lines," "points," and
> "planes" as there are specific sensible modalities, which is also to
> say, forms of sensibility, and there is never anywhere a general
> sensibility – in essence, *aisthesis* is differential.) (*P* 52–3/41)

25 One thinks of course of land art, where drawing involves the
marking of a landscape but, as de Zegher aptly remarks: "But every
drawing is also a landscape of its own, and unframed, open space – a
form of land art in response to the surrounding world" (*L* 99).

26 Paul Klee, "Contributions to a theory of pictorial form: lecture notes
from the Bauhaus at Weimar and at Dassau," 1921, in *Paul Klee*

Notebooks, vol. 1, *The Thinking Eye*, ed. Jurg Spiller (London: Lund Humphries, 1961), 103; quoted by de Zegher, *L* 39.

27 "A kinesthetic practice of traction – attraction, extraction, protraction – drawing is born from an outward gesture linking inner impulses and thoughts to the other through the touching of a surface with repeated graphic marks and lines" (*L* 23). This definition is close to Nancy's own phrasing of the line as a trait retracing/retracting itself.

28 Color, one knows, has always been considered a threat to the clarity and intelligibility of drawing that, by its schematic qualities, was alone "lucid" and essential to the Idea, drawing/intention deriving from pure ideality, whereas color remained impregnated by materiality and corporality: a "supplement" to exclude, then. The *Oxford English Dictionary* rightly underlines this division, which is also a power struggle: a drawing is defined as "'any mode of representation by lines in which delineation of form *predominates* over consideration of color'" (quoted in *L* 23; my emphasis). Besides, color evidently opposes itself to drawing in that it is on the side of painting (tone, texture, surface, volume).

29 "[. . .] Nor is it a question of taking up the long history of disputes over the *supremacy* of drawing or color," writes Nancy (*P* 21, n. 1/11, n. 8; my emphasis). Earlier, also in a note, he had insisted upon the general contagion between the arts, and so upon this strictly speaking untenable line between painting and drawing: "*Drawing* affects music in the same way as *timbre* affects the graphic arts. *Color, model, brilliance, note, touch, leap, figure,* and *rhythm,* are some of the terms from which this contagion or general communication of the arts draws [. . .]" (*P* 13, n. 1/110, n. 3). Finally, in a third note, Nancy specifies that this exclusion of color quickly becomes complicated and does not resist a careful examination of the trait, drawing "including color, as needed": "Though I will not address the question of color further, it is important to emphasize that, even on an empirical level, all drawing is colored (at least, color as from pencils). If drawing *opens* [*ouvre*] space, color *covers* [*couvre*] this opening (this is its primary meaning). It is not that it closes it off but rather that it keeps it secret" (*P* 82, n. 1/115, n. 34).

30 Interestingly, both de Zegher and Nancy quote this passage from Badiou's text "Drawing" [*Lacanian Ink* 28 (Fall 2006): 42–3]:

It is that sort of movable reciprocity between existence and inexistence, which constitutes the very essence of drawing. The question of drawing is very different from the question in Hamlet. It is not 'to be or not to be,' it is 'to be and not to be.' And that is the reason for the fundamental fragility (and femininity) of drawing: not a clear alternative, to be or not to be, but an obscure and paradoxical conjunction, to be and not to be (*L* 119; *P* 34).

De Zegher adds the parenthesis "(and femininity)," which is not in Badiou's text but nonetheless implied by the context.

31 See J.-L. Nancy, *L'Adoration*, 107. In his recent dialogue with Aurélien Barrau in *Dans quels mondes vivons-nous ?* [*In What Worlds Are We Living?*] (Paris: Galilée, coll. "La philosophie en effet," 2011; hereafter *M*), Nancy elaborates on this important notion of *struction* – a better word than "*déclosion*," he conceded in a discussion at the colloquium "*Jean-Luc Nancy, figures du dehors*" held in 2008, a while after the publication of *La Déclosion* (Paris: Galilée, coll. "La philosophie en effet," 2005) [*Dis-Enclosure. The Deconstruction of Christianity*, trans. Bettina Bergo, Gabriel Malenfant, and Michael B. Smith, New York, Fordham University Press, coll. "Perspectives in Continental Philosophy," 2008], in which he declared that he had, at the time, chosen the term "*déclosion*" to avoid direct confrontation with the all-too-charged Derridean "*deconstruction*." "*Struction*," considered in aesthetic terms, is close to the thought of the line elaborated in *Le Plaisir au dessin*:

The struction offers a dis-order that is neither the opposite, nor the downfall of an order; it situates itself elsewhere, in what we call contingency, fortuity, dispersion, erring, which merits just as much the names of surprise, invention, chance, encounter, passage. It is a matter of nothing but the co-presence, or, better still, the co-appearance [*com-parution*] of all that appears, that is, of that which is. (*M* 97)

This contingency must equally be understood in its philosophical and political consequences:

What I call here "struction" would be the state of the "with" deprived of the value of sharing, putting in play just the simple contiguity with its contingency. It would be, to recall the terms Heidegger wants to distinguish in the apprehension of the "with" (of the *mit* in the *Mitdasein* as the ontological constitution of the existent), an only categorial and not existential "with"; the pure and simple juxtaposition that does not make sense. (*M* 90–1)

32 J.-L. Nancy, "*Politique et/ou politique*," unpublished, 3, conference delivered in German on March 15, 2012 in Frankfurt at the Derrida-Konferenz of the Goethe Universität. I am grateful to Jean-Luc Nancy for giving me access to this text and for allowing me to quote him here. Hereafter *PP*.

33 "[. . .] one can at least introduce a distinction between politics understood as assumption of 'the being of man in his relation [*rapport*] to being' and politics understood as the particular sphere in charge of keeping access to that relation [*rapport*] open" (*PP* 8–9).

34 J.-L. Nancy, *Vérité de la démocratie* (Paris: Galilée, coll. "La philosophie en effet," 2008), 51–2 [*The Truth of Democracy*, trans. Michael Naas, "Just Ideas" (New York: Fordham University Press, 2010)]: "Democracy is not figurable. Better, it is not by essence figural" (27). Like art, the line of drawing.

35 J.-L. Nancy, *Identité. Fragments, franchises.* Paris: Galilée, coll. "La philosophie en effet," 2010, 34. Hereafter *I*.

36 Cornelia H. Butler, "Walkaround Time: Dance and Drawing in the Twentieth Century" (*L* 158).

37 J.-L. Nancy, "'Éloquentes rayures,'" in Adnen Jdey (ed.), *Derrida et la question de l'art. Déconstructions de l'esthétique* (Nantes: Éditions Cécile Defaut, 2011), 16.

38 J.-L. Nancy, *Les Traces anémones*, op. cit.

Chapter 6 Differing on Difference

1 The proceedings of this conference are collected in Francis Guibal and Jean-Clet Martin (eds), *Sens en tous sens. Autour des travaux de Jean-Luc Nancy* (Paris: Galilée, 2004).

2 'Responsabilité – du sens à venir,' in *Sens en tous sens*, 165–200.

3 *Sens en tous sens*, 165.

4 *Sens en tous sens*, 168.

5 *Sens en tous sens*, 168.
6 Simon Critchley, *Ethics, Politics, Subjectivity* (London: Verso, 1999), 239–53. See in particular 242, 251.
7 See Derrida, *On Touching – Jean-Luc Nancy*, trans. Christine Irizarry (Stanford: Stanford University Press, 2005), 41, 110.
8 Derrida, *On Touching – Jean-Luc Nancy*, 95.
9 See Bernard Stiegler, *Technics and Time 1: The Fault of Epimetheus*, trans. Richard Beardsworth and George Collins (Stanford: Stanford University Press, 1998); and *Technics and Time 2. Disorientation*, trans. S. Barker (Stanford: Stanford University Press, 2009).
10 Derrida, *On Touching – Jean-Luc Nancy*, 113.
11 Derrida, *On Touching – Jean-Luc Nancy*, 229.
12 Derrida, *On Touching – Jean-Luc Nancy*, 229.
13 Derrida, *On Touching – Jean-Luc Nancy*, 288.
14 Derrida, *On Touching – Jean-Luc Nancy*, 287.
15 Derrida, *Writing and Difference*, trans. Alan Bass (London: Routledge, 2001), 97–192.
16 On the exchange between Levinas and Derrida after "Violence and Metaphysics," see Colin Davis, *Levinas: An Introduction* (Chicago: Notre Dame, 1996), 66–7.
17 On this point, see Ian James, "Bernard Stiegler and the Time of Technics," *Cultural Politics* 6(2) (2010): 207–28.
18 Derrida, *Of Grammatology*, trans. Gayatri Spivak (Baltimore: Johns Hopkins University Press, 1998), 74.
19 Derrida, *Of Grammatology*, 79.
20 Derrida, *Of Grammatology*, 84. This passage is also a key point of departure for Stiegler in the first volume of *Technics and Time*.
21 It is interesting to note that the exchange between Derrida and Nancy cited above concludes with a discussion of their different perspectives on the human. It may be that Nancy's emphasis on bodies leads him to a greater focus on human bodies (although this should not necessarily be the case) and that Derrida's understanding of the trace takes his thought well beyond the orbit of the human.
22 Derrida, *Of Grammatology*, 62.
23 Derrida, *Of Grammatology*, 47.
24 Nancy, *Corpus*, trans. Richard Rand, New York, Fordham University Press, 2008, 87–9.
25 Nancy, *Corpus*, 89, trans. modified.

26 Nancy, *Corpus*, 89, trans. modified.
27 Nancy, *Corpus*, 89.
28 Nancy, *Corpus*, 89.
29 Nancy, *Corpus*, 89, trans. modified.
30 Nancy, *Corpus*, 89.
31 Nancy, *Corpus*, 91, trans. modified.
32 Nancy, *Corpus*, 43.
33 Nancy, *Corpus*, 43.
34 Nancy, *Corpus*, 43.
35 Nancy, *Corpus*, 43.
36 This is a risk that is highlighted in the responses to Derrida made by both Stiegler and Catherine Malabou, one of Derrida's last students. On this point see Ian James, *The New French Philosophy* (Cambridge: Polity, 2012), 61–109.

Chapter 7 *(Mis)Reading in* Dis-Enclosure

1 *Dis-Enclosure: The Deconstruction of Christianity* (New York: Fordham University Press, 2008), 9. Citations from this text will subsequently be indicated by page numbers in parentheses.
2 *Memoires for Paul de Man* (New York: Columbia University Press, 1986), 48.
3 *The Work of Mourning* (Chicago: The University of Chicago Press, 2003). This book was first published in English and later augmented in French.
4 Speech delivered at the colloquium "Judeities. Questions for Jacques Derrida" organized by Joseph Cohen and Raphael Zagury-Orly in 2000 in Paris.
5 "And if I wanted to pass from one James to the other [to Jacques Derrida], I would say that faith, as the *praxis* of *poiesis*, opens in *poiesis* the inadequation to self that alone can constitute 'doing' ['*faire*'] and/or 'acting' ['*l'agir*']." In this case, Jean-Luc Nancy translates into Jacques Derrida's language the speech of James – the author of the Epistle (*Dis-Enclosure*, 52).
6 "Circumfession," *Jacques Derrida* (Paris: Seuil), 1991.
7 *The Gift of Death* (Chicago: The University of Chicago Press, 2008), 119.
8 "According to Paul, what is important is that Abraham believed

that God could give him a son, against all natural evidence." (*Dis-Enclosure*, 53)

9 "What *anastasis* would designate – in the essay I wrote to deconstruct it or to turn around its value, understood as 'resurrection' – is nothing other than redress (*anastasis*), this raising up [*cette levée*] (and not a sursumption or a relay [*relève*]) of ruined sense like a truth cast forth, appealed to, announced, and saluted" (*Dis-Enclosure*, 101).

10 Matthew 16: 18–19.

11 N. 430, Special Issue, "Jacques Derrida," Paris, April 2004.

12 Geoffrey Bennington and Jacques Derrida, *Jacques Derrida* (Chicago: The University of Chicago Press, 1993), 148.

13 *Archive Fever* (Chicago and London: The University of Chicago Press, 1996), 48.

14 *Archive Fever*, 50.

15 *Archive Fever*, 45–6.

16 "Exactitude is a word that he generously credited me with having 'resuscitated'": 103.

Chapter 8 Sovereignty Without Subject

1 See especially Bennington's "The Fall of Sovereignty," *Epoché* 10(2) (2006): 395–406.

2 See her *Walled States, Waning Sovereignty* (New York: Zone Books, 2010).

3 For all the above, see Bennington's "Sovereign Stupidity and Autoimmunity," in Pheng Cheah and Suzanne Guerlac (eds), *Derrida and the Time of the Political* (Durham and London: Duke University Press, 2009), 97–113.

4 Bennington, "Sovereign Stupidity and Autoimmunity," 99.

5 Brown highlights the case of the wall at the US–Mexican border, where not much concrete state control or authority seems to be in place since it is very often the case that right-wing militia groups have been tasking themselves to conduct border patrols to prevent the penetration of these walls by illegal or clandestine immigrants.

6 This text has been translated as "Psychoanalysis Searches the States of Its Soul: The Impossible Beyond of a Sovereign Cruelty," in *Without Alibi*, ed., trans., and intro Peggy Kamuf (Stanford: Stanford University Press, 2002), pp. 238–80.

7 Translated as *Rogues: Two Essays on Reason*, trans. Pascale-Anne
   Brault and Michael Naas (Stanford: Stanford University Press), 2005.
8 To be precise, the "apparent retreat of powers of surveillance" does
   not refer to structures or apparatuses of surveillance, for it is only
   evident that the presence of CCTVs at almost every corner of a
   street in almost every city is a common sight today. It refers, instead,
   as Foucault also makes clear, to surveillance powers as embodied by
   human agents, for example, law-enforcement personnel who, as in
   the recent past, would keep watch behind onsite surveillance posts.
9 See "War, Right, Sovereignty – Technē" in *Being Singular Plural*,
   trans. Robert D. Richardson and Anne E. O'Byrne (Stanford:
   Stanford University Press, 2000), 138. An earlier translation
   appeared in Verena Andermatt Conley (ed.), *Rethinking Technologies*
   (Minneapolis and London: University of Minnesota Press, 1994.
10 Schmitt, *Political Theology: Four Chapters on the Concept of Sovereignty*.
   [1922/1934]. Trans. and intro. George Schwab. Foreword Tracy B.
   Strong (Chicago and London: University of Chicago Press, 1985), 7.
11 *The Sense of the World*, trans. with foreword by Jeffrey S. Librett
   (Minneapolis and London: University of Minnesota Press, 1997), 90.
   Trans. modified.
12 On the question of the modern *subject* in Schmitt, see Nancy's
   intervention in *Démocratie à venir: autour de Jacques Derrida*, ed. Marie-
   Louise Mallet (Paris: Galilée, 2004), 348. The sovereign *subject* who
   decides on the exception indeed becomes clear toward the end of
   Schmitt's *Political Theology*, where he argues that the rise of dic-
   tatorship is only the projection of the undeniable and irreducible
   presence of a sovereign *subject* behind all state apparatuses. As to the
   question of the "fiction" of the *subject-subjectum* that has its source
   in Descartes's philosophy, see Nancy's *Ego Sum* (Paris: Flammarion,
   1979).
13 Nancy posed that question in a letter addressed to his contempo-
   raries such as Maurice Blanchot, Gilles Deleuze, Jacques Derrida,
   Alain Badiou, Étienne Balibar, and Jacques Rancière, among others.
   The letter and their responses were published in the special issue on
   "Who Comes After the Subject?," *Topoi* 7(2) (1988). The original
   French version appeared later in *Cahiers confrontation* 20 (Winter
   1989), under the title "Après le sujet qui vient." The English version
   was republished in Eduardo Cadava, Peter Connor, and Jean-Luc

Nancy (eds), *Who Comes After the Subject?* (New York and London: Routledge, 1991). The later English volume included additional contributions from Sylviane Agacinski, Sarah Kofman, and Luce Irigaray.

14 See Nancy's "Un sujet?" in *Homme et sujet: la subjectivité en question dans les sciences humaines*, conférences du Centre d'Études Pluridisciplinaires sur la Subjectivité, ed. Dominique Weil (Paris: L'Harmattan, 1992), 47–114.

15 See Jean Bodin, *On Sovereignty: Four Chapters from the Six Books of the Commonwealth*, ed. and trans. Julian H. Franklin (Cambridge and New York: Cambridge University Press, 1992).

16 See *Rejouer le politique* (Paris: Galilée, 1981), 23, my translation. In addition, for Nancy's discussion on a "politics without *subject*," see also *The Creation of the World*, 106.

17 *The Creation of the World*, 101.

18 Having said that, one does not forget Nancy's essay on war, technē, and sovereignty in *Being Singular Plural*. The question of cruelty is not foregrounded there, but it surely is a concern given that the essay was partly a critique of the war on Iraq in 1991, where western sovereign powers celebrated their minimum casualty count thanks to the superiority of their high-tech weapons, in contrast to the greater number of their vanquished Iraqi adversaries using more primitive weapons. According to Nancy there, such cruel, if not nihilistic, ends through wars are but the logical conclusion of Schmittian sovereignty, where one sovereign seeks to obliterate another so that he remains the sole, absolute sovereign. In response to that, Nancy would call for the resistance to such sovereign drive to unleash overwhelming power or "sovereign ends" (see especially "War, Right, Sovereignty – Technē," 114–28).

19 Following Heidegger's notion of *Mitsein*, Nancy would also call such existing "being-with" or *être-avec*. And to anticipate a little the following discussion on the "deconstruction" of the *subject* in Nancy, I also note here that Nancy in "Rives, bords, limites" will write that all existents, just by the fact of their existences, without any subjective decision, are already "sovereign" (*Le Poids d'une pensée, l'approche*, (Strasbourg: Phocide, 2008), 136).

20 According to Nancy, that is the question, or even the challenge, of the "in" in "being-in-common" (see the section "De

l'Être-en-commun" in *La Communauté désoeuvrée*, rev. and enlarged edn (Paris: Christian Bourgois, 2004), 230)

21 *The Inoperative Community*, ed. and trans. Peter Connor, Minneapolis and London: University of Minnesota Press, 1991, 27, trans. modified.

22 See *The Sense of the World*, 93, where Nancy argues that, with regard to relations that are infinitely open to both their renewals and dissociations, "the model of the contract remains [. . .] insufficient, even impoverished [*indigent*], in that it presupposes contracting parties or subjects" (trans. modified).

23 It is in *The Sense of the World* where Nancy calls for the rethinking of sovereignty as "naked existence" (93). See *The Creation of the World*, 103–7, for the question of being "sovereign otherwise" as without foundation or hierarchy. There, Nancy also makes the claim that any sovereignty that is structured on a vertical hierarchy cuts itself off from all senses of a relation (see 96–8).

On another note, such sovereignty can also be considered "sovereignty in sharing or *shared sovereignty*" (*The Inoperative Community*, 25, trans. modified), which Derrida in *Voyous* and in his final lecture at Strasbourg in 2004 has recognized as impossible (not only because of the historiography of sovereignty as indivisible in Bodin, Rousseau, and Schmitt, but also because of the very real fact that states would safeguard their monopoly on sovereign, violent force) but necessary. According to Nancy, this "shared sovereignty" is "shared [. . .] between singular existences that are not subjects" (*The Inoperative Community*, 25).

24 *The Sense of the World*, 110.

25 Already with Nancy's project to think "who comes after the subject," one witnesses the quick return of the *subject*. The responses by Balibar, Badiou, and Rancière evidently expressed a resistance to depart from the *subject*. For Rancière, the *subject* remains critical for his political philosophy of "disagreement" [*mésentente*] or "dissensus," as he believes that it is the *subject*, in control of or responsible for his or her self-representation in the world, that will be able to articulate or expose the "wrong" [*le tort*] in politics. Balibar believes that the modernist project of establishing the *subject-subjectum* remains unfinished, as long as the attribute of citizenship is denied to some of these *subjects*, and hence will call for the "citizen subject." Badiou, never

on the side of "deconstruction" as Nancy and Derrida have been, has never thought of doing away with the *subject*. Having published his *Théorie du sujet* in 1981 prior to Nancy's project (c. 1986), Badiou insists, up till today, on thinking of the *subject* whose formation is not due to a discovery of his or her individual consciousness (as in Cartesian subjectivity) but is given by an *event* the elements of which have so far been considered "inexistent" or "impossible" in the world. For Badiou, it is this *subject* as such, unlike Descartes's *subject*, that is able to attain truth without the help of God. In Badiou's case, one could therefore say that we are dealing with a hubristic hyper-Cartesian *subject*. And as recent critics, including Peter Hallward who was among the first besides Žižek to champion Badiou's thought in the Anglo-American world, have sensed, this hubris has a sovereign will to power, which is really indifferent to differences, as it militantly declares his faith to the event and demands that all follow likewise in this faith. See the collection *Who Comes After the Subject?*; Badiou's *Being and Event, Second Manifesto for Philosophy*; and Hallward's "Sujet et volonté dans la philosophie d'Alain Badiou," trans. Isabelle Vodoz, in *Autour d'Alain Badiou*, ed. Isabelle Vodoz and Fabien Tarby (Paris: Germina, 2011), 303–31.

26 See for example my "Rejecting Friendship: Reading Derrida's *Politics of Friendship* Today" (*Cultural Critique* 79 (2011): 94–124), and *The Reject: From Contemporary French Thought to "Post-Secular" and "Posthuman" Futures* (forthcoming, Fordham University Press).

27 See note 23.

28 See "'Eating Well,' or the Calculation of the Subject: An Interview with Jacques Derrida," trans. Peter Connor and Avital Ronnell, *Who Comes After the Subject?*, 96–119.

29 The above is not to suggest that a perfectly timely justice is attainable with the *reject*. I recognize that justice is always untimely, but I keep with the Derridean endeavor nonetheless, which recognizes that timely justice is "impossible but necessary." That is to say, I believe in pursuing as best as possible a more timely justice. As a step toward that, I have suggested in the above recognizing *rejects* as equally deserving as *subjects* of justice. That is meant to reduce the untimeliness of justice brought about by bureaucratic hoops in existing legal institutions which have hierarchical and prejudicial bias against non-*subjects* built into their structures. In transforming

legal or juridical systems such that *rejects* can equally demand justice without becoming-*subjects*, one must also ensure that the process does not re-empower existing *subjects*, as if they are the ones deciding on according justice to *rejects*. On the contrary, what must be underscored is that the demand for justice comes from *rejects* themselves, by which existing *subjects* will also come to acknowledge that they are not the only ones privileged to have the right to justice.

30 As Derrida acknowledges in *Rogues*, his engagement with *voyous* is motivated by the proliferation in American politics, especially from the Clinton administration to the Bush administration that inaugurated the "war on terror," of the word "rogue" to label states that not only deviate from but also go against American political ideology. *Voyous* in Derrida's case therefore is more properly the translation into French of "rogues."

31 See Hardt and Negri's *Multitude: War and Democracy in the Age of Empire* (London and New York: Penguin), 2004, and *Commonwealth* (Cambridge, MA: Belknap), 2011.

32 *The Creation of the World* or *Globalization*, trans. and intro. François Raffoul and David Pettigrew (Albany: SUNY Press, 2007), 109. Trans. modified.

33 See Žižek's *The Year of Living Dangerously* (London and New York: Verso, 2012); Hardt and Negri, "The Fight for 'Real Democracy' at the Heart of Occupy Wall Street: The Encampment in Lower Manhattan Speaks to a Failure of Representation," *Foreign Affairs*, October 11, 2011. Available at www.foreignaffairs.com/articles/136399/michael-hardt-and-antonio-negri/the-fight-for-real-democracy-at-the-heart-of-occupy-wall-street, last accessed March 13, 2014; and Butler and Athena Athanasiou, *Dispossession: The Performative in the Political*, Malden, MA: Polity, 2013.

34 See the *New York Times* article, "For Annoyed Neighbors, the Beat Drags On," November 13, 2011.

35 See the *New York Times* article, "Dissenting, or Taking Shelter? Homeless Stake a Claim at Protests," October 31, 2011.

36 See "Un sujet?"

37 Hardt and Negri, "The Fight for 'Real Democracy' at the Heart of Occupy Wall Street: The Encampment in Lower Manhattan Speaks to a Failure of Representation," *Foreign Affairs*, October 11, 2011. Available at www.foreignaffairs.com/articles/136399/

michael-hardt-and-antonio-negri/the-fight-for-real-democracy-at-the-heart-of-occupy-wall-street, last accessed March 13, 2014. For a more sympathetic reading of the political experimentation of Occupy, see also W. J. T. Mitchell, Bernard E. Harcourt, and Michael Taussig's *Occupy: Three Inquiries in Disobedience* (Chicago and London: University of Chicago Press), 2013.

38 Of course, the poor and the homeless are not necessarily *voyous*. However, when they partake in the Occupy movement, moving and taking shelter within the camp sites of the movement, there is no doubt that the state sees them as much as *voyous* as the movement's participants or activists.

39 "Church, State, Resistance," in Hent de Vries and Lawrence E. Sullivan (eds), *Political Theologies: Public Religions in a Post-Secular World*, trans. Véronique Voruz (New York: Fordham University Press), 2006, 110.

40 "Church, State, Resistance," 109.

41 "Church, State, Resistance," 112.

42 "Church, State, Resistance," 112.

43 *The Sense of the World*, 103, 111.

44 *The Sense of the World*, 112.

45 *The Sense of the World*, 103.

46 *The Sense of the World*, 103. Trans. modified.

47 *The Sense of the World*, 103.

48 *The Sense of the World*, 111. Trans. modified.

49 *The Sense of the World*, 113, 111. Nancy's notion of relation is perhaps closer to Deleuze and Guattari's assemblage, which, as they explicate in *Mille plateaux*, is something that, depending on one's desire, one is always free to enter or depart from, than to Rousseau's social contract.

50 Here, one could perhaps hear the echo of Agamben's *other* potentiality to "not-be," which is also, given his *Coming Community*, his critique or move away from the *subject*.

51 See "War, Right, Sovereignty – Technē," 141.

52 Blanchot's "right to disappear" appears in *Michel Foucault tel que je l'imagine*, (Paris: Fata Morgana), 1986. The question of disappearing would be particularly close to Nancy's notion of relation or tie or knot (*nouage*) that is of "proximity and separation, attachment and detachment" if, following the counsel of Nancy's friends such as Agamben, Hamacher, and Lacoue-Labarthe, one hears the subtle

difference, if not *différance*, of *nuage* in *nouage*. *Nuage* is cloud in French, and clouds appear, come together to form larger clouds, disperse, and disappear. The "right to disappear" is obviously in contradistinction, without being entirely opposed, to Butler's argument, following the Occupy movement, of and for a "right to appear."

53 *The Experience of Freedom*, trans. Bridget McDonald and foreword by Peter Fenves (Stanford: Stanford University Press, 1993), 57, 138.

54 *The Experience of Freedom*, 141.

55 *The Experience of Freedom*, 166.

56 *The Experience of Freedom*, 163.

57 *The Experience of Freedom*, 142.

58 *The Experience of Freedom*, 142.

59 *The Experience of Freedom*, 129.

60 *L'Équivalence des catastrophes* (Paris: Galilée, 2012), 66, my translation. I would argue that the turn to adoration, respect, and esteem, rather than to remain with any notion of decision, further reduces the trace of the *subject*.

61 On the resistance that is critical for a "being-with" of "being-in-common" that is "sovereign otherwise," Nancy would suggest that "we should [. . .] give up [. . .] the desire for a politics that could put to work this affect and its heteronomy" ("Church, State, Resistance," 110–11). In a more recent text, Nancy would also say, "politics must not define itself but be determined by a fidelity to that which surpasses it" ("Hors colloque," in *Figures du dehors: autour de Jean-Luc Nancy*, Paris: Cécile Defaut, 2012, 531, my translation).

62 *The Creation of the World*, 101.

Chapter 9 Dialogue Beneath the Ribs

1 I am extremely grateful to Verena Andermatt Conley and Jean-Luc Nancy for all the help in translating this piece.

2 Translator's note: One might be inclined to translate *greffon* as graft, and that tendency can even be justified, acoustically and orthographically, when Nancy later in the dialogue compares *greffon* to the name *Griffon* and the French term *greffier*. However, I note that the context here concerns a heart transplant, and it is rare to refer to the organ transplanted (i.e. the heart) to a graft. Instead, the term "transplant" is given to the organ, in its entirety, in question. Furthermore, except

in the case of a liver graft, graft does not typically refer to an entire organ. For example, in skin grafting, it often involves the grafting of *parts* of skin from another part of the body to the part of the body that needs them. This is also the case of coronary artery bypass graft surgery, where arteries or veins from other parts of the body are grafted to coronary arteries to prevent angina or coronary artery diseases.

Index

Nancy's works are indexed under their English titles if they have been published in English, and under their French titles otherwise.